SOCIETÀ ITALIANA DI FISICA

RENDICONTI

DELLA

SCUOLA INTERNAZIONALE DI FISICA

"ENRICO FERMI"

CXCII Corso

a cura di F. Carminati e L. Betev

Direttori del Corso

e di

A. Grigoras

VARENNA SUL LAGO DI COMO

VILLA MONASTERO

25 – 30 Luglio 2014

Grid e Cloud Computing: Concetti e applicazioni

2016

SOCIETÀ ITALIANA DI FISICA
BOLOGNA-ITALY

ITALIAN PHYSICAL SOCIETY

PROCEEDINGS

OF THE

INTERNATIONAL SCHOOL OF PHYSICS

"ENRICO FERMI"

COURSE 192

edited by F. CARMINATI and L. BETEV

Directors of the Course

and

A. GRIGORAS

VARENNA ON LAKE COMO

VILLA MONASTERO

25 – 30 July 2014

Grid and Cloud Computing: Concepts and Practical Applications

2016

IOS
Press

AMSTERDAM, OXFORD, TOKIO, WASHINGTON DC

ISSN 0074-784X (print)
ISSN 1879-8195 (online)

ISBN 978-1-61499-642-2 (print) (IOS Press)
ISBN 978-1-61499-643-9 (online) (IOS Press)
ISBN 978-88-7438-100-5 (SIF)

LCCN 2016937539

jointly published and distributed by:

IOS PRESS
Nieuwe Hemweg 6B
1013 BG Amsterdam
The Netherlands
fax: +31 20 687 0019
info@iospress.nl

SOCIETÀ ITALIANA DI FISICA
Via Saragozza 12
40123 Bologna
Italy
fax: +39 051 581340
order@sif.it

Distributor in the USA and Canada
IOS Press, Inc.
4502 Rachael Manor Drive
Fairfax, VA 22032
USA
fax: +1 703 323 3668
sales@iospress.com

Supported by

    Camera di Commercio di Lecco

    Istituto Nazionale di Fisica Nucleare (INFN)

    Consiglio Nazionale delle Ricerche (CNR)

    Istituto Nazionale di Ricerca Metrologica (INRIM)

    Museo Storico della Fisica e Centro Studi e Ricerche "Enrico Fermi"

    CERN

Produced by the SIF Editorial Staff

Production Editors: Marcella Missiroli and Elena Baroncini

Cover: see I. C. Legrand, *Monitoring and control of large-scale distributed systems*, p. 129

Graphic elaboration by Simona Oleandri

Printed in Italy by Labanti e Nanni Industrie Grafiche S.r.l. - Crespellano (BO)

CONTENTS

The electronic version is available online at the IOS Press web site

http://ebooks.iospress.nl/bookseries/proceedings-of-the-international
-school-of-physics-enrico-fermi

Figures with colour source files will appear in colour in the online version.

Preface

The distributed computing infrastructure known as "The Grid" has been undoubtedly one of the most successful science-oriented large-scale IT projects in the past 20 years. The basic idea of the Grid is to take individually managed, network-connected computing centres to the next evolutionary level —a "self-managing, seamless large computer entity" sharing various types of resources and open to all research communities. This is done through simple user interfaces and web portals, successfully hiding the underlying structure of the individual computing centres, and owing to a fast network, making access to the resources independent of their geographical location. These once bold-sounding promises and ambitious goals are today a reality and the Grid is viewed as an ordinary, albeit quite powerful, computational tool by its users.

The Grid had the usual growth pattern of a large project —many years elapsed from its inception to full-blown operation status. A rich development history [1] goes back to the Condor project [2] first steps in 1988, passing through several important milestones —the Globus project in 1997, the European Union DataGrid in 2001 and its successor the EGEE project, gLite Grid middleware release in 2006 [3-5], and beyond. Today, after a decade of physical growth —enlarging the existing computing centres and constantly adding new ones— it is a fully operational international entity, encompassing several hundred computing sites on all continents, giving access to hundreds of thousands CPU cores and hundreds of petabytes of storage, all connected through robust national and international scientific networks. It has evolved to become the main computational platform for many scientific communities —mathematical sciences, physics, geology, earth-observation and number of life-science disciplines.

There are several essential key elements that have contributed to the success of the Grid. The primary one is the early adoption of standard interfaces and open-source technologies, allowing contribution from a variety of development groups and individual programmers to build a common Grid middleware. Its functionality is further enriched by specific tools serving the needs of individual groups but all using the common middleware to access to the underlying resources. The second element is its fully distributed nature, presenting no single point of failure and permitting new computing centres to join, or old ones to leave the Grid, with minimal effort and minimal impact to the overall operational status. The third one is the commitment of the national and international funding agencies to support the operation and growth of the individual computing centres comprising the Grid, as well as the middleware developer groups. This has resulted in a robust capacity growth: the year on year increase of CPU and storage has been of 25% and 20%, respectively, able to fulfil the ever-increasing computing needs of the user communities. It also allows the Grid software to continuously evolve, readily and rapidly absorbing new technologies and computational models, for example Cloud and Supercomputing resources, even being able to utilise volunteer desktop spare CPU cycles through projects like LHC@Home [6]. The fourth element is the network, both in the sense of LAN and WAN. The ever increasing network hardware capabilities —NICs, switches and routers— allows the design and deployment of computing centres with high local throughput between CPU and storage nodes, using readily available off-the-shelf components. The performance characteristics of such centres reach and sometimes surpass dedicated, purpose-build high performance computing clusters at a fraction of the price. The WAN aspect has been even more astonishing —through national investment in scientific networking, the computing centres have now unprecedented data connectivity. International projects facilitate network peering between countries, thus enabling movement of petabytes of data between computing centres with dedicated links, or terabytes between any pair of computing centres around the world. The fast progress of the network was not foreseen in the original Grid charter where the network paths were functionally linked with specific roles of the computing facilities, thus introducing the Tiered centre structure.

This last deserves a bit of elaboration. The MONARC model [7] assigned a specific tiered hierarchy to the individual computing centres. At the top of the pyramid are the Tier 1s with fastest network connection, serving as data collection and distribution points. Going down the structure are Tier 2s and Tier 3s serving progressively less-data intensive tasks and linked to specific regional centres, usually the country Tier 1. All data paths were strictly prescribed in the model, creating a complex hierarchical infrastructure and requiring special data management tools. The rapid network capacity growth which served the Tier 1s, 2s and 3s with fast networks both within a region and internationally, considerably reduced the task dependency on the tiered structure diminished. All centres could effectively execute any task, almost independent of the data volume involved. Operationally, the Grid structure became almost flat.

The availability of fast networks contributed to two additional positive aspects of the Grid. Bridging the "Digital divide": already weakened by the open model of software development, ubiquitous network allows many new and emerging countries to deploy and operate Grid-enabled computing resources, thus further erasing the boundaries between regions with strong computing traditions and newcomers to the field. The second aspect is related to the establishment of network-related projects, for example the LHCONE [8], aimed at further improving the connectivity and collaboration across country borders. These projects use extensively Virtual Routing and Forwarding (VRF) technology to create direct, efficient and secure network for the Grid centres across the globe.

Ample CPU, storage and network resources as well as mature and simple to use Grid middleware allow the execution of a wide and complex variety of data- and CPU-intensive tasks. Taking as an example the CERN Large Hadron Collider [9] experiments, since the start of operation in 2010, the processed amounts of data has reached volumes of few XB/year (1018 bytes) and hundreds of centuries of wall CPU time. This moved the Grid CPU and data management into the realm of "Big data", fully consistent with the characteristics [10] applied to this term. The amount of data stored and analysed by other scientific projects has also seen a manifold increase over the past years. Furthermore, the future-generation experiments like the Square Kilometre Array (SKA) radio telescope project and High Altitude Water Cherenkov (HAWC) Experiment [11, 12] will produce and process unprecedented by today standards data volumes of hundreds PBs yearly. These experiments are poised to use Grid technology for storage and processing adequately evolved for the future. This assures the existence of the Grid as a main platform for scientific computation well into the next decade and likely beyond.

The rapid growth of the individual computing centres forming the Grid presents new challenges for resources management. The standard batch systems and storage management solutions are no longer able to cope with the sheer number of CPU cores and petabytes of disk deployed at each of these centres. Emerging new technologies, usually associated with Cloud computing, are being actively adopted on the Grid. OpenStack [13] and OpenNebula [14], to mention few of the most actively used Cloud management solutions, are used today to orchestrate the installations of large and small data centres. These open-source projects allow not only overcoming the limitations of the traditional batch systems, but open new possibilities in resources provisioning with increasing complexity and functionality. Coupled with VM and container technology, they allow the centres to offer "on demand" capabilities, from providing different OS images, memory and disk capacities to specific security and network settings, fulfilling diverse user requirements at the same time and on the same physical hosts. Just few years ago, some of these capabilities did not exist or required complex expert-intensive interventions. The ease of deployment of the new management technologies allows resources providers to switch from traditional to Cloud capabilities with minimal downtime, assuring continuous and efficient use of the installed hardware.

On the storage side, the advent of distributed object store solutions like HADOOP and CEPH [15, 16] allow for better scaling of the installed storage capacities and, at the same time, minimizes the possibility of data loss. This is achieved by using block device images, striped and replicated across the entire storage cluster. Both capabilities are becoming increasingly important as storage continues to grow and is still the most expensive item in the computing centres installations. Simple methods for data redundancy like RAID arrays or multiple file replicas are no longer affordable. Other novel approaches to storage include federated installations, where the individual storage capacities of many computing centres are managed together and present a single point of entry to the Grid middleware. This is also a Cloud-inspired approach which simplifies the structure of the Grid. The software tools used for federated storage are also part of the Cloud software stack or purpose-build storage solutions like xrootd and EOS [17, 18], developed and deployed by the High Energy Physics community.

The ever increasing need for computing resources turned the attention of Grid developers and user community to industry resource providers and more specifically to the Elastic Clouds like Amazon Elastic Compute Cloud, Google Cloud Platform and European Cloud resources providers. There are several projects aiming at providing Grid middleware interfaces to the various Cloud solutions and successful pilot runs using Cloud resources have taken place in the past two years. The intended use of these resources is to bring further "elasticity" to the capacity of the Grid, especially in periods of high resource demand. Clouds are also used by the scientific project directly though the Cloud interfaces, usually implemented according to the Open Cloud Computing Interface (OCCI) standard. The computing centres nowadays provide both Grid and Cloud interfaces to their resources as the software maturity is such to minimise the burden of supporting various high-level interfaces to the underlying computing capacity.

To assure the working status of the computing resources, their efficient use and to help trace and fix operational issues, the Grid requires comprehensive and real-time monitoring. Several packages, different in scope and complexity are in use today. They monitor basic parameters of the installed hardware, the running applications, storage status and the network. The full list of the monitored parameter in today's Grid would be quite long and after ten years of continuous operation, is stored in many large, TB sized, relational databases. The challenges for the monitoring software are many —it must be unobtrusive, secure, scalable and configurable. The common approach to monitoring is to deploy it at several levels —the computing centres use fabric monitoring tools, the user communities have higher level tools for the running applications, the network operators deploy monitoring along the data paths. Further monitoring aggregation is done for resources accounting purposes. New projects are exploiting the possibilities to use Elasticsearch [19] techniques and tools to go beyond the limitations of the traditional monitored data representations.

The Varenna Course 192 "Grid and Cloud computing: Concepts and Practical Applications" aimed to cover in-depth the conceptual and practical aspects of the Grid and Cloud computing, briefly outlined above. The present volume is divided into 8 chapters:

1. *LHC computing (WLCG): Past, present, and future*, by Ian G. Bird
2. *Scientific Clouds*, by Davide Salomoni
3. *Clouds in biosciences: A journey to high throughput computing in life sciences*, by Vincent Breton *et al.*
4. *Monitoring and control of large-scale distributed systems*, by Iosif Charles Legrand
5. *Big data: Challenges and perspectives*, by Dirk Duellmann
6. *Advanced networking for scientific applications*, by Artur Barczyk
7. *Networking for high energy physics*, by Harvey B. Newman *et al.*
8. *Towards an OpenStack-based Swiss national research infrastructure*, by Sergio Maffioletti *et al.*

Chapters 1, 2, 3 and 8 cover general application of Grid and Cloud computing in various scientific fields; chapters 4, 5, 6 and 7 discuss specific technical areas of the Grid and Cloud structures.

Happy reading!

F. CARMINATI, L. BETEV and A. GRIGORAS

REFERENCES

[1] FOSTER I. and KESSELMAN C., *The History of the Grid* (IOS Press, Amsterdam) 2013.

[2] THAIN D., TANNENBAUM T. and LIVNY M., *Distributed Computing in Practice: the Condor Experience*, in *Concurrency and Computation: Practice and Experience*, Vol. **17**, issue No. 2-4 (Wiley) 2005, pp. 323–356.

[3] The Globus project, project web site
https://www.globus.org/about

[4] The DataGrid project, project web site
http://eu-datagrid.web.cern.ch/eu-datagrid/

[5] European Middleware Initiative, project web site
http://www.eu-emi.eu

[6] Volunteer Computing for the LHC, project web site
http://lhcathome.web.cern.ch/

[7] Model of Networked Analysis at Regional Centres (MONARC), project web site
http://monarc.web.cern.ch/MONARC/

[8] LHC Open Network Environment, project web site
http://lhcone.net/

[9] The Large Hadron Collider, web site
http://home.cern/topics/large-hadron-collider

[10] MAYER-SCHOENBERGER VIKTOR and CUKIER KENNETH, *Big Data* (Houghton Mifflin Harcourt) 2013.

[11] Square Kilometer Array, project web site
https://www.skatelescope.org/

[12] The High-Altitude Water Cherenkow Gamma-Ray Observatory, project web site
http://www.hawc-observatory.org/

[13] OpenStack software, project web site
https://www.openstack.org/

[14] OpenNebula software, project web site
http://opennebula.org/

[15] CEPH storage, project web site
http://ceph.com/ceph-storage/

[16] Apache Hadoop, project web site
http://hadoop.apache.org/

[17] XRootD project, project web site
http://xrootd.org/

[18] EOS, project web site
http://eos.web.cern.ch/

[19] Elasticsearch project, project web site
https://www.elastic.co/products/elasticsearch

Italian Physical Society
INTERNATIONAL SCHOOL OF PHYSICS «E. FERMI»
COURSE 192
25 - 30 July 2014
VILLA MONASTERO – VARENNA, LAKE COMO

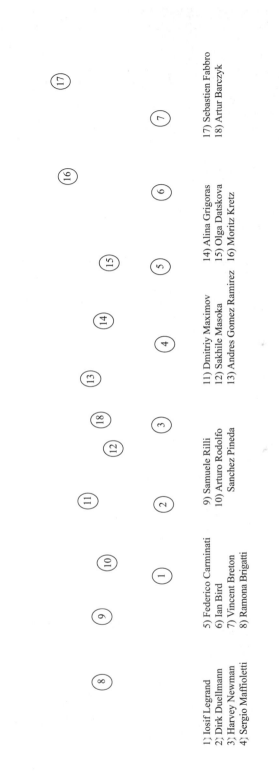

1) Iosif Legrand
2) Dirk Duellmann
3) Harvey Newman
4) Sergio Maffioletti

5) Federico Carminati
6) Ian Bird
7) Vincent Breton
8) Ramona Brigatti

9) Samuele Rilli
10) Arturo Rodolfo Sanchez Pineda

11) Dmitriy Maximov
12) Sakhile Masoka
13) Andres Gomez Ramirez

14) Alina Grigoras
15) Olga Datskova
16) Moritz Kretz

17) Sebastien Fabbro
18) Artur Barczyk

Proceedings of the International School of Physics "Enrico Fermi"
Course 192 "Grid and Cloud Computing: Concepts and Practical Applications",
edited by F. Carminati, L. Betev and A. Grigoras
(IOS, Amsterdam; SIF, Bologna) 2016
DOI 10.3254/978-1-61499-643-9-1

LHC computing (WLCG): Past, present, and future

I. G. BIRD

CERN - CH-1211 Geneva 23, Switzerland

Summary. — The LCG project, and the WLCG Collaboration, represent a more than 10-year investment in building and operating the LHC computing environment. This article gives some of the history of how the WLCG was constructed and the preparations for the accelerator start-up. It will discuss the experiences and lessons learned during the first 3 year run of the LHC, and will conclude with a look forwards to the planned upgrades of the LHC and the experiments, discussing the implications for computing.

1. – Introduction

The challenge of LHC computing arises from several factors. In summary these factors are:

- the physics itself: the LHC is searching for very rare processes against a background of many well-known processes;
- the LHC accelerator reaches very high energy and luminosity, providing a large number of interactions;
- the scale and complexity of the detectors;
- the huge volumes of data that are produced by the detectors;
- the need to distribute all this data to a global community of many thousands of physicists.

The standard model of particle physics has proven to be very good at describing the observed universe, and has been confirmed to better than the 1% level. However, a significant missing piece has been the mechanism through which mass is generated. The Higgs boson was proposed in the 1960's as such a mechanism, and was one of the physics drivers behind building the LHC. However, the cross sections for processes likely to produce Higgs bosons, are extremely rare, at the level of some 1 in 10^{13} of the total number of interactions. Since typical particle physics analyses are statistical in nature, a very large number of "uninteresting" collisions must be collected in order to observe any candidates for potentially interesting or new processes. The LHC obtains a high rate of collisions by circulating large numbers of protons in the accelerator—typically in 2012 some 1400 proton bunches, each with 10^{11} protons, accelerated to 3.5 TeV per beam and brought into collision at each of the 4 interaction points. This results in a crossing rate of up to 40 MHz, and a collision rate between protons of 10^9 Hz in the large detectors.

These collisions are made to occur at the centres of four large detectors, built and operated by the experiment collaborations with the same names. ATLAS and CMS are very large general-purpose detectors with goals of searching for new physics phenomena. They are complementary in that the two detectors are very different in design and construction and use quite different detector technologies. Both detectors have a very large number of electronics channels, some 150 million, that are read out for each collision. The size of data for each collision event is around 1–2 MB in each of these large detectors, but given the very high event rate, the full detector data rate approaches 1 PB/s. There is additional complexity in that due to the high intensity of the proton beams, many interactions may overlap in time—in the running conditions of 2012, up to about 20 collision events could appear together in each read-out event.

The other 2 detectors have more specialised physics goals. The ALICE detector is designed specifically to study heavy-ion collisions, when the LHC accelerates lead ions in place of protons. This generates very high energy densities at the collision point, and allows the reproduction of states of matter close to those of the very early universe. A characteristic of these heavy-ion events is a very large number of particles generated at the collision, and a consequent very large data rate out of the detector. The fourth detector, LHCb, is designed to study the asymmetries of matter and anti-matter. It is a relatively small experiment with a much lower data rate than the others, but since the LHCb event size is very small, the collision rate can be extremely high, and LHCb is able to measure very small effects extremely precisely with very high statistics.

The very high data rates that come from the detectors must be filtered with hardware "triggers"—selections of characteristics of interesting events, initially done in custom electronics, close to the detector, and then secondly in large computer clusters that look in some more detail at the events, again selecting those that potentially exhibit characteristics of interest. These hardware and software filters result in data rates that are manageable and can be written to magnetic tape for later analysis. These resulting data rates are typically the following:

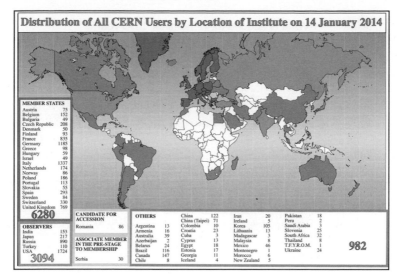

Fig. 1. – Global distribution of CERN users.

- ATLAS and CMS: around 1 GB/s,

- ALICE: 4–5 GB/s during heavy-ion data taking,

- LHCb: around 200 MB/s,

The data itself is digital information recording which detector elements were hit, how much energy was deposited, timing signals, and perhaps information on particle types. The first stage of processing is to "reconstruct" the particle traces using these raw data, to find the momenta of the tracks (4-vectors), the origin of the collisions, determination of energy of clusters of tracks (jets), determination of particle types, and various calibration data.

The collaborations that built and operate these large detectors are global collaborations of up to 4000 physicists. Figure 1 shows the truly global nature of CERN users.

One of the challenges of computing for LHC is enabling this global community to have easy and direct access to all of the data generated by the LHC and the detectors. Given all of these challenges, building a globally distributed computing system was seen as a potential method by which to harness the available funding, resources, and expertise. That eventual system—the LHC Computing Grid—is what is currently being used to process and analyse the LHC data. However, consideration of computing needs for LHC started much earlier.

2. – The past—the LCG project and the WLCG

The LHC project was first approved in 1994, with the experiment detector projects being approved over the following few years. the first estimates of the computing needs

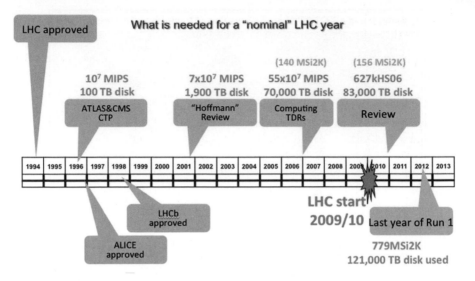

Fig. 2. – Evolution of computing needs.

of ATLAS and CMS were produced at the time of the initial design studies in 1996, although the first serious estimates were not until a review of the computing needs held in 2001. At that point the requirements had evolved significantly from the first estimates, and it was clear that the computing challenge of LHC was significant, and far in excess of anything that had been achieved in the past. The estimated data volumes were around 15 PB per year of new data that would be added to the system. That data includes the raw data, and other key data sets such as simulated data that would need to be stored and processed. Figure 2 shows the evolution of requirements over time, and by the time of the Technical Design Reports [1] of the computing projects produced in 2005, the stated needs for processing and storage capacity were several orders of magnitude greater than the original estimates!

At the time of the review in 2001, the scale of the overall challenge for LHC computing could be summarised as the following:

– signal-to-noise ratio between all proton collisions and those potentially exhibiting new physics: $1{:}10^{13}$;

– data volume of some 15 Petabytes per year of new data due to the high rate of collisions and the large number of detector elements, and four detectors;

– compute power required of the equivalent of 200000 of the fastest CPU of the time, driven by the event complexity and the amount of data;

– storage requirement for staging and processing in addition to the archiving of some 45 PB of new disk each year;

- the need to serve a global user community and to be able to deliver data and allow access to the computing resources to that community;

- funding likely to be locally available in each collaborating country, but not available to build a large central facility.

These challenges led to a computing model that would be highly distributed over the worldwide user community in order to be able to make use of available funding. It was clear that the CERN computer centre could only provide some 20% of the overall requirement, not only because of the funding mechanisms but also because the size of the facility was inherently limited. It was at that time that grid technology was being used in various computer science experiments, and it looked as though the technology may be a good fit for implementing the LHC distributed computing system.

In order to be able to systematically build and prototype such a system, and to be able to get it funded, a project was proposed to the CERN Council, and approved in September 2001 [2]. The LHC Computing Grid (LCG) project began in 2002, with support from CERN and several countries in the form of dedicated funding. That support was critical to get the project started.

The model that had been proposed in late 1999 [3], and that formed the basis of understanding how a distributed computing service could work, is that illustrated in fig. 3 and introduces the concept of different Tiers of computer centres with different roles and capabilities.

Since several European and US projects had prototyped aspects of grid computing for use in high energy physics, it was a natural way to implement this model. The working assumption of the LCG project was that it would build on the results of those prototypes. The higher level goals of LCG was prototype and deploy the computing environment for the LHC experiments, including the aims to set up a production-quality service and to validate the distributed LHC computing models. The LCG project was conceived in two phases:

- Phase 1 from 2002 to 2005: build a service prototype, based on existing grid middleware; to gain experience in running a production grid service; and the produce the Technical Design Report for the final system;

- Phase 2 from 2006 to 2008: Build and commission the initial LHC computing environment for LHC start-up foreseen for 2008.

LCG was not intended as a development project, and relied upon other grid projects for grid middleware development and support. To give some context to those other projects, fig. 4 shows the grid project landscape at this time.

Some of the more specific aims of the LCG project were really to make this new technology usable within our existing computing facilities and to ensure that such a global distributed system could actually be run and operated by the available staff. Some if the initial goals included providing a close-to-real production level service for experiment data challenges foreseen for 2003 and 2004, focusing on batch work. Of

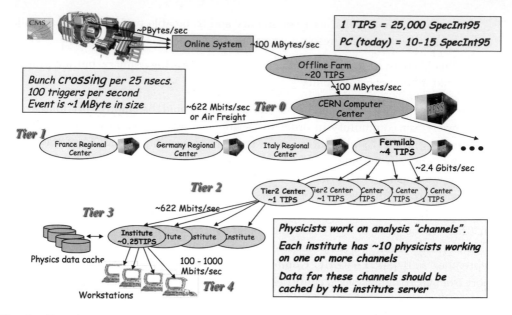

Fig. 3. – Initial computing model of 1999.

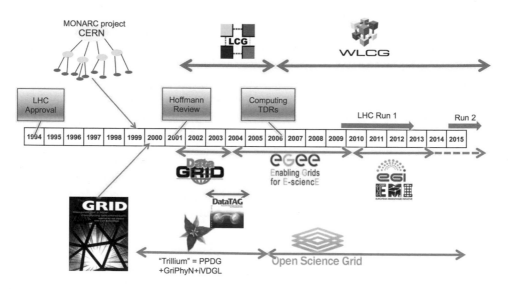

Fig. 4. – Landscape of grid projects.

course building experience and expertise in collaboration between the regional computing centres would be essential at this point, so it was important to have a large participation of more than a few centres. It was also important to ensure that this novel service could be integrated into the existing physics computing services, as until then all of the grid projects were treated as experimental and special. From the beginning, a focus

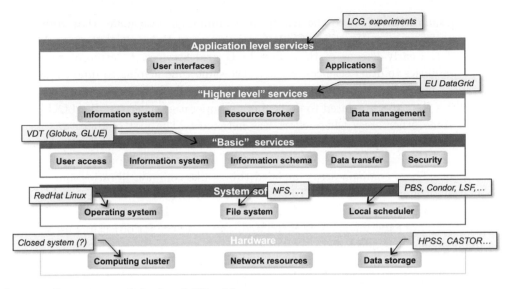

Fig. 5. – Components of the first LCG grid.

on things like robustness, fault tolerance, predictability and supportability were seen as more important than additional functionality in order to be able to achieve the above aims. Of course functionality was also important but in retrospect some of the apparent essential requirements of the applications were very unrealistic.

The initial service started with around 25 participating sites began in 2003 providing facilities and support for the experiments testing some simulation challenges and data scaling exercises. The project itself had several areas of effort in order to actually run the service. These included:

– Middleware: a testing and certification activity to ensure that the middleware was of sufficient quality and robustness. The middleware coming from various development projects was tested together and then packaged to create a distribution that could be deployed around the participating sites. This team also provided support and assistance to the remote grid site operators.

– Operations: services for running the infrastructure; prototyping the first grid operations centre, to help with trouble and performance monitoring and problem resolution, aiming for 24×7 response globally. RAL (the UK Tier 1) prototyped the first such operations centre.

– Support: a team working with the experiments to integrate the middleware with experiment software. A prototype user support service led by KIT (the German Tier 1) who developed a global ticketing system (GGUS)—still in use today.

Figure 5 illustrates the main building blocks of the initial grid system at that time.

At this time a proposal to the European Commission was made that resulted in the large EGEE project (Enabling Grids for E-science in Europe) [4] that would build on some of the early lessons of these first LCG grid services, to attempt to provide similar capabilities to other sciences, while at the same time helping to fund some of the development work that was clearly needed to build a real robust production service.

As well as the aspects related to deploying and operating a service, the LCG project itself had some other areas where effort was necessary. The first of these was an Applications area that was responsible for building common software applications needed by all of the LHC experiments, together with the supporting development and support environment. These common areas included things like common libraries, but also the coordination of effort around GEANT4 [5]—the simulation system, and around ROOT [6] that was use for I/O and analysis by all of the experiments. In addition common projects between 2 or more experiments were incubated, and a service for object persistency and data management was developed.

The Fabric area focussed on automating systems to be able to build large scale data centres since the scale that would be required for the Tier 0 was unprecedented, and the tools for management at scale did not exist at that time. It was also essential that the project had a good handle on technology in order to be able to foresee costs, and set up a technology tracking activity. This was essential in order to be able to cost the service in preparation for LHC start-up.

2˙1. *Grid Services*. – The term "computing grid" came to have many meanings, but for LHC it really meant a "federated, distributed, infrastructure", with a vision close to that of the inventors of the Grid—Ian Foster and Karl Kesselman [7]. Their definition was "coordinated resources sharing and problem solving in dynamic, multi-institutional virtual organisations". The implication is that services cross the administrative boundaries of institutions, but that appear as a single service to the user. The concept of a Virtual Organisation (VO) is also key—a group of people who collaborate to address a specific problem. This maps naturally onto the HEP experiment collaborations in our case. A fundamental concept is that a user only requires one set of credential in order to be able to use services available to his VO—no matter at which physics institution they may be provided. Practically that means a user does not have to register with each resource provider, or even to know where his compute task may run. It is also important to understand that the computer centres are autonomous and have full control over their systems, and who is permitted to use them.

Figure 6 shows the main components of the grid software services that were initially set up and deployed.

The grid has to cope with a number of constraints. One of these is the inherent heterogeneity of the resources that it tries to integrate. Since sites are autonomous, the resources and services running at a site may be very different one from another. Examples of this include the wide variety of batch systems used to manage compute resources, large variety of different storage system technologies and management services. Each of these may be constrained by local considerations, history, available expertise,

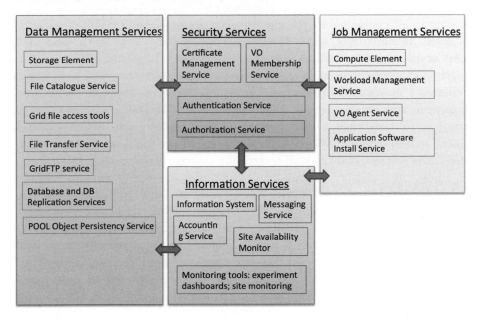

Fig. 6. – Original set of grid services of WLCG.

need for compatibility with other applications at the site, and so on. At least for LHC we have agreed on using a limited set of Linux versions as the operating system. In addition available skills at sites may vary a lot, at large data centres are very experienced professionals, while at some smaller sites operating the grid services may be reliant on physicists and students with very different skill sets. At a high level, the approach of the grid is to define abstraction layers to resources such as compute and storage in order to connect to the specific local implementation. This is coupled with a system for Authentication, Authorisation, and Auditing (AAA) that is common for the grid, does not require local registration, and delegates management details to the VOs. The information system provides a way of advertising the resources available at a site. There may be higher level services that provide brokering or other workflows to make use of the underlying systems, these high level services are often integrated into the applications. Figure 6 illustrates these various grouping of services and abstractions. Complexity arises from the need to support the huge variety of heterogenous systems, and the middleware must interface between all of them in a seamless way. This results in many adaptors, that need continual support as the end-systems evolve. This also lead to a significant challenge in testing and ensuring all of this works correctly. In addition, there was a general move to make the middleware layer support a lot of functionality, which added to the complexity (and often to instability in the early days), while experience has shown that a lot of that complexity is better dealt with at the application layer.

In the next few paragraphs we detail a few of the key components of the grid as deployed in Europe. Other countries and areas (*e.g.*, USA) deployed very similar sets of services (for example in the USA via the *open science grid*—OSG [8]), although not always with the same technology. However, for all collaborating grids used for LHC, the AAA framework has been unique (as it must be). It should also be noted that when the LCG project began in 2002, grid technology was nowhere near usable for production, it was a more than 5 year process to achieve that at the scale needed for LHC. The European and US broader grid projects (*e.g.*, EGEE, OSG, etc) were enormously important in fully developing the operational infrastructure for LHC. That included investment in middleware development, and in operations tools, support tools, security response processes, etc. and the staff to actually manage the operation.

2˙1.1. AAA and Security. Authentication is based on the X.509 PKI (public key) infrastructure. Certification Authorities (CA) issue long-lived certificates identifying individuals (like a passport). These certificates are what is commonly used in web browsers to authenticate to web sites. There is a trust relationship established between CA's and sites. In order to reduce vulnerability, actual work on the grid is done using short-lived proxies of the users' certificates. The certificate or the proxy can be used to identify a user to a service, be delegated to a service to act on a user's behalf, be renewed by an external services (necessary since the lifetime is short), and can include additional attributes. In the grid these additional attributes are used for Authorisation.

The VO Management Service (VOMS)—a de-facto standard, is the mechanism by which these additional attributes are managed, and can provide users with additional capabilities, as defined by the VO. This is the basis for the authorisation process. At a site users are mapped to a local user on a resource.

The network of trust that must exist between the CA's themselves and between them and the sites, is key to this entire process being able to work. To this end an International Grid Trust Federation (IGTF) [9] has been set up to maintain a list of accredited CAs, with their public keys and pointers to their certificate revocation lists. In order to be accredited a CA must publish a conforming policy and set of processes, and be reviewed by the peer CA's. In this way trust is established. There are regional trust federations in Europe (EUGridPMA), in the Americas (TAGPMA), and in Asia-Pacific (APGridPMA). The sites are then able to trust that these conforming CAs will give the level of assurance necessary to accept validated users to access resources at their sites.

This trust network is the mechanism by which a user needs only a single credential to be able to access the worldwide pool of resources.

2˙1.2. Computing. The abstraction for the computing service is the so-called "Compute Element" (CE). This is essentially a gateway to a site that interfaces to the local batch system, and allows a remote user to submit a job to the site. The CE takes care of the differences between various batch implementations. It also provides a connection to the grid accounting system that provides data on grid jobs run at each site.

Today, most grid jobs for LHC are actually "placeholder" jobs, often referred to as "pilot jobs". Once such a job begins to execute on a local batch system it connects to a service run by the VO (LHC experiment), that then sends the highest priority task to be executed. In this way, the experiment is able to manage the priorities of its tasks in a centralised way, and ensure that those workloads are executed immediately. The analogy to this is queues in a bank. It is inefficient to have a queue in front of each teller, while a single queue that dispatches to the next available teller ensure that all tellers are occupied and the queuing time minimised. These pilot job services are now ubiquitous for all of the LHC experiments, and have really allowed the full occupation of all resources. Today, the system regularly runs more then 2 million such pilot jobs per day globally, with many more individual tasks executed.

A further refinement of this approach is the ability to change the identity of the task within the pilot job to be the actual owner of the task (rather than the identity running the pilot itself) on demand.

2˙1.3. **Storage.** The abstraction for the storage systems is the "Storage Element" (SE). Again this is the interface to the underlying storage systems at a site. A standard interface is used for this based on the "Storage Resources Manager" (SRM) [10] concept. This hides the storage implementation (disk, tape), handles the authorisation process, and translates Storage URLs (which are fixed and stored in catalogues) to a "Transfer URL" (TURL) (which may change according to the underlying system). There are both disk based and tape based implementations of the SRM. The SRM interface has to provide all of the necessary user functionality and control, as well as managing the data transfers. It is a complex system, and must be tightly integrated to the underlying storage service.

The SRM is the control interface, while the actual file I/O is a posix-like access from local nodes or from the grid.

The implementation of storage services was quite lengthy and complex. There are many existing and heavily used systems locally at sites, that represent (often) decade-long investments, and tightly integrated with other site infrastructure and local users.

A file catalogue was developed for LHC (the LCG File Catalog—LFC). The LFC stored mappings between the users' file names and the locations of the corresponding files on the grid, of which there may be many replicas. This catalog was also a distributed service with many catalogue instances, and a continual synchronisation between them.

One of the key technologies for LHC is the ability to transfer massive amounts of data between grid sites, and being able to make full use of the available bandwidths. For this the File Transfer Service (FTS) was developed. The FTS provides a reliable, scalable and customisable service. It manages multiple VO's and can balance the usage of site resources and networks according to SLAs between sites and the VO's. The FTS uses gridftp as the underlying transfer mechanism, but provides a way to fill the available bandwidth b scheduling multiple transfers. It also provides a retry in case of failure. These features were essential in being able to achieve the needed data transfer rates for LHC.

2˙1.4. **Information System.** Finally, the information system is the mechanism by which service endpoints can be discovered, and by which the available resources at as its can be advertised. It is a lightweight database making use of the LDAP protocol, and the

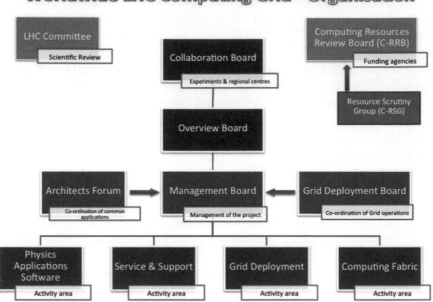

Fig. 7. – The WLCG Collaboration management and review structure.

information is stored according to a schema that was developed in the context of the grid projects and become a standard. The amount of data describing the grid is around 200 MB.

2˙**2.** *The WLCG.* – As described above, the first phase of the LCG project resulted in two products, the first of which were the Computing Technical Design Reports (TDR), of which there was one per experiment and one for LCG. The second outcome was the set up of the long-term structure for managing LHC computing. This structure is the Worldwide LHC Computing Grid (WLCG) Collaboration [13].

The WLCG Collaboration is formed by a Memorandum of Understanding (MoU) between CERN and the contributing funding agencies. Today (2014) there are close to 50 funding agencies supporting WLCG. The MoU specifies the services, and service levels of the Tier 0, 1, and 2 sites, and the process for managing the collaboration. It also includes a process to manage the resource requirement and pledge balance. This process has a yearly cycle, with an outlook for 3 years, and includes mechanisms for reviewing the requests for compute and storage resources by a group of experts (the Resource Scrutiny Group). The WLCG is reviewed scientifically by the CERN LHC Committee [14] that also reviews the LHC experiments in all aspects, and financially by the Resource Review Boards which have funding agency membership. Figure 7 shows the management and review structure of the WLCG Collaboration.

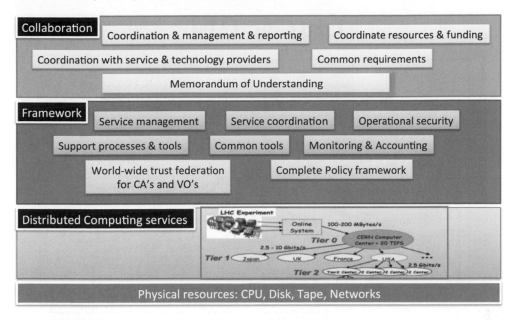

Fig. 8. – The WLCG Collaboration services and scope.

The scale of the WLCG infrastructure in 2014 is significant, and can be characterised by the following parameters:

– 1 Tier 0, and 13 Tier 1 sites;

– 160 Tier 2 sites in 35 countries;

– more than 350000 computing cores;

– 200 PB of disk, and 200 PB of tape storage;

– more than 2 millions jobs per day are processed;

– many 10 Gb (and recently 100 Gb) links.

Figure 8 illustrates the layers of service that WLCG provides, from the physical hardware to the collaboration.

Since the volumes of data, and the ability to enable global access to that data were primary concerns of the project, the connections between CERN and the Tier 1s was addressed by provisioning dedicated 10 Gb links between CERN and each of the Tier 1s. This Optical Private Network (LHCOPN) [15] grew over several years with secondary connections between sites, in order to provide a robust and redundant network. The LHCOPN connectivity of today is illustrated in fig. 9. For connectivity between Tier 1 and Tier 2 sites, WLCG relied upon the National Research and Education Networks (NRENs) in most countries, in Europe coordinated through GEANT [16], and in the

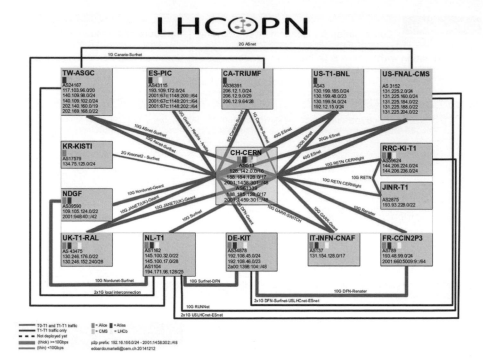

Fig. 9. – The WLCG LHC Optical Private Network (LHCOPN).

USA making use of ESNET [17] and the Internet2 facilities. Transatlantic networking has been assured until 2014 by a joint project [18] between the US ATLAS and CMS projects and CERN. In a later section we describe how this networking is evolving.

WLCG relies on a reliable and robust infrastructure. That is the only way by which it is possible to achieve the scale and performance that is necessary. In such a large distributed system, small problems can be magnified and affect many other things. For this reason there has always been a significant emphasis on requiring high standards of reliability and availability, performance, and manageability. The infrastructure never stops, it has run permanently since it started. Upgrades must be performed during production running. There is no concept of maintenance periods for the infrastructure as a whole. Of course individual services must undergo some periods of interruption, but usually redundancy is required to avoid this creating problems. Today the large sites (Tier 0, Tier 1) do not go down for maintenance, but ensure continual service even while upgrading software and services.

There is also a long term commitment from the Tier 0 and 1 sites—that is to ensure the storage of LHC data for at least the lifetime of the accelerator, 20 years or more. This is not a passive requirement, but requires significant investment in skills and equipment. For example, storing data on tape for any length of time requires active reading and migration from one generation of media to the next to ensure data integrity and availability.

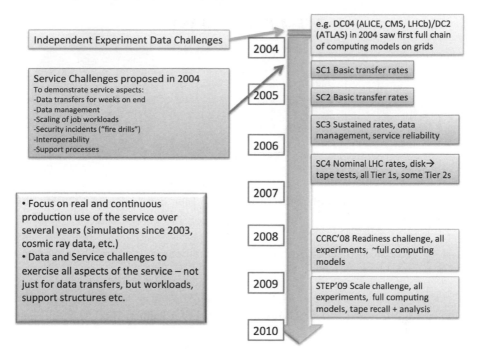

Fig. 10. – The path from prototypes to data: testing and data challenges.

It is vital for WLCG that the system is reliable and fault tolerant. For this reason monitoring and operational tools and procedures are as important as middleware. The collaboration has published availability and reliability metrics to the funding agencies for many years, in order to push sites to improve the overall service levels to build a reliable service. The situation today is that the majority of sites are extremely reliable, but it has taken many years to achieve this. Today most problems arise from real infrastructure problems such as power or cooling failures, and equipment failures. The level of these failures are probably now at the level that is irreducible, but is certainly acceptable.

In order to build the grid to the scale, functionality and performance required, a multi-year programme of testing and data challenges was developed and exercised. This is shown schematically in fig. 10. These challenges were key to pushing the boundaries of the performance, and driving the development of the necessary software. The exercises were an important mechanism by which priorities could be managed, for example stressing data transfer performance, over additional job submission features.

2˙2.1. Policies. An aspect of a production grid that is not often mentioned is that of the necessary policies. These have been shown to be essential to being able to operate across different legal system, and in being able to establish the necessary trust between all parties involved. This policy set has been built over several years, in cooperation with many of the national and international grid projects. The policies related to AAA

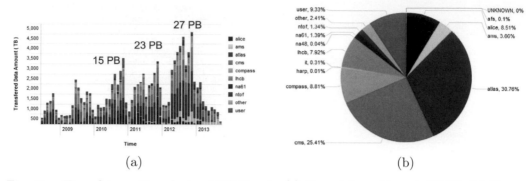

(a)   (b)

Fig. 11. – Tape data written during LHC Run 1. (a) Tape data written at CERN. (b) Tape usage breakdown.

and the CAs have been discussed above. In addition there are the following set of key policies:

- Grid Acceptable Use Policy (AUP): common across all collaborators, and is general and straightforward. It is common for all VO members and the different grid infrastructures.

- Incident handling and response: specifying how such incidents will be managed.

- Audit requirements: detailing the information that must be stored by sites, for how long, and its intended use.

- Publication of accounting data, what data is gathered, how it should be used, and who is able to use it.

These are supplemented by a number of others detailing the users' responsibilities, etc. In particular, the VOs specify their own acceptable use policies. This set of policies is under continual evolution and adaptation. It is fair to say that without these, the deployment of the LHC grid would not have been possible.

3. – The present—experiences in LHC Run 1

The WLCG grid as described above has been shown to be highly successful in providing the computing environment and resources for the first physics run of the LHC from 2010 to 2013. It was instrumental, together with the LHC itself, and the LHC detectors, in the successful hunt for the Higgs boson, the discovery of which was announced in July 2012. The following figures show some of the performance metrics of the WLCG grid during this time.

3'1. *Performance during LHC Run 1*. – Figure 11a shows the amounts of data written to tape during the three years of the first LHC run, and fig. 11b the total amount of data acquired during that time shown by experiment. We recall that the planned data rate for

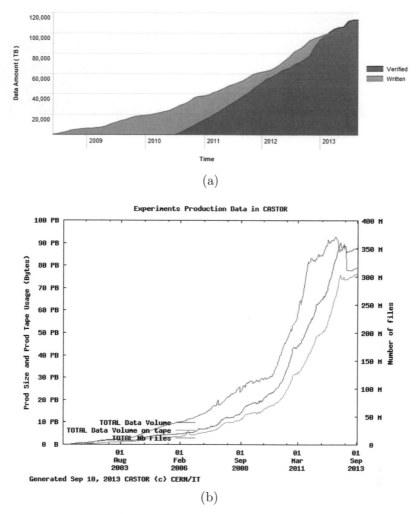

(a)

(b)

Fig. 12. – CERN tape archive. (a) CERN tape data verification. (b) CERN tape archive reaches 100 PB.

a *nominal* year of data taking was anticipated to be 15 PB. This rate was easily achieved even in the first year, and doubled by the end of the third year. The LHC was also far from its nominal energy and intensity during this time. It was thus very important that the system had been tested to ensure that such data volumes were supportable.

By the end of the three year run, the Tier 0 data archive had reached 100 PB, shown in fig. 12b (albeit with a small reduction as the experiments performed some clean ups). As can be seen this corresponds to nearly 0.5 billion files. The scale of the archive is important as the process of ongoing verification and repacking of data to new media takes several years, as is shown in fig. 12a. As noted earlier, this is an essential aspect of long term bit preservation of the data, and is non-negligible in terms of human and physical resources. The process also illustrates the excellent reliability of tape, during

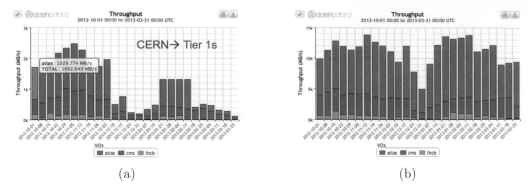

(a)   (b)

Fig. 13. – WLCG data transfer performances. (a) Data exported from CERN. (b) Global data transfers.

the verification only some 65 GB of the 100 PB total was not readable. This is a bit failure rate of less than 1 in 10^6.

The ability to transfer data worldwide at sufficient bandwidths was one of the main points of concern for the original design of the LHC computing project. The LHCOPN was put in place to ensure that data could be transferred from CERN to the Tier 1s at the anticipated nominal aggregate data rates of 650 MB/s with enough capacity to double that in case a Tier 1 was down for some time and needed to catch up. Figure 13a shows the actual rates of export from CERN of well in excess of 2 GB/s, showing not only that the system was perfectly capable, but also that the experiments were taking far more data than originally planned. The right part of that plot is the period of the start of the long shutdown, where the data acquisition had ended. Figure 13b shows the aggregate global data transfer rates. Here this is independent of the LHC running or not, and is fairly continuous in the range 10–15 GB/s.

In terms of the computing resource usage, the plots in fig. 14 show the continual growth in usage of the grid, in both numbers of jobs run, and in terms of the CPU

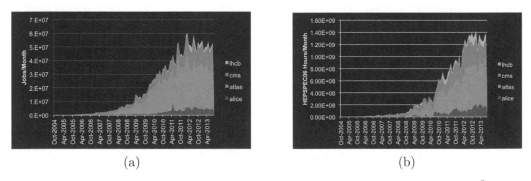

(a)   (b)

Fig. 14. – Processing on the grid: more than 2 million jobs per day, and 1.4×10^9 HEP-SPEC06/month equivalent to 210000 CPU used continuously. (a) Grid jobs run per month. (b) CPU time used globally.

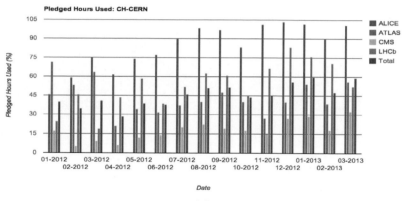

(a)

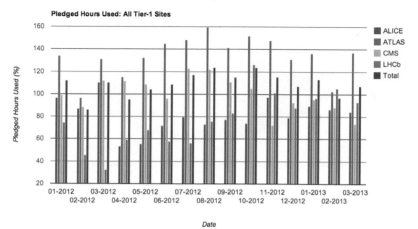

(b)

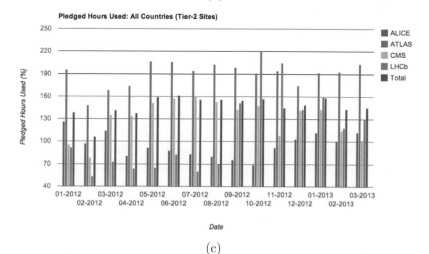

(c)

Fig. 15. – Comparison of CPU usage to pledges. (a) Tier 0. (b) Tier 1. (c) Tier 2.

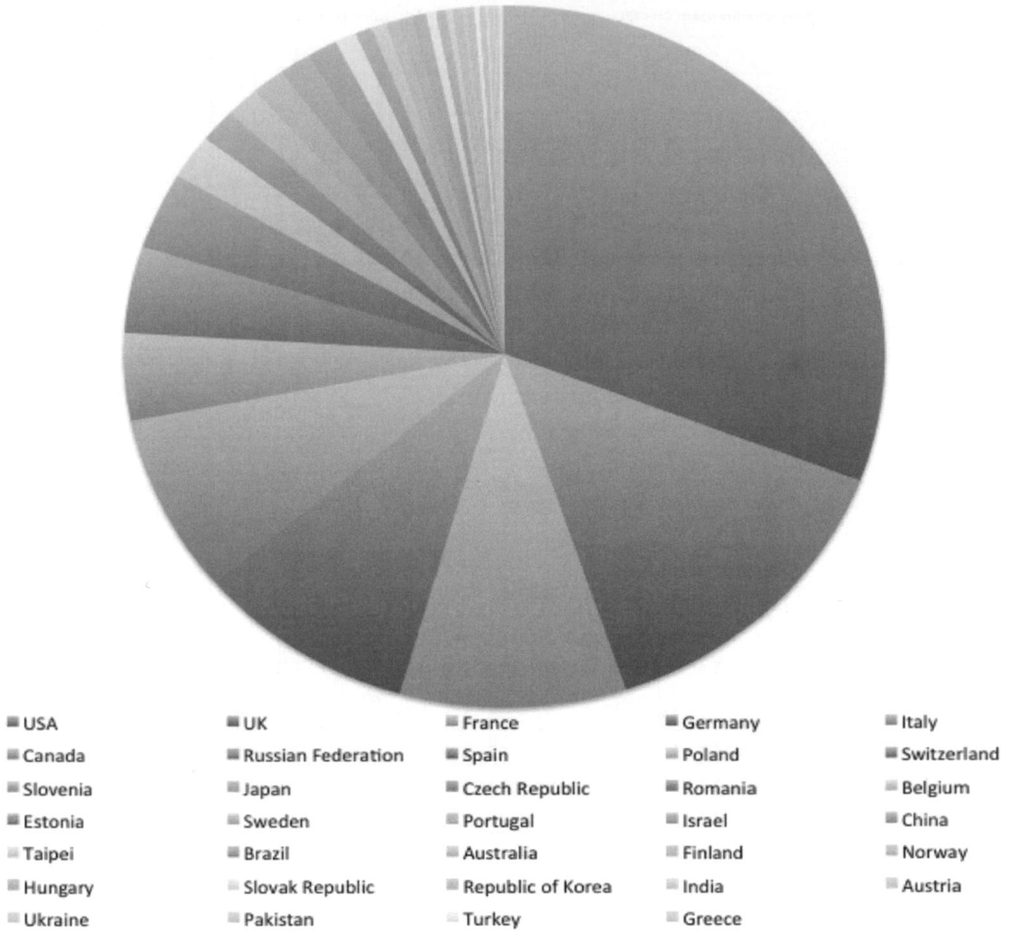

Fig. 16. – Tier 2 CPU delivered by country, according to the MoU.

delivered. This continues to grow, and today corresponds to around 250000 CPU cores in continual use.

This high usage level may be better seen in comparing the actual CPU delivered grid-wide to the CPU pledges from the funding agencies. Figure 15 illustrates this for the various Tiers. Both Tier 1 and Tier 2 sites actually are able to deliver more than promised, and the experiments are using the resources. This shows the CPU requests have been realistic, and necessary. The Tier 0 is slightly different, in that during data taking it is sized to ensure the peak needs of the experiments, so at times may not be so well used. That situation is being addressed for the future.

Finally, in terms of CPU delivery, the pie chart in fig. 16 shows the CPU delivered by each country. It is important to recognise that this is a validation of the grid model. Every country no matter what size of resources it is able to afford, can both contribute, and provide access to LHC data to its physicists.

3˙2. *First evolution of the computing models*. – Even during this first LHC run, there were some very clear lessons that became apparent with real LHC data, despite the extensive testing beforehand. Although the networks were very capable, as demonstrated above, it was clear that the experiments were moving a lot of data around unnecessarily. In addition, the networks were observed to be extremely reliable, and the available bandwidths much better than had been foreseen 10 years earlier.

Even after the first year of data taking the experiment computing models started to evolve as regards data placement and transfer. The strict hierarchical system of data moved between Tier 0 to Tier 1, and then from Tier 1 to dependent Tier 2s only, was seen as too restrictive and inefficient. The desired model was more of a mesh than the hierarchy, with data transfers between any Tiers more desirable. This would mean that the need to pre-place many replicas of important data sets could be avoided if they could be fetched when needed. This actually had the effect of reducing the overall network traffic as it turned out that many data sets were being replicated but then never used.

This changing model raised some concerns over the need to build network connections to support it. The concept of LHCONE [19] was born to provide a network infrastructure between Tier 2 and Tier 1 sites, that left the LHCOPN dedicated to priority Tier 0 - Tier 1 traffic. The concept of LHCONE is a network to serve LHC sites, to share the cost and use of expensive network resources, and importantly to allow the NRENs to potentially separate LHC traffic from other data, and to be able to provide a resource allocated and fund by HEP. The services of LHCONE are the L3VPN and a perfsonar monitoring infrastructure.

The L3VPN is a layer 3 virtual private network providing a dedicated worldwide backbone connecting all LHC sites, and reserved to LHC data. The advantages are a bandwidth dedicated to LHC, not contending with other researchers; a well defined cost for LHC, and trusted traffic allowed to bypass firewalls.

3˙3. *Lessons learned*. – During the first run of the LHC there were a number of lessons learned, and several significant achievements. On the positive side these included:

- the LHC community was able to solve its computing challenge and to make effective use of the available distributed resources;

- the grid could be made to work at huge scale;

- it was extremely effectve in enabling all collaborators worldwide to have access to the LHC data and resources;

- networks became a significant resource that allowed more effective use of other resources (disk);

- the federation of trust and policies is a significant achievement and will continue to be important in future.

However, from our work with other sciences it became clear that grids and cluster computing are not always very suitable for many use cases, and indeed we saw a move away from grids in other communities. We have also seen that the operational cost of such a grid is very high, and reducing this must be a goal for the future. During Run 1 it became clear that a lot of the complexity of the middleware was not necessary, and that there had been an over-insistence of putting too much intelligence (complexity) into the middleware. In many cases that is better managed at the application layer. Finally many of the tools we developed were too HEP-specific to be able to be re-used by other communities. On one hand that is a pity, but expedience and the need for extreme performance led in this direction. Again this is something that could be addressed in future.

4. – The future—the next 10 years

The first Run of the LHC which ended in early 2013 showed that the distributed computing system of WLCG could well deliver in terms of resources and performance. During the long shutdown (LS1) 2013-14, the LHC itself is being upgraded to be able to reach close to its nominal energy and design luminosity. This upgrade, together with advances in the capabilities of the data acquisition systems of the experiments is expected to result in a significantly higher data rate during Run 2 (2015-2018), anticipated to reach up to 50 PB of new data per year. The needs for processing power are expected to be double the scale in Run 1. Figure 17 shows the timescales of LHC upgrades and luminosity expectations for CMS and ATLAS (LHCb and ALICE follow different strategies).

As can be seen in the figure, the integrated luminosity (total number of collected events) is expected to increase significantly with each upgrade, culminating in a major upgrade to HL-LHC for Run 4 which will produce and order of magnitude more data. The sequence of upgrades is the following:

- Run 2: upgrade to design energy and nominal luminosity; factor 2 more data overall;

- Run 3: Phase 1 upgrades to the LHC, to double the luminosity; ALICE and LHCb foresee major detector upgrades and corresponding increases in data rates; ALICE data rate up to 75 GB/s during heavy-ion running; LHCb up to 2 GB/s;

- Run 4: Phase 2 upgrades (HL-LHC); significant increase in luminosity, major upgrades to ATLAS and CMS significantly increasing their data rates; ATLAS anticipates rates of 10–20 GB/s and CMS up to 40 GB/s.

Figure 18 shows the likely increases overall in data volumes and CPU requirements for each of these LHC run periods. It is clear that LHC computing will face some challenges over the next decade in being able to manage this evolution. LHC will remain at the forefront of scientific computing in terms of scale of data and processing over this timescale.

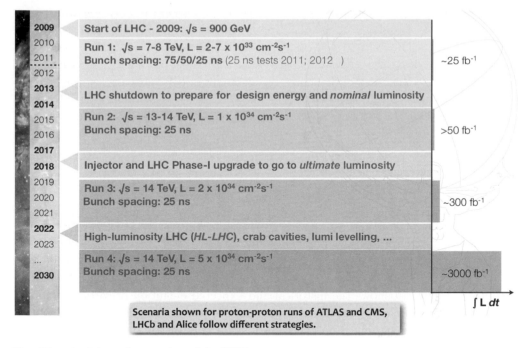

Fig. 17. – Anticipated upgrades of the LHC.

4˙1. *Run 2.* – In early 2014 WLCG published a document [11] describing the evolution of the experiment computing models. That evolution is both a consequence of lessons learned in Run 1, discussed above, and strategies for being able to manage the increased needs in Run 2. In that document a study was made of the expected evolution of key technologies over the coming years, in order to be able to estimates likely costs of

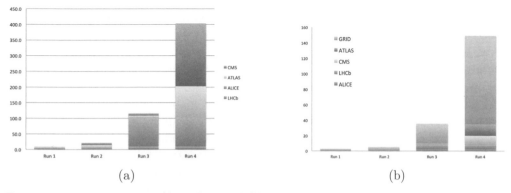

(a) (b)

Fig. 18. – Rough estimates of how data and CPU needs will evolve with the LHC and detector upgrades. (a) Estimates of raw data growth. (b) Estimates of evolution of CPU needs.

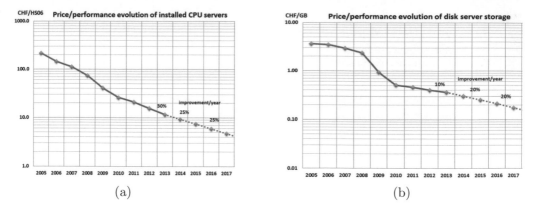

Fig. 19. – Rough estimates of how data and CPU needs will evolve with the LHC and detector upgrades. (a) Price/performance evolution of CPU servers. (b) Price/performance evolution of disk servers.

computing. Figure 19 shows the historical and expected evolution of costs of disk and CPU. Taking into account that some fraction of computing budgets must be invested into replacing old equipment, and other costs such as infrastructure, networking, and increasing power costs, we have estimated that an effective yearly growth that can be achieved with constant budgets is around:

- CPU: 20%,

- Disk: 15%,

- Tape: 15%.

The evolution of CPU and storage needs during Run 2 discussed in [11] is shown in fig. 20. The straight lines on the histograms represent and extrapolation of historical resource purchases during 2008–2012 (so in a sense represent a realistic actual budget), while the curves represent what could be afforded given the yearly growth of technology discussed above, with constant spending. As can be seen the stated requirements fit quite well with the likely budget scenarios at least in 2015 and 2016, but it should be noted that those requirements already included very significant performance improvements in experiments' reconstruction and simulation software.

As noted earlier, available networking has been an enabler of building highly performant distributed systems. Today scientific networks benefit from commercial development driven by services such as video streaming etc. The academic world benefits directly from the increases in capacity and decreases in overall costs as advanced networking becomes commodity. Over the next decade we foresee academic networks to continue to benefit and to follow the same growth pattern observed in the last 10 years. Thus we can anticipate adequate bandwidth at affordable cost, reaching commodity of 10 Tb/s or more in 10 years. The continued evolution of LHC computing depends on this.

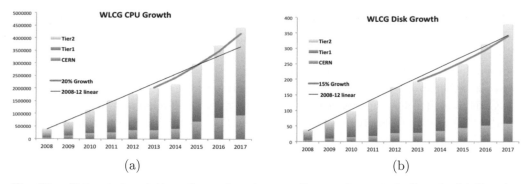

Fig. 20. – Estimated evolution of experiment computing requirements in Run 2. (a) Requirements for CPU. (b) Requirements for disk storage.

In broad terms the strategy for LHC computing in the medium term is to be able to live within budgets that are essentially flat in real terms, whilst being able to gain up to an order of magnitude in event processing throughput. This latter must come either through finding additional resources via new collaborators, and through making much better use of the existing resources. It is important to note that this can only be achieved through an overall systematic optimisation of cost of CPU, storage, networking, and power. Improving CPU performance alone, for example, would likely result in increased I/O needs which may directly impact the storage costs. Today WLCG spends some 60% of its global budget on disk. Strategies to reduce overall cost must take this into account.

Additional strategies must include reducing the cost of operating the grid, and being able to easily make use of opportunistic resources that may become available, without the need for complex and lengthy preparations.

These considerations imply that we must simplify the grid model and the middleware to as thin a layer as possible, focussing on the key functionalities and being able to simplify operations and support. Centralising services at a few large centres also improves reliability and reduces operational effort, while maintaining robustness and performance. Networks again are key here. It is important to insist that all Tier 2s are connected at reasonable bandwidths.

For Run 2 some of the other areas where it is important to improve performance and costs, include improving on software performance (sect. 4˙2), addressing areas where there are potential synergies between experiments, and simplifying the overall system wherever possible. One change compared to Run 1 is the use of the Tier centres according to capabilities rather than according to their strict roles. The peer-peer data access patterns help to do this.

The data management is a very important aspect of the overall system. We observe that we have locally very large storage systems at large centres, with 100 PB archives on tape, with key data stored in several places, and large multi-10's of PB disk caches. Globally the LHC experiments have started to introduce the concept of "data federations" and remote data access. These federations permit wide-area access to data, and allow the experiments to optimise data access from jobs, being able to access files remotely and to fetch them as needed, or in some cases to really do remote I/O across the wide area. This strategy avoids the need to copy files in many situations. Of course, the massive, policy driven predictable data distribution for bulk processing workloads will continue. However, other use cases are becoming increasingly important—for example discovering idle CPU at a site, and then replicating data from a remote site on demand to be able to use the CPU; or real time remote access to data. These strategies have been used when bulk CPU resources (e.g. in commercial cloud providers) have been made available for relatively short periods. Remote data allows us to use the resources simply without the need for complex disk caches. Of course adequate network access is a prerequisite, but for simulation workloads even this is simple to satisfy.

Evolution of how we provision the computing resources is being driven by the costs of the operational effort, and the need, as mentioned earlier, to be able to simply access opportunistic or non-grid resources. The grid middleware layer is much simpler today, as complexity has moved closer to the application layer where it properly belongs. On the other hand model cloud technologies give us a way to implement job submission and management without the need to maintain special grid software with its associated costs. Grid sites today are already deploying cloud management software and using virtualisation to improve their cluster management and efficiencies. An example can be seen with the CERN data centre. Due to space and power limitations a second computer centre for the Tier 0 has been procured in Budapest, some 1000 km from CERN. This remote centre is connected via 2×100 Gb/s dedicated network connections, and is treated as a logical extension of the CERN centre. In order to do this CERN has deployed Openstack [20] cloud software to manage and provision the resources. It is also using the same data management software noted above (data federations) to be able to move data between jobs in the two centres.

Many both WLCG sites are also deploying Openstack or the cloud software, and through the CERN openlab, CERN is engaged on a project to be able to federate these different clouds, including the ability to access commercial Openstack clouds. This is a first step towards a full implementation of a grid structure using cloud software.

4'2. *Software.* – The original requirements as software was developed for LHC included a concern that the software should be easy to use as it was very complex. The users wanted to hide the complexity and wanted stability. Performance and efficiency were not initially the main concerns. During the same period CPU technology trends reached the limit of being able to continually increase clock speeds, since the power demands became unmanageable. Around 2004, clock speeds no longer increased, and additional transistors on chips were used to provide additional cores, or in specialised processing facilities. Consequently most HEP code, that had for many years been scaling in performance with clock speed reached a limit. The introduction of parallelism was key to obtaining improved performance in this new scenario. As we noted above, improved software performance is absolutely essential in being able to continue to increase the ability to make the best use of the available resources.

There are several strategies that can be used to address this problem, and to improve performance:

- Use of many nodes: the current strategy, running many processing on different machines or CPUs. Very effective until now, but does not address the efficiency of use of the individual cores;

- multi-socket and multi-core: a single job using many cores or CPU on the same machine, coupled with intelligent memory management (*e.g.* by the Linux kernel) can reduce the overall memory footprint, and improve the time to solution, but does not improve the overall throughput;

- use of paralellism through the use of Vector facilities, instruction pipelining, instruction-level parallelism, or hardware threading gives potential gains in throughput and in time-to-solution.

It is this last strategy that holds the prospect of significantly improving the software performance. However, the implications, and potential costs are significant. It probably eventually requires re-engineering of the frameworks, data structures and algorithms in order to make real progress. HEP must re-develop a lot of the necessary expertise in concurrent programming, and such a program requires significant investment of effort. However, WLCG has initiated a HEP-wide software foundation [12] to try and address this. Work in this area is just beginning.

4˙**3.** *Longer-term outlook.* – For the longer term future, it is quite likely that the computing needs of LHC Run 3 will be achievable through systematic and painstaking improvements in the existing computing models, algorithms, and techniques currently planned for Run 2, albeit undergoing evolution over that timescale. However, Run 4 represents a very significant step up in data volumes and computing complexity. It is not clear that evolution of today's models can scale to that challenge, and that perhaps a more dramatic re-think is needed. Such a reflection would also be an opportunity to reconsider how HEP experiments can benefit from each other and from experiences in large-scale computing in other sciences. Some of the trends that may become important in the future are noted here.

Already for Run 3, ALICE and LHCb are adapting their computing models to try and put more intelligence closer to the detectors, in order to be able to do more processing earlier, and thus to be able to make decisions on which data to keep. Ultimately storing less data may be a solution to the problem.

The way computing and storage is provisioned may also change significantly. Firstly, it may be more cost-effective to consider having some types of specialised but dedicated resources for certain tasks. An example could be the use of GPU (or other specialised architecture) clusters for workloads such as simulation. If it were the case that the performance gain would be on the scale of an order of magnitude or more compared to a generic cluster, this may well be cost effective. Since simulation is some 50% of the total CPU load this may well be a useful strategy. Along the same lines, commercial or opportunistic resources may web more easily suited to providing simulation capacity, with relatively lightweight needs for data management, leaving dedicated resources to handle the raw data processing and analysis where large scale and highly performant I/O is necessary.

On this timescale we may also see the costs of purchasing computing services drop significantly, so that we may not need to operate our own large compute facilities. Data management will remain an essential core task for HEP data centres, since we will be responsible for the long term curation, but the compute tasks could well be outsourced to large-scale hosting or cloud services. That may give us the benefit of economies of scale without the need to build large private compute clusters, where it will be difficult to pool resources.

Being able to aggregate compute services may then open the way to more advanced analysis models, such as the ability to make use of map-reduce or search-like technologies for physics analysis.

The LHC computing community has demonstrated very large scale data management capabilities. Building on this is essential to improve our own efficiency, testing new models of data placement, caching, and access. It is also important to bring this experience to the wider scientific community to build solutions that can be re-used across disciplines and to move towards open standards. Consequently, and to help improve our own sustainability we should explore collaborations with other data intensive sciences and industry.

The other aspect of data is that of long-term data preservation and open access. This is now very important and highly visible to the public. LHC can provide leadership to build a set of policies and strategies to address this for the broader HEP community, and again in collaboration with other big data sciences.

LHC has had great benefit from the funding made available to develop general purpose e-infrastructures. It is important that HEP maintains its relevance in the broader community by thinking about how the HEP and other data intensive science solutions can converge, From the facilities viewpoint, networking and federated identity services will underly future solutions, together with the provision of an academic (cloud) resource usable by sciences in general. HEP leads the way with experienced and sustainable data archive centres.

Software tool development is essential to allow science communities federate their own resources (in the way that LHC has done). Common tools for data management tasks, workflows and application support will form the basis of a common toolbox. Together with software tools to help communities build citizen-cyberscience infrastructures will help sciences exploit all available resources as well as being an active mechanism for outreach and public engagement. HEP also needs investment in software to make sure that we can adapt our core software and algorithms to make the best use of all possible resources.

4˙4. *Conclusion.* – WLCG has had a great success in building a globally distributed, federated, computing environment (the Grid) that has been the enabler of the production of outstanding physics results. This was the result of a 10-year programme of development, and large scale testing, prior to production running. First contact with real data led to immediate evolution of the computing models and procedures, exploiting technology and real-world experience.

Growing data and processing requirements in a financially-constrained world will be difficult to satisfy in the future without significant changes to the computing models. The evolution of technology helps in this, although software challenges are more complex.

It is clear that despite the coming challenges, there are exciting opportunities to really change the way that HEP does computing and data analysis.

REFERENCES

[1] *ALICE Computing TDR*; CERN-LHCC-2005-018; *ATLAS Computing TDR*; CERN-LHCC-2005-022; *CMS Computing TDR*; CERN-LHCC-2005-023; *LHCb Computing TDR*; CERN-LHCC-2005-019; *LHC Computing Grid TDR*; CERN-LHCC-2005-024, LCG-TDR-001.

[2] *Proposal for Building the LHC Computing Environment at CERN*; CERN/2379/Rev., 2001, http://cern.ch/LCG/PEB/Documents/c-e-2379Rev.final.doc.

[3] *MONARC: Models of Networked Analysis at Regional Centres for LHC Experiments*; http://cern.ch/MONARC.

[4] *Enabling Grids for E-sciencE project*; http://eu-egee.org.

[5] *Geant4 Simulation Toolkit*; http://geant4.cern.ch.

[6] *ROOT: A Data Analysis Framework*; http://root.cern.ch.

[7] FOSTER I. and KESSELMAN K., *The Grid: Blueprint for a New Computing Infrastructure* (Addison-Wesley) 1995.

[8] *The Open Science Grid*; http://opensceincegrid.org.

[9] *The International Grid Trust Federation* (now the Interoperable Global Trust Federation); http://www.igtf.net.

[10] SHOSHANI A., *Storage Resource Managers*; https://sdm.lbl.gov/srm-wg/papers/SRM.book.chapter.pdf.

[11] *Update of the Computing Models of the WLCG and the LHC Experiments*; CERN-LHCC-2014-014; http://cds.cern.ch/1695401.

[12] *The HEP Software Foundation*; http://hepsoftwarefoundation.org.

[13] *The Worldwide LHC Computing Grid Collaboration*; http://cern.ch/lcg.

[14] *The LHC Committee*; http://cern.ch/Committees/lhcc.

[15] *The LHC OPN*; http://cern.ch/lhcopn.

[16] *GEANT Network Project*; http://www.geant.net.

[17] *Energy Sciences Network*; http://www.es.net.

[18] *US LHC Net*; http://cern.ch/lcg/uslhcnet.

[19] *LHCONE*; http://lhcone.net.

[20] *Openstack*; http://www.openstack.org.

Proceedings of the International School of Physics "Enrico Fermi"
Course 192 "Grid and Cloud Computing: Concepts and Practical Applications",
edited by F. Carminati, L. Betev and A. Grigoras
(IOS, Amsterdam; SIF, Bologna) 2016
DOI 10.3254/978-1-61499-643-9-31

Scientific Clouds

D. Salomoni(*)

INFN CNAF - Viale Berti Pichat 6/2, 40127 Bologna, Italy

Summary. — This paper describes some of the main characteristics of Cloud Computing, in particular when used for scientific purposes, highlighting current technologies and possible future developments.

1. – Introduction

Distributed computing has been successfully employed in scientific domains for many years. Specifically, the form of distributed computing called *Grid Computing* [1, 2] was the computational pillar of important scientific discoveries such as the Higgs Boson at the Large Hadron Collider [3]. It enabled the use of computing, storage and network resources distributed around the world by thousands of scientists and made it possible to access and work on large pools of commodity equipment and data in a coherent and effective way.

A description of the Grid Computing architecture is beyond the scope of this paper. However, it is important to note that several international collaborations driven by research institutions started from the early 2000's to first define the needs and then develop the building blocks of such an architecture for scientific applications. Grid-related

---

(*) E-mail: davide.salomoni@cnaf.infn.it

organizations, standardization bodies, projects and infrastructures such as the Open Science Grid [4], the Open Grid Forum [5], DataTag [6], DataGrid [7], Globus [8], EGEE [9], SIENA [10], the European Middleware Initiative [11], the European Grid Infrastrucure [12], and many other national or international initiatives were funded.

This work led to the definition and implementation of essential interoperable blocks for Grid computing and data infrastructures, such as federated authentication mechanisms through the Virtual Organization Membership Service or VOMS [13], computing elements (CE) acting as interfaces to local computing resources such as CREAM [14], ARC [15] and HTCondor [16], storage elements (SE) for distributed data access such as XRootD [17], StoRM [18] and dCache [19], services for the distributed allocation of job requests like the Grid Workload Management System or WMS [20]. These building blocks were then progressively refined and brought to full maturity by many scientists around the world, eventually contributing to realize important scientific discoveries.

As successful as Grid Computing may have been in some scientific domains, it is remarkable that the installation, operation and maintenance of the complex Grid software from both a system administration and a user point of view was never particularly easy. This, and the difficulty in accessing the Grid because of complex and often not very user-friendly interfaces, the partial support for evolving and sophisticated use cases, the need to dedicate sizable human resources to support Grid environments, all this had the consequence that only scientific endeavors with sufficient critical mass and self-organized enough to truly operate in a distributed way were able to fully exploit the power of Grid infrastructures. Other, smaller or less coherent scientific collaborations typically continued to use mainly local hardware, or had to write their own specific software to get access to some form of distributed resources.

Also, Grid Computing never really took off in the industrial sector. This was due to multiple factors, such as the technical complexity of creating federations of commercial providers, the doubts about the strategic sustainability of these federations for the providers themselves, the unclear definition of use cases seen as attractive by private companies, the limited development of distributed technologies exploiting commodity hardware, the fragmentation of both user communities and of potential providers and their data centers, and last but not least the widespread adoption in the commercial world of proprietary, incompatible interfaces and protocols used to access computational and storage resources.

The rise of Cloud Computing, starting from roughly the second decade of this century and driven mostly by the IT industry, is substantially changing the landscape of distributed computing and challenging many of the assumptions that were at the base of Grid Computing, technically and economically.

This paper will give an overview of what we could call *Scientific Clouds*, *i.e.* Cloud services used for scientific applications, and is structured as follows: sect. **2** will list some of the key characteristics that define Cloud Computing, applying them specifically to scientific domains. Section **3** will examine some of the pros and cons of Cloud computing, and is followed by sect.**4**, that will briefly discuss how can applications be written to run on Clouds. Section **5** will then examine open issues that still hinder the full

Fig. 1. – A useless plywood box.

exploitation of Cloud-based resources. Finally, sect. **6** will conclude the paper, providing some suggestions toward possible solutions and potential future work.

So, how is Cloud Computing defined, and what relevance has it got today for scientific work?

2. – Cloud computing: Definition and technology recap

2‛1. *The problem of getting predictions right.* – It is often difficult and perhaps sometimes embarassing to evaluate in advance the promises of new, emerging technologies.

There are abundant occurrences of this fact in history, and even known, well-educated people were often unable to predict the success of now popular inventions or discoveries.

For example, Darryl Zanuck (see fig. 1), co-founder of 20th Century Pictures, when asked in 1946 about a new device, the TV set, was rather direct in stating that

– Television will not last because people will soon get tired of staring at a plywood box every night [21].

Breakthrough ideas indeed do not always derive linearly from the *status quo*. Take for example the famous quote allegedly uttered by Henry Ford (see fig. 2) who, speaking of cars, is supposed to have said (although he may not have actually ever said it):

– If I had asked people what they wanted, they would have said faster horses [22].

Sometimes not only is it difficult to predict the *success* of a certain technology or invention, it is also complex to understand its future *impact* when it is eventually fully applied and understood. With Cloud Computing in science, we are perhaps at a stage where we are still trying to understand whether this is really a viable technology, whether it is really needed, and maybe we still do not clearly see its potentially disruptive model in all its implications.

Fig. 2. – Horses on a Cloud.

2`2. *How to define Cloud Computing*. – The most used definition of *Cloud Computing* is given by the US National Institute of Standards and Technology (NIST) [23]. We can summarize it by saying that

> Cloud Computing supplies information and communication technologies (ICT) as a service.

There are three components that it is interesting to highlight in this definition. Cloud Computing:

– *Supplies something*. This implicitly refers to the existence of one or more Cloud Computing suppliers or providers, immediately pointing to the core fact that a *contract* between a supplier and a consumer exists. What is supplied, in particular, are ...

– *Information and communication technologies*. It is important to underline that Cloud Computing does not necessarily provision just *hardware* (be it virtual or physical), or *infrastructures*, although in the scientific world we are often accustomed to require or directly manage lower-layer details such as CPUs, disks, network connections, etc. It provisions, more generally, *technologies* linked to the handling or processing of information, and to its communication. Finally, it provisions these technologies ...

– *As a service*. The fact that what customers of Cloud Computing technologies see are *services*, points again to a clear definition of a contract between suppliers and users. We shall define more specifically which services we are talking about in sect. **2`3**.

The NIST text in [23] expands this definition into some more details, and in the end one could say that Cloud Computing may be summarized in *five postulates*, according to which Cloud Computing is based on:

1) Self-service, on-demand requests

The customer autonomously ask what he needs, when he needs it (and eventually hopefully gets it). In other words, there is typically no need to define or approve specific provisioning contracts to get the requested services once a relationship with a Cloud provider is in place. What is also implicitly meant by this point is that Cloud Computing provides access to resources through user-friendly interfaces.

2) Access through the network

This will be further discussed later on when covering the differences between virtualization and Cloud Computing. Let us note here that, as obvious as it may seem, this point takes for granted that some sort of (usually broadband) intranet or internet networking is available to the customer. This might not necessarily be the case in all environments or countries [24].

3) Resource pooling

On the one hand, customers of Cloud Computing services do not care about resource details, because these are managed by the Cloud resource providers. On the other hand, Cloud resource providers exploit economies of scale by pooling resources, limiting their under-utilization.

4) Elasticity

By *elasticity* we mean here that a Cloud service should rapidly scale, according to customer needs. Actually, we could say that the theoretical Cloud model foresees *unbounded elasticity*, *i.e.* an infinite capacity to react to and satisfy any customer need. As we shall discuss later, this might not necessarily be the case in the real world, though.

5) A *pay-as-you-go* billing model

In such a model, a Cloud customer only pays for resources that are being or have been used by him, without the strict need to introduce flat-payment models.

These postulates may still seem abstract, but one could derive a metaphor based on a real-world example (keeping in mind the inherent limitation of all metaphors): *a car rental business* (see fig. 3). Looking at car rentals, they indeed seem to expose a set of characteristics similar to those of Cloud Computing [25]:

1) Self-service, on-demand requests

We do not need to set up complex contracts in advance, when we need a rental car: we just pick up the phone, book online or simply show up at a car rental booth.

Fig. 3. – Car rental as a metaphor for the Cloud.

2) Access through the network

Car rental is ubiquitous, in the sense that normally one can rent a car almost everywhere. There are of course some places where car rentals is not available or very expensive. The metaphor here would be that the Cloud Computing business model too is absent or limited when a network is not available, or when its costs are too high.

3) Resource pooling

From the point of view of a customer, it is often more convenient (normally both financially and with regards to possible choices) to select car rental businesses having a large pool of cars. From the point of view of a resource provider (*i.e.* the car rental business), pooling of rental cars is more efficient when acquiring cars, or when answering to user requests.

4) Elasticity

The car rental business is *elastic*, in the sense that the number of available cars usually depends on market requests. So, for example, if there is a scheduled market fair in a given city that could lead to a higher number of car rental requests than usual, the car rental owner may decide to be elastic in its provisioning and move cars from another site where they are not in high demand. But, as we noted when commenting the definition of elasticity in Cloud Computing, elasticity is normally not an unbound property, and rental cars may eventually run out, leading to service disruption.

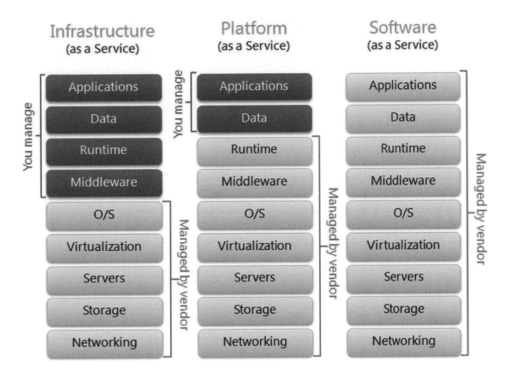

Fig. 4. – The Cloud Service Levels [27].

5) A "pay-as-you-go" billing model

In the car rental business, customers only pay for the time they are using the car. They may subscribe to some *quality of service agreement* such as purchasing an extra insurance, or using facilities such as automatic transmission and air conditioning, but these are items that are paid only for the time the good, *i.e.* the rented car, is used, and not for the entire lifetime of the car.

2˙3. *Who does what?.* – When defining Cloud Computing more in detail, it is useful to explain *who does what* in terms of service and resource provisioning.

In the end, *what is important is how a technology such the Cloud answers concrete user needs*, *i.e.* how it handles *applications*. The stack of components shown in fig. 4 decomposes a generic use case into several blocks, and categorizes Cloud Computing into three *service levels*. For each of them, fig. 4 shows how a given service level maps to some components provisioned or managed by a Cloud provider *vs.* other components provisioned or managed by a Cloud customer. In other words, the keyword *service* is applied in this taxonomy to increasing levels of delegation (from the user to the provider), as we move from left to right.

Let us now proceed to briefly explain the main characteristics of each service level.

a) IaaS, or Infrastructure as a Service

In IaaS, the basic service for Cloud Computing, resources are provisioned in the form of an *infrastructure*. Concretely, a IaaS Cloud could provide a set of machines (be they physical or virtual), some storage space (again, physical or virtual), some form of network connectivity between these resources, and operating systems to run higher-layer services on top of them. A Cloud customer, in a IaaS cloud, retains full control and responsibility for installing, maintaining and operating these services, *i.e.* he is supposed to handle himself topics such as data management services, runtime libraries, databases and applications.

b) PaaS, or Platform as a Service

In a PaaS Cloud, the Cloud not only provides infrastructural resources, but it also gives its customers the possibility to request (using some well-known format) and obtain resources such as application servers (for example, a Java EE application server [26]), databases, or sets of connected resources where some middleware is running (for example, a Hadoop cluster [28]). The customer responsibility is, in this case, to connect its own data and applications to these Cloud-provided services through, for example, Cloud APIs.

c) SaaS, or Software as a Service

With SaaS, a Cloud provider gives its customers ready-to-use applications. These applications will of course utilize some lower layer resources such as databases, operating systems, storage space, etc., none of which is the responsibility of the customer. What a customer does is in this case to simply operate the provisioned applications. A concrete example of SaaS Clouds might be a Cloud-based email service: the user does not need to understand or even know how is email handled, which programs are needed to store and relay emails, and so on: he only uses the service (perhaps through a convenient web-based or mobile interface) for his own purposes.

The three service levels shown above give some insights about what type of resources Cloud Computing may provide. However, they do not say anything about important aspects such as the resiliency, performance, security, etc. of these resources. For a proper categorization and understanding of Cloud Computing, therefore, the *service models* of IaaS, PaaS and SaaS have to be complemented by other models, namely *deployment models* and *isolation models*, as shown in fig. 5.

The deployment models define *where* Cloud services are distributed. Based on these models, Clouds can typically be categorized into four types:

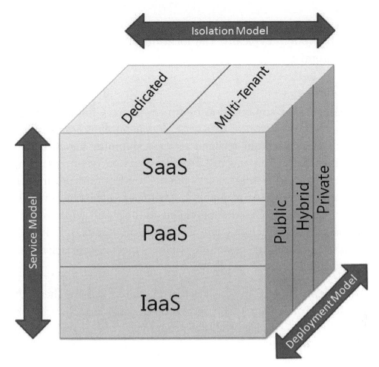

Fig. 5. – The three Cloud dimensions [27].

– *Private Clouds*

In a Private Cloud, services are procured and provisioned for the exclusive *use* of a single organization. We are explicitly talking of use here, because ownership, management, location of the private cloud do not necessarily have to coincide with those of the organization using the Cloud services. An example of a private Cloud is a corporate Cloud, which is meant for exclusive use by a given corporation.

– *Community Clouds*

In a Community Cloud, services are procured and provisioned for a community of organizations typically sharing common goals or regulations. For example, a scientific community might be spread across several countries, and have the single objective to analyze some data in a coordinated way. It might therefore create a community cloud to exploit this through the definition of common services, that could be commonly provisioned by Cloud Computing.

– *Public Clouds*

A Public Cloud is a Cloud service that is offered to the public at large. As in the case of private clouds, we are talking here of the *use* of services offered by the Cloud. Management of these Clouds, on the other hand, could be either private or public. Typically, the location of public clouds is at some Cloud provider premises.

– *Hybrid Clouds*

A Hybrid Cloud is a combination of two or more Clouds of different type; for example, a combination of a private and a public Cloud. A hybrid cloud is useful when, for example, resilient services spanning Cloud belonging to different administrative domains are needed, or when resources such as hardware, application or data available on a given Cloud infrastructure need to be complemented by resources available on another infrastructure. It is the most complex form of the Cloud deployment models and while so far there are not many concrete, production examples of hybrid clouds, it is likely to assume increasing importance in the coming years, especially for scientific applications, for both organizational and financial reasons.

Isolation models define *how* Cloud services are isolated among them. Although very important, this point is often not taken into proper consideration, for example in the selection process of a Cloud service or Cloud provider.

According to isolation models, Clouds can be based on:

– *Dedicated infrastructures*, where resources are reserved, and isolated, for certain uses or customers.

– *Multi-tenant infrastructures*, where several customers, or several types of similarly grouped customers, share some resources. For example, in a multi-tenant Cloud, a database service offered to two different customers might be based on some common back-end. This point, often known only to the Cloud provider and transparent to the user(s), may have an important impact of the quality on the service that is being offered.

The isolation type of Clouds is indeed essential in many regards. For example, issues such as disaster recovery, segmentation or resources, data protection, security of applications, auditing of critical logs, are all items that are typically impacted by Cloud isolation models. Normally, establishing and operating a dedicated Cloud is understandably more expensive than establishing and operating services provisioned through a multi-tenant Cloud.

2˙3.1. The Cloud Hype. A very popular picture, often presented to illustrate how Cloud Computing is actually composed of many technologies, and how each of them typically has a different level of maturity (and of hype), is shown in fig. 6.

In fig. 6, one can appreciate the typical pattern of technologies: they often start up rapidly thanks to novel ideas, intuitions or developments, then go through a period of inflated expectations. Not all expectations are normally realized, so there might later be a time of failures and disillusionment, which is essential, because it allows the technology

Figure 1. Hype Cycle for Cloud Computing, 2012

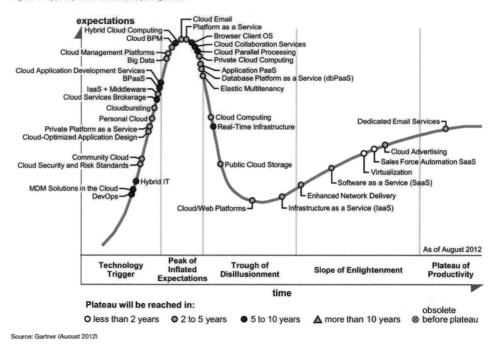

Fig. 6. – A most popular picture about Cloud hype [29].

to mature and properly assess its limits. Finally, the refined or surviving parts of the technology come to fruition in what is called the "Plateau of productivity".

2˙4. *Virtualization or Cloud Computing?*. – A frequently asked question is what is the relationship between virtualization technologies and Cloud Computing.

Virtualization predates the Cloud, and is often seen as the technological foundation for Clouds. However, strictly speaking, Cloud Computing can be provisioned also *without* resorting to virtualization technologies. At the same time, virtualization often allows to reduce both operational and capital costs and, in general, may lead to greater efficiency in resource utilization (barring potential performance issues, which will be covered later on).

At the same time, a reality check on the service provider side is often useful, especially when thinking about virtualization applied to private infrastructures such as those operated by many scientific communities. As obvious as it may seem, being able to rapidly provision many virtual machines (VMs) is *per se* not very efficient, if *procurement processes* for the provisioning and installation of the physical servers needed to host the VMs take months to finalize.

Also, hypes aside, one should alway ask himself whether the time spent for installing and managing a virtualization layer is recovered by the savings associated to not having to work with physical resources only, since this time might not be negligible. Especially when dealing with many resources (although this really applies to infrastructures having as little as some tens of physical servers), it is therefore essential that automated installation, configuration, monitoring and accounting tools connected to a virtualization infrastructure are fully adopted.

Having said that, virtualization technologies do provide a substantial number of *advantages* over directly using physical resources:

– *Server consolidation*. VMs allow to better use physical servers. Several VMs can run on a single host, and often not all of them will be fully using server resources at the same time, so it is convenient to multiplex a physical host into multiple virtual hosts. Reducing the number of physical hosts also reduces procurement overhead, and *may* also simplify activities such as system management and monitoring, if coupled with efficient, easy-to-use workflows.

– *Sandboxing*. VMs allow to *sandbox*, or isolate, applications. This is useful in many cases like, for example, when doing software development, testing and debugging. Or for security reasons (but see also later words about VM security), because applications running on VMs are isolated and do not normally interfere with each other. Last but not least, sandboxing is useful also when creating customized VMs for dedicated environments dictated by special customer needs.

– *On-demand creation of VMs*. VMs can be easily created or destroyed. This dynamic nature of VMs is what makes it possible to instantiate and offer resources on-demand, be they just plain VMs, or more complex services created on top of them.

– *Decoupling between hardware and software*. VMs decouple hardware and software layers. This makes it possible for example to dynamically suspend or resume a VM independently from what happens to other VMs on the same physical host, or to migrate VMs across physical hosts, with various degrees of sophistication.

– *Testing, Data Preservation*. Effective testing of new operating systems or of new versions of applications can profit from the prompt availability of VMs. Moreover, in the scientific world, special importance can also be attributed to running *old versions* of applications, for example to satisfy the need to access scientific data that was collected perhaps decades ago through old programs or platforms (data preservation and access).

– *Emulation services*. VMs can help in cases where there might be the need to execute applications that are not compatible with the operating system installed on the physical host, or when certain hardware might need to be emulated, because native systems are not readily available or convenient to use.

Together will the advantages brought by virtualization technologies, it is important to also mention some of their *potential disadvantages*:

– *Security*. With VMs, the same physical hardware handles several operating systems. This inherently increases the probability of having bugs and the potential number of *attack vectors*. These are several ways through which a bug can spread from one place to another, possibly compromising the security of the entire system. VMs indeed introduce a number of these vectors, that could by exploited by malicious users:

- VM-to-VM network attacks, where VMs typically installed on the same physical hosts, or in the same network subnet shared by different physical hosts, can be compromised through network communications.

- VM-to-Hypervisor attacks. We will not discuss here the technology used to manage VMs on a physical host in any detail, but normally VMs are handled by a software layer called *hypervisor*, such as KVM [30], Xen [31] or VMware [32]. The hypervisor is often a process running with special privileges. For example, in Linux, KVM is a kernel module, and Xen is a software directly connected to the hardware resources of the physical host. If an attacker manages to gain some control of the hypervisor, everything running on the host (*e.g.*, all VMs) can be compromised.

- VM-to-QEMU attacks. Sometimes VMs are mediated by a piece of software called QEMU [33]. QEMU is a complex and large software, and because of that the chances for it to have bugs are not negligible. If QEMU gets compromised, an attacker can potentially reach the operating system layer and take control of all processes or resources available there, including VMs.

- *Performance*. Normally, having an intermediate layer in software causes performance penalties. Since typically virtualization is a software layer, performance penalties can indeed occur, first of all for the physical machine, due to some overhead induced by VM management. Then, processes running on VMs may have lower performance than corresponding processes running on physical resources. From a practical point of view, the performance penalty for CPU-bound processes on VMs is nowadays rather low and in the order of some percentage points [34,35]. Less negligible, however, is often the performance penalty associated to I/O-bound processes [36].

Coming back to VM security, it is essential to stress that this is not something to be taken lightly. There are naturally security issues linked to wrong configurations or human errors, for example for what regards network isolation. This problem is made more likely by the fact that properly configuring VM networking and other VM-related characteristics is potentially a very complex area.

But all virtualization layers are also susceptible to explicit malicious attacks. Here are some examples of recent security exploits involving common hypervisors:

- CloudBurst, 2008. Target: VMware, result: full breakout.

- Xen Ownage Trilogy, 2011. Target: Xen, result: full breakout.

- VirtuNoid, 2011. Target: KVM, result: full breakout.

– SYSRET-64, 2012. Target: Xen, result: full breakout.

– VMDK Has Left The Building, 2012. Target: VMware, result: data leakage, loss.

– KVM IOAPIC, SET MSR, TIME, 2013. Target: KVM, result: DoS, potential breakout.

First of all, it is important to note that all exploits above were fixed by appropriate security patches. But the list shows that exploits target *all* common hypervisors and that protecting them from exploits must be an ongoing task. A useful text describing problems and mitigation measures is the OpenStack Security Guide [37], born out of the popular OpenStack framework [47] but containing security concepts of general usefulness.

Concluding this short consideration of security issues, it is important to note that there is a clear positive impact on security brought by the adoption of *efficient provisioning and configuration systems*. In fact, such systems can contribute to mitigate configuration errors and to consistently and automatically apply patches to all systems as soon as they are available.

In summary, how can we compare virtualization and Cloud Computing? Looking at what was discussed above, *installing / reinstalling servers or applications using VMs is not per se Cloud Computing.* We can easily verify this statement checking if and how the characteristics of plain virtualization technologies fit with the five postulates of Cloud Computing described in sect. **2˙2**:

1) Self-service, on-demand requests?

   No. Typically, VMs are not directly provisioned by end users, but rather by IT departments.

2) Access through the network?

   No. Plain deployment of VMs is normally limited to local, internal customers who do not remotely access them.

3) Resource pooling?

   Yes. As a matter of fact, resource pooling and server consolidation is one of the main traits of virtualization.

4) Elasticity?

   No. Virtualization by itself is just a way of providing emulated or virtual environments. They are often provisioned by IT departments, not necessarily in dynamic nor scalable ways.

5) A "pay-as-you-go" billing model?

   No. With plain virtualization, billing is often defined according to tradition flat bills rather than to "pay-as-you-go" models.

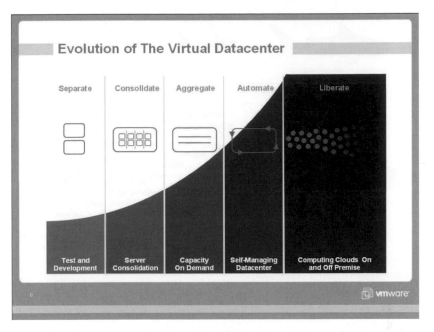

Fig. 7. – The evolution of the virtual datacenter [38].

As one can see, therefore, virtualization only partially fulfills the five Cloud postulates.

Figure 7 shows the evolution of a data center adopting first simple virtualization technologies, and then Cloud Computing services. As we move from left to right in the figure, the data center becomes more and more sophisticated, and what started as a simple testing virtual environment becomes a fully distributed infrastructure ("Computing clouds on and off premises"). The picture also shows the evolutionary and increasing importance of points that were mentioned earlier, such as dynamic, on-demand allocation of resources, full automation of provisioning and monitoring procedures, and distributed access.

3. – Pros and cons

Having now defined the main characteristics of Cloud Computing, it is important to understand its main advantages and disadvantages. Starting from the five Cloud postulates discussed above, one can definitely derive a large set of pros and cons. Here, we shall be concentrating on just some topics that can be considered of relevance specifically for scientific applications and users.

Let us start first with the observation that Cloud computing is normally based on the exploitation of commodity hardware, *i.e.* hardware found at massive scale on the market.

This, coupled with the increasing performance of such hardware, contributes to drive prices down and, as fig. 8 shows, also contributes to reverse a pattern in distributed computing: while in the past decades large mainframes based on proprietary hardware and

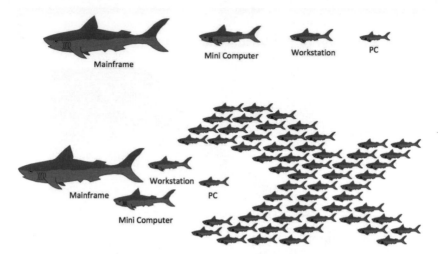

Fig. 8. – Sharks in distributed computing.

software technologies were considered as the only serious option for heavy computational tasks, the combined power of many distributed commodity CPUs, storage and networks challenges this assumption. We are not arguing here that mainframes designed to run specific High-Performance Computing (HPC) applications are to be completely and readily supplanted by Cloud-based services; however, there is a definite trend that shows how Cloud-provisioned resources can be a viable option (technically and financially) for many High-Throughput and also for some High-Performance Computing applications.

This fact is also testified by the abundant investments that major corporations are making on Cloud infrastructures and Cloud software. A typical example, recent at the time this paper was written, is given by Cisco, that in March 2014 announced that together with it partners it would build "the largest global intercloud" [39].

According to that announcement, Cisco intended to invest *over $1 billion* "to build its expanded cloud business". A stated goal of the Cisco intercloud, in particular, is to allow the combination and movement of data and applications across hybrid Clouds. Figures given by Cisco report a target market for the company and its partners increasing in value roughly four times (from $22 billion to $88 billion) between 2013 and 2014 [40].

An interesting picture showing how typical budget for IT departments is used in traditional environments is shown in fig. 9. One could see here that more than half the budget is used to maintain the infrastructure, followed by another third used to maintain existing application. Only about a tenth of the budget is used to actually develop *new* applications or products. In a fast-moving and highly competitive world this is clearly a problem. Cloud Computing, with its promise to offload the burden of maintaining infrastructural services, and with the offer of user- and developer-friendly ways to interface to its services, aims to substantially change the ratio between the various IT spending chapters.

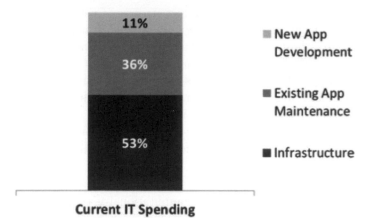

Source: Microsoft.

Fig. 9. – How is money spent in a traditional IT department.

3˙1. *Pros.* – The pros for Cloud Computing that we shall consider in this section mainly center around economic sustainability (cost reduction), ease of use (flexibility and scalability), ease of access, and finally around the Cloud as an enabling technology to create opportunities for new developments or ideas.

3˙1.1. **Cost reduction.** Pooling resources, one of the Cloud Computing foundation principles, allows providers to *lower per-server costs*. With Cloud Computing hardware procurement costs may often become lower, because of economies of scale (the more resources I centrally buy, the more I am likely to get better prices).

Aggregating resources into a limited number of sizable data centers, rather than distributing them across many small centers, also normally allows to *reduce and optimize manpower costs*. The more customers there are, the less overhead there is on per-customer management costs. And the same economies of scale that apply to resources and manpower can also lead to *lower energy bills*, typically one of the largest shares of costs in IT budget. Finally, resource aggregation normally leads to an *increase in efficiency utilization*; and resource aggregation, if coupled with good planning and organization, can also lead to *lowering the relative complexity of the infrastructure*.

From the users' point of view, the cost reductions that a provider can realize thanks to the Cloud normally translate directly into lower costs to access and use Cloud resources, when compared with the cost of traditional, non Cloud-based resources.

3˙1.2. **Flexibility and scalability.** These benefits directly derive from some of the core Cloud principles.

For example, Cloud-based *self-service provisioning* should be compared with typical procurement time in a traditional data center. With the possibility to *scale out requests*, a provider could avoid to purchase new resources if they can be provisioned (perhaps even temporarily) through other Cloud infrastructures. Customer-wise, this scalability feature of Clouds is what, at least in theory, allows one to neglect details about where and how are resources provisioned, and focus simply on the needs.

But flexibility in Clouds also brings other advantages, for example in the *mitigation of growth uncertainties*. Both in the business and in the research worlds, growth patterns are often unknown for a long time. With traditional computational infrastructures, this translates (for both business and research use cases) in the need to make guesses that can lead, if proven wrong, to either under- or over-provisioning of resources. In both instances this can be very inefficient, technically and financially. The dynamic nature of Clouds allows to overcome this difficulty.

Growth uncertainties can also be more technology related. For example, when undertaking a scientific challenge involving computational needs, it might not be known from the onset whether the typical computational workload type to be considered will be mostly CPU-intensive or mostly I/O-intensive. The two workload types are often exploited through different types of resources. Cloud Computing allows to avoid static provisioning of resources belonging to one or the other type. Tests could be carried on with for example Cloud resources optimized for CPU-intensive work; in case they do not fit well, this choice can be dynamically changed, and tests could go on using instead Cloud-provisioned resources optimized for I/O-intensive work. In other words, the dynamic nature of Cloud Computing allows one to avoid too much early commitment to technology or financial exposure.

3˙1.3. Democratization of resources. One could say that Cloud Computing provides easier, cheaper access to distributed resources, and therefore is an ideal *conduit for a more widespread access* to them. For instance, a Cloud infrastructure may facilitate access and utilization to resources by SMEs or by small scientific experiments, which otherwise might have been unable to engage in problems because of time- or cost-related limits.

In general, Cloud computing, especially with its promise of infinite resources, tends to *shift problem models from batch to real-time or to quasi-real-time*. And, in particular with SaaS solutions (*e.g.*, Google Apps, Dropbox), Cloud Computing can provide access to ubiquitous resources on multiple platforms, including mobile platforms, without the need to install applications, operating systems, costly licenses, etc.

3˙1.4. Business opportunities. For what regards *business opportunities*, Cloud Computing offers both private or public companies the possibility to make profits that are not linked simply to reselling software frameworks developed by big corporations. For example, using an open source Cloud framework, it is possible to create and offer a portfolio of Cloud services linked to fields such as integration into existing apps, training, customization, support, etc. The open source model is in this case particularly attractive because it does not require purchasing licenses and because if provides open interfaces. It is indeed already being exploited by several companies offering Cloud-related services, such as, for example, RedHat, Canonical, Mirantis, IBM, HP and many others.

This is still a sort of a greenfield that could be exploited even by public institutions (for example, by research institutions) willing to take some risks in order to make money that could actually be reinvested for their own business. On the other hand, it is important to realize that traditional computational services are nowadays quite efficient, and that it is therefore very difficult to differentiate and make money out of them. Hence, when evaluating these potential business opportunities one should:

– Leverage state-of-the-art technologies. This normally comes at some non-negligible cost, and a conscious investment is therefore needed.

– Profit from big economies of scale, for example consolidating data centers and servers.

So, how can you differentiate yourself in the Cloud world? The key point is to leverage new services and new ways to consume them [41].

Now, *why is this relevant for scientific clouds?* Because a key question to be asked is *whether current commercial clouds are capable of properly supporting scientific needs.* As will be shown in a subsequent section, there are still a number of technological gaps that may make commercial clouds not ideal for scientific work. So, what could be done is to *extend* what is available, providing these extensions as a service to ours or other communities. The slogan here would be something like *scientists for scientists*, and a business case could be created out of this. Maintenance and sustainability of new features created by scientists for scientific clouds, in other words, might in some way be offloaded away from scientific users, for example through commercial (paid) support.

3˙2. *Cons.* – There is of course the other side of the coin, *i.e.* the cons of Cloud Computing, some of which we already mentioned, for instance when we spoke of security issues. In this section we shall cover some other points that might especially be important if, for example, one wanted to do away with privately-owned resources, and adopt Cloud resources provisioned through a commercial Cloud provider.

In many of the sections below we shall use as an example the Terms and Conditions that at the time of this writing govern the use of the Amazon Web Services (AWS) [42], one of the most popular Cloud services in the world. However, similar terms and conditions are defined by many other Cloud providers and should not be taken as pointing to issues that are peculiar to Amazon only.

For the sake of conciseness, we shall call the AWS Terms and Condition document *TC* in subsequent sections.

3˙2.1. Non-exclusive rights. The TC text says (§13.3), that Amazon could develop products directly competing with what you yourself develop on AWS, or adopt technologies that you are using. You could do the same and compete with what Amazon develops, but of course one might be worried that Amazon enjoys substantial more insights than you into what is put on their servers than viceversa.

Amazon need not do the work itself, though. The same paragraph states that Amazon could assist somebody else (maybe your own competitors) in developing products competing with yours.

What in the end this means is that you basically lose full ownership for "products, services, concepts, systems, or techniques" that you develop when using AWS.

3˙2.2. Unavailability. The TC says (§11) that Amazon is not liable for unavailability of data or services. These could be due to "power outages, system failures or other interruptions". Therefore, you should protect your own data or services and not count on the Cloud provider to do it for you. Even more worrisome is perhaps the fact the Cloud provider is according to this TC not liable even for "unauthorized access to, alteration of, or the deletion, destruction, damage, loss or failure to store any of your content or other data".

3˙2.3. No guarantees. The TC has also an interesting section (§10) on Disclaimers. There, one can read that there is not any warranty that the service offerings of the Cloud provider will be "uninterrupted, error free or free of harmful components" (whatever these harmful components might be).

The TC goes on then to say that there is also no warranty that "any content, including your content or the third party content, will be secure or not otherwise lost or damaged".

Now, what if we decided to use this Cloud provider to store some tens of petabytes of unique scientific data? We might make a backup at our own premises, but what would be the point then of using the Cloud provider in the first place?

3˙2.4. Responsibility. The point above related to the need to having one's own backup is stated indeed very clearly in the TC in §4.2, when it says that "You are responsible for properly configuring and using the Service Offerings and taking your own steps to maintain appropriate security, protection and backup of Your Content".

On the one hand, this means that, again, one should not count on the reliability of the service (and, again, what if we had, as is often the case, petabytes of data to store?); on the other hand, we as users are fully *responsible* to take appropriate steps to avoid unauthorized access to our content. However, the systems that ultimately serve our content and not under our full control: they are owned by the Cloud provider and, as stated in sect. **3˙2.2**, the Cloud provider is not liable for any authorized access to our content.

3˙2.5. Data privacy. Data privacy is not an easy topic. What happens, for example, when a contract with a Cloud provider gets cancelled, either by us or by the Cloud provider? How can we make sure that all our data is removed? This is perhaps an even more complicated question when the content is stored on social media such as Facebook.

The TC states (§7.3) that the provider "will not erase any of Your Content", at least during the 30 days following termination. But what happens after these 30 days to our content is unclear. Who will handle it and how?

Also, how can we avoid vendor lock-in? An answer to this question would be that we should only be using Cloud providers offering open interfaces to move data, code or services in and out their infrastructure. But do we really know whether this can be done, and done securely?

An even trickier question is about data location: *where is my data*? It might be stored in locations that are not subject to the jurisdiction of my own country. And, do we know whether it is subject to scrutiny or tapping by external agents [43]?

3˙2.6. Maturity. Cloud Computing is a set of modern technologies sometimes not completely stable or reliable, due to their relative youth. This means that many times involving experts for tuning of both private Clouds and of Cloud applications is needed. One should actually foresee that, in particular for fields that do not precisely map with what the market is mostly asking for (*e.g.*, scientific needs), the help of a set of competent professionals may often be necessary.

However, exactly in order to avoid complex configurations, sometimes shortcuts are taken, even with commercial Clouds. This could have an impact for example in areas linked to security or performance. These shortcuts may even go unnoticed unless something special happens: think about a weak network configuration that might allow silent wiretapping of your communications. Even applying the relatively frequent security patches could be seen by a Cloud provider as a burden, and as a consequence it can happen that task is skipped to avoid complex reconfigurations, thus endangering the Cloud customers.

On the other hand, in order to avoid missing a customer or a use case, sometimes "non production-ready" solutions are offered, without considering the necessary steps needed to properly address these cases.

3˙2.7. The big misunderstanding. One of the core Cloud postulates is (see sect. **2˙2**) that the Cloud should be *elastic*. This theoretically means that, whatever amount of resources a customer is willing to ask (and pay for) to a Cloud provider, he will get them.

But in the real world capacity is not infinite (nor are credit card limits, in general). Hence, unless maybe we are willing to pay some hefty over-provisioning costs, resources might not be available when we actually need them. Or, if available, they might not have all the technical features we need. How would we cope with such an occurrence?

3˙3. *Private vs. public Clouds*. – Looking at the pros and cons described above, a natural question seems to be: is it then more reasonable to adopt a Private or Public Cloud infrastructure?

The answer is again not easy, because it depends on the use cases and on the importance attributed to some of the points that were discussed earlier. Figure 10 is a useful categorization of Private Cloud Preference *vs.* Public Cloud Economics. An interesting thing that can be glanced from the figure is the perhaps obvious consideration that for small, isolated communities (or for small scientific experiments, although one could question how much would these be considered isolated) the burden of running a private cloud does not pay off, unless other considerations such as security or performance are given particular relevance. In those cases, a public Cloud infrastructure might be the best solution.

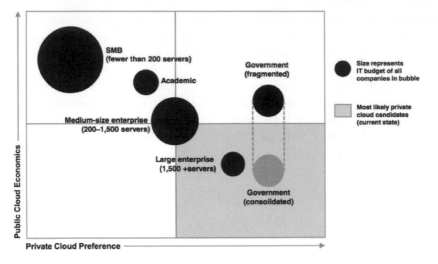

Fig. 10. – Private *vs.* Public Clouds.

3˙4. *More pros or cons then?* – If we had to strike a balance of pros and cons of Cloud Computing, what would it be the conclusion in the end?

From the discussion above it appears that first and foremost we need to understand what exactly a Cloud is, and in particular what are its various dimensions. The choice of which type of dimension to favor, for example when considering deployment or isolation models, ultimately depends by the importance we attribute to the consequences that are attached to each choice.

As long as we understand the characteristics of these dimensions, for instance with regards to choosing a public Cloud *vs.* establishing a private one (or selecting a hybrid model), the economic and sustainability advantages associated to Cloud Computing seem to easily outweigh the cons.

However, we still need to assess what it means to run Cloud applications, and whether there are gaps that prevent full exploitation of Cloud services for scientific tasks. This is what we shall do in the next sections.

4. – Apps in the Cloud

A key question, assuming that our choice of a Cloud Computing provider can answer issues such as vendor independence, use of standard interfaces, cost savings, etc., is: *how to migrate applications to the Cloud?*

Let us consider what this means from the start. *What are the technical or business reasons leading to this migration?* Are they sound?

Typically, answers could span one of more of these areas:

- Cost reduction, due for example to resource pooling and pay-per-use.

- "Business agility", due for example to simplification of application deployment. Think about a PaaS service automatically provisioning redundant application servers.

- Management savings, due for example to performance improvements (thanks, *e.g.*, to high-performance platforms or to the auto-scaling of resources), or to the simplification of system administration duties (thanks, *e.g.*, to the outsourcing of operational responsibilities).

Then, what type of Cloud are we considering for our migration, *e.g.* are we targeting a private of public Cloud infrastructure? Answers in this case should consider for instance these points:

- Will my application generate a substantial amount of wide-area network (WAN) traffic? WAN traffic is typically very expensive, especially when going to/from public Clouds.

- What type of security am I expecting from the Cloud services? (see the previous points on Cloud security)

- Is there any integration of my app with other legacy applications? For example, some applications have a strong coupling with other applications running on AS400 or similar platforms that normally will not run on a public Cloud. What will this imply?

This first level of analysis is very important to avoid or at least mitigate false expectations. Similarly, it is key to realize what the benefits and limitations of each solution for our specific application would be. This task is normally not trivial, and adequate time and effort should be dedicated to get reasonable clarity on this.

Let us now proceed to consider possible simple migration strategie for SaaS, PaaS and IaaS Clouds:

- Migration to a SaaS service

    Are there readily-available SaaS alternatives to our application, that can be run through some Cloud provider? In reality, this is not a migration, but rather a transposition of applications. It is worth considering, though.

    Note that even with a SaaS solution, application data might need to be actually migrated to the Cloud, and this could mean some further costs. It is also important to consider long-term expenditures, that might be related to the number of users accessing the application: is there a per-user licensing agreement with the Cloud provider? Does the SaaS cost depend on network traffic generated to/from the application? Does the application handle sensitive data? If so, security characteristics offered by the Cloud provider should be closely evaluated.

– Migration to a PaaS service

Is a PaaS model applicable to our application?

This might be the case if *e.g.* the application were based on standard application servers, such as Java EE or .NET, since these could be available through some PaaS service. A Cloud provider might also provide other popular PaaS services, such as database back-end systems (be they SQL- or noSQL-based).

An important fact to consider, for both performance and security reasons, is whether the application server infrastructure (and / or the back-end databases) are shared with other customers, since this may or may not be acceptable, depending on the concrete use case. Also, it might happen that not all the PaaS features needed to our application are available through the selected Cloud provider, so a careful evaluation is needed here as well.

– Migration to a IaaS service

Are there any hardware or software compatibility issues of the application *vs.* what the Cloud provider offers as IaaS? For example, an application might be constrained to run on ARM, or on a given operating system running on an x86-compatible platform: are these supported by the Cloud provider?

Other IaaS-level questions must also be asked: for example, it might happen that our VM, provisioned by a certain Cloud provider on some physical hardware, shares the same subnetting policies of VMs belongings to other customers. Is this case problematic for what regards security? Also, what scalability is there? How is load-balancing implemented (if implemented) for instance when auto-scaling resources on the Cloud? Actually, is there any auto-scaling feature available, and what would be its policies?

4˙1. *A typical application architecture.* – Let us assume that our application cannot easily be instantiated on a simple IaaS Cloud. We may need to rethink the overall architecture, adopting well-known typical computer science patterns in designing the "new app". First and foremost, when dealing with multi-tiered applications one should normally consider three tiers:

– The *data management tier*, dedicated to managing databases, be they relational or not.

– The *business logic tier*, typically through application platforms such as Java EE or .NET.

– The *presentation tier*, interfacing the application with the user or with other external components.

If the application were well structured according to this pattern, it might be possible to migrate individual tiers independently to the Cloud. For instance, one could start by

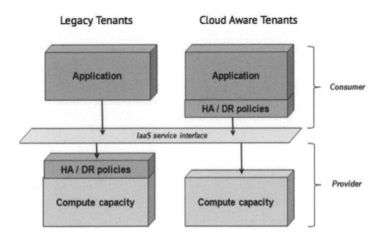

Fig. 11. – Cloud awareness.

moving to the Cloud the presentation layer only. However, it is not a given that this is effective nor that it is advantageous, for example when there is high network traffic across tiers. Thorough *application profiling* is therefore needed to evaluate potential associated costs and requirements for what regards CPU, RAM, storage (*e.g.* IOPS) and network needs.

4˙2. *Is my application cloud-friendly?*. – If from previous steps we have determined that we could move our application to the Cloud (perhaps considering some code or architectural rewriting), what would be the best way of doing that?

Should we just encapsulate the application in a VM, provision that VM from a IaaS cloud, and be done with it? Or is there a better way of defining what is a *cloud-friendly application*?

Figure 11 shows in a simple schematic way the difference between legacy and cloud-aware applications, while table I lists some of the characteristics of the two models.

TABLE I. – *Legacy vs. Cloud Applications.*

Legacy applications	Cloud applications
Client-server	Distributed
Monolithic, no horizontal scalability	Stateless
Fail-over in the infrastructure	Fail-over in the app
Scaling in the infrastructure	Scaling in the app
Scale up	Scale out

In summary, Cloud applications should keep as less state as possible, and in general their services should also depend as less as possible on features provided by a given Cloud infrastructure. Cloud infrastructures, in this sense, offer much simpler services than those offered by complex virtualization frameworks. If an application really wants to exploit Cloud features such as for example vendor independence, auto-scaling, distributed access and deployment, it should behave so as not to depend on infrastructural details.

There is an analogy that is often used when discussing the difference between legacy and Cloud applications [44]. *Legacy applications are treated as pets*: they are unique and irreplaceable. On the other hand, *Cloud applications are treated as cattle*: when for example a cow falls ill, we replace it with another one taken from the pool we have at our disposal. All of them share the same identical technical function. Also, if we want to produce more milk, we just use more cows: this is what in Cloud terms is called to *scale out*, while in legacy apps what is normally done is to *scale up*, *i.e.* obtain more powerful resources (perhaps a bigger pet, if we wanted to stick to the analogy).

4˙3. *Which adaptation?*. – While each application should be examined on its own merit when considering its migration to the Cloud, the following list providers some general implementation characteristics to be considered when rewriting (or writing from scratch) an application for the Cloud [45]:

– Applications are often to be offered with web-based front-ends, and there are ways to write increasingly sophisticated user interface just using standard browsers.

– Application deployment should be thought as the deployment of a set of "instances" rather than of a monolithic piece of code.

– It should be possible to replicate each instance, in order to realize the scaling out of the application when necessary. The scaling policies should be clearly defined.

– The application in itself should be designed so that it can be decomposed into a set of services.

– If the application can have one instance per service, then scaling out can be applied not simply to the entire application, but to each of its services. in order to scale a service, therefore, one could replicate only the instance that provides that service.

– It is often necessary to keep *some state* for an application. In that case, this state, for example a shared configuration across all instances of an application, should be kept in a distributed database (which should have some internal replication features), in order to avoid dependencies on a particular Cloud infrastructure.

This procedure of thinking at applications so that they are somewhat infrastructure-independent and inherently scalable often requires a thorough rewrite of the internal logic and expert advice. But it is only in this way that we can start using Cloud resources exploiting their benefits, instead of just limiting ourselves to see the Cloud as just a virtual hardware provider (although already considering Cloud infrastructures this way has some benefits, compared to traditional infrastructures).

5. – Is anything missing?

Having now described the key characteristics of Cloud Computing, its main pros and cons, and the way of seeing applications so that they can fully exploit it, we now turn to looking at whether there is something that we are still missing from the Cloud, especially for what regards scientific applications.

5˙1. *Federated identities*. – As mentioned in sect. **1**, Grid Computing solved the problem of federated identities developing VOMS [13]. A similar solution is needed in Cloud Computing. While the Grid used X.509 digital certificates to map identities, though, the Cloud should be using this but also other forms of identification for scientists, such as those supported by federated identity services like eduGAIN [46]. However, this requires proper integration of these mechanisms into the authentication services offered by popular Cloud frameworks, such as OpenStack [47].

5˙2. *Local scheduling*. – As mentioned in sect. **3**˙2.7, real-world data centers (be they Cloud-based or not) have the problem of managing workload scheduling in a resource-constrained environment. In other words, there is no true, infinite elasticity.

How can therefore a Cloud provider offer resources to a given user (or set of users), while at the same time maintaining *average* provision levels for other users, avoiding resource starvation? This problem was solved long ago at the local level in traditional data centers through the use of batch systems. Something similar, *i.e.* a form of smart, fair queueing mechanism, should be introduced into common Cloud frameworks in order to support this use case.

The current solution for big scientific experiments is that they write their own workload management systems to handle job submissions to both Grid and Cloud infrastructures. However, this solution is not really sustainable in terms of code maintenance, duplicates work across several experiments, and typically only applies to big collaborations, who have the necessary manpower to developed such experiment-specific software.

5˙3. *Networking and storage strategies*. – When using public Cloud providers to handle computational and data transfer tasks generated by international scientific collaborations, it is extremely important to carefully check network bandwidth and latencies.

For example, a popular Cloud provider such as Amazon has multiple data centers, spread across many geographic *regions*. One would expect that network connections between data centers located in a single country like, for example, the United States, were of better quality (in terms of bandwidth and latency) than connections between countries far apart. However, as Maheshwari *et al.* show, "A cluster of 1000 nodes between Japan and Singapore might be faster than one between US-east and US-west" [48] (the latter two being two Amazon regions in the US). The conclusion they reach is that there is a wild variety of quality in network connections within Amazon services: Europe seems well connected to US-East, but not so much to US-West; Japan and Singapore are well connected among themselves, but are poorly connected with the rest of the world. And so on.

This is very relevant for scientific use of Cloud Computing, because it means that *smart storage strategies are needed*, and that one should exploit locality, replication and caching, choosing the *best* (for a specific application, that is) storage servers and Cloud centers.

However, fundamental questions remain: how can one do this dynamically, and in a general, provider-independent way? How can we actually *control* networking?

A current trend is that network behavior could be directly programmable through Software-Defined Networks (SDN), with network services being separated from the network forwarding plane. The control and forwarding planes are supposed to be connected through the OpenFlow protocol [49].

However, should we assume we have *infinite bandwidth* for this mechanism to properly work? This may or may not be true (it generally is not). And, how constrained are we by the specific support offered to this technology by Internet Service Providers (ISP)? What if our data has to cross multiple ISPs and some of them do not support these features? (Most currently do not.)

5`4. *Dynamically extending layer 2 networks*. – Given the constant increase and commoditizing of network bandwidth, it would be useful to be able to *dynamically* exploit hybrid Cloud deployments. This would mean to transparently extend data centers to remote locations, to realize what could be called *dynamically distributed virtual data centers*.

This could be useful, for example, to handle so-called *flash requests*, *i.e.* requests for resources that exceed the capacity of a given Cloud infrastructure, designed to locally handle workloads most of the time. If one could transparently connect data centers to remote locations for example at the data link layer (layer 2) of the OSI stack [50], IP addressing could be extended to these remote locations, thus potentially realizing also a much simpler connection to storage subsystems than what could be achieved with "traditional" Cloud federations (in case these existed).

5`5. *Using VMs in existing data centers*. – As mentioned in sect. **1**, in the past fifteen years scientific communities have created sizable and successful computing infrastructures. These are often based on traditional data centers; now, it is often the case that not every data center is ready to migrate (or even willing to do so) *all* its resources to Cloud computing.

Indeed, there is often the need to maintain current operational workflows, customers, etc. that rely on batch systems to prioritize scientific workloads. Several systems exist, allowing to manage VMs through some integration with an already deployed batch system. One of them is WNoDeS (Worker Nodes on Demand Service), developed and deployed by INFN in Italy since 2008, and used to handle VMs in a large computing production farm alongside (*i.e.*, in the same cluster of) normal, non-virtualized workloads. Scalability is proven to many thousand of running VMs, together with several tens of thousands of non-virtualized workloads [51].

The importance both of queuing services and of integrating Cloud and non-Cloud resources is apparent looking at fig. 12, showing the typical utilization pattern of a scientific computing center (in this case, the main Italian computing center for physics

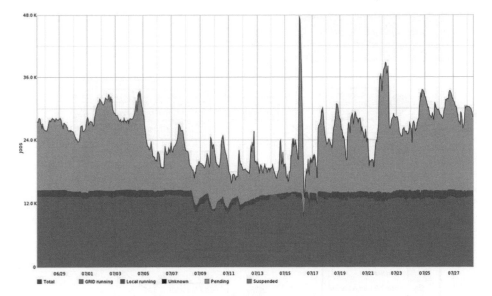

Fig. 12. – Typical batch resource utilization at a scientific data center.

experiments, run by INFN at CNAF in Bologna). There, as in many other similar cases, for optimal resource utilization there is a single large shared cluster, serving tens of scientific collaborations. Resource utilization is normally 100% all the time (violet area), with thousands jobs waiting for their turn for execution at any given time (green area).

If we had to set up separate clusters to handle Grid, Cloud and local workloads, with or without VMs, this could substantially decrease resource utilization. What a solution like WNoDeS does is indeed to integrate Grid or local access with VM and Cloud support, *as long as Cloud requests goes through WNoDeS itself.* This is realized through for example Cloud interfaces such as OGF OCCI [52] or Amazon EC2 [53]. But, as fig. 13 shows, this is really still implementing a partial integration of resources.

Also, WNoDeS by no means provides a general integration mechanism, because it is dependent on a specific batch system, or set of batch system.

There should therefore be a true, scalable, general infrastructural integration between Cloud management frameworks (like OpenStack [47]) and local or Grid Computing use cases. Referring to OpenStack components as an example, VM image management could be accomplished through Glance [54], virtualization could be directly handled by Nova [55] instead of calling lower layer virtualization mechanisms, and fig. 13 should be modified accordingly.

This would make it possible to support the following use cases in a *traditional computing center*:

– traditional workloads,

– customized VMs running jobs,

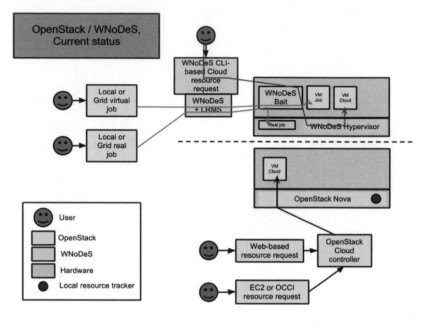

Fig. 13. – Cloud *vs.* rest of the world(s).

– cloud instantiations through OpenStack APIs.

All this within a common cluster, therefore ensuring resource optimization, and letting physical resources to run both traditional workloads on the "bare metal" and VMs at the same time.

This implementation requires a certain amount of components that are still to be fully developed, and assumes as mentioned above that we are dealing with a *traditional* resource center, running for example a batch system as a core part of its infrastructure.

But what if a data center wanted to get rid of its traditional queueing systems altogether? As mentioned in sect. **5**˙2, some currently missing queuing features must be introduced into Cloud scheduling mechanisms. We shall only add here that, from an implementation perspective, one should probably avoid rewriting a scheduling algorithm from scratch, reusing instead an open-source one such as, for example, Slurm's [56].

5˙6. *Virtualization penalties*. – Section **2**˙4 mentioned that virtualization introduces some penalties, especially with regards to I/O performance. It also often introduces the impossibility to effectively exploit some specialized hardware devices, such as Graphical Processing Units (GPUs) used for computational tasks, or fast network interconnections like InfiniBand. A more lightweight way of supporting virtual-like services that might overcome these issues, therefore, would be really welcomed.

Docker [57] is a project for the creation of lightweight *containers*, intended as portable and self-consistent units capable of wrapping up any application. A container encapsu-

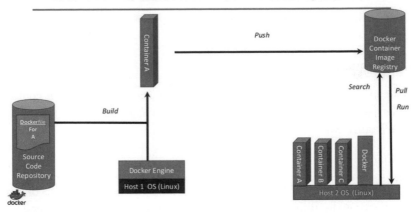

Fig. 14. – Docker basics.

lates everything that is needed for some code to be run, such as the code itself, its dependencies, system libraries, etc.

It is important to note that the focus here is on *applications*, not on the infrastructure, nor on "virtual machines". The latter, indeed, are much more heavyweight than containers since each VM replicates an entire execution environments, including a full operating system, while Docker containers rely on common blocks provided by the host system and not replicated on each container [58].

On a Linux server, a basic building block common to all containers running on that host is the kernel. It has been said that Docker containers, which to an application look similar to a VM, could be defined as *chroot on steroids*; in practice, they are a group of processes in an isolated environment where controlled use of resources such as CPU, memory and I/O is implemented through well-known Linux features like `cgroups` [59].

The basics of a Docker system are shown in fig. 14. In summary, a container (called Container A in the picture) is built through a *Docker engine* running *e.g.* on a Linux system, starting from a `dockerfile` stating in a human readable way how it should be defined. This container can then be pushed to a Docker Container Image Registry. The Registry can be searched, and a container stored there can be pulled, and run on some other host in a portable way.

There are various benefits of using containers; they can be summarized as follows:

– Portable deployment across machines

Docker defines a format for bundling an application and all its dependencies into a single object which can be transferred to any docker-enabled machine, and executed there, with the guarantee that the execution environment exposed to the application will be the same.

– Application-centric

> Docker is optimized for the deployment of applications, rather than of much more complex virtual machines.

– Automatic build

> Docker includes tools for developers to automatically assemble a container from their source code, with full control over application dependencies, build tools, packaging etc.

– Versioning

> Docker includes git-like capabilities for tracking successive versions of a container, inspecting the difference between versions, committing new versions, rolling back etc.

– Component re-use

> Any Docker container can be used as a "base image" to create more specialized components.

– Sharing

> Docker has access to a public registry (see `http://index.docker.io`) where thousands of people have already uploaded useful containers.

– Tool ecosystem

> Docker defines an API for automating and customizing the creation and deployment of containers.

Containers could be the future for software delivery and for ultimate portability. However, in order to exploit these benefits, it is important that on the one hand the format for containers is somewhat standardized across the whole industry and, on the other hand, that containers can be properly and reliably instantiated by popular Cloud computing frameworks such as, for example, by Nova in OpenStack.

5'7. *Distributed authorization*. – As already mentioned in sect. **1**, the Grid Computing world long ago defined ways to create and manage *Virtual Organizations* (VO), for example through VOMS [13], and to create, propagate and manage distributed access control policies, for example through Argus [60].

We still need something similar for Cloud computing, without being limited by the technologies used in the Grid world. A proprietary example of what could perhaps be used as a starting point is given by the Identity and Access Management (IAM) mechanism available on Amazon Web Services [61].

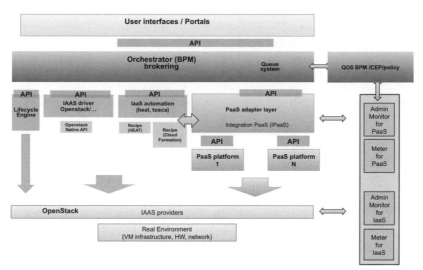

Fig. 15. – Some missing PaaS components (in blue, purple, green, yellow) [62].

5˙8. *PaaS architectures*. – PaaS was defined in sect. **2˙**3. Is it enough to use what the market already provides us with, in order to be able to use all resources that might be available to us?

Let us assume for example that IaaS offerings are pervasive, simple enough, and based on well-known standards. Which components would still be needed for scientific applications?

Figure 15 shows some building blocks that could be useful to define and implement to provide scientists with a flexible Cloud programming environment and IaaS allocation mechanism.

What fig. 15 says is that already today we can use several open source PaaS platforms such as Cloudify [63], Cloud Foundry [64], WSO2 [65] and OpenShift [66], on top of IaaS providers. What is missing, though, is an adaptation layer (called *Integration PaaS* in the picture), mediating across these platforms. This adaptation layer should then interface to a PaaS provisioning system (called *Orchestrator (BPM) brokering* in the picture) supporting also PaaS-level queuing of resource allocation requests. The orchestrator should also interface to a *QoS BPM policy system* (shown on the right), which on its turn is connected to a comprehensive set of monitoring and metering modules for both PaaS and IaaS (called *Admin Monitor* and *Meter* in the picture.) On the left we have components that exist already, such as *OpenStack Heat* (described below), and that partially implement some IaaS automation features bordering on PaaS features. However, these components would also need integration into a PaaS-level orchestrator engine.

In practice, the blocks in blue, purple, green and yellow in the picture are what would allow scientists to express requirements such as the following.

A common need for some scientific communities is the procurement of *ready-to-use, customized virtual cluster.* There are open source products such as Hadoop [28], Nimbus [67] and commercial products that can partially handle this use case. However, what is normally missing are easy ways to:

- Dynamically create these virtual clusters. In other words, handling elastic adaptation to the workload submitted by users, adding or removing nodes.

- Move beyond job-level solutions. How could one get access to his nodes?

- Avoid dependencies on specific batch system implementations.

- Avoid dependencies on specific Cloud infrastructures such as Amazon EC2, for example.

- If required, take into account something more sophisticated than number of VM instances, through for example cost-aware schedulers.

- Easily express requirements that define what a cluster of resources (not necessarily coincident with just VMs) should look like and what should it contain (or do not contain).

Extending the PaaS layer in ways similar to what is shown in fig. 15 would allow one to support a similar use case.

Another simple example of what could be done with a PaaS layer is given by OpenStack Heat [68], a component of the OpenStack Orchestration program. While OpenStack is normally considered a IaaS Cloud framework, some of its components like Heat cover some PaaS features as well.

Schematically, Heat allows creation of Cloud applications defined by *templates*, and Heat resources (which are not necessarily just VMs) communicating among themselves define *stacks*. Stacks, then, can be integrated in configuration management systems such as Puppet [69]. Through Heat, also, one can automatically manage high-availability and auto-scaling configurations.

Now, it is to be noted that the Heat native format for templates is undergoing some changes. The idea, however, is to make it compatible with Amazon CloudFormation templates [70]. It is interesting to note that Heat implements direct support for auto-scaling instances. Unfortunately, due to differences between OpenStack versions, Heat uses different constructs depending on the OpenStack version being used.

So, for example, with OpenStack Havana auto-scaling is supported by Heat through calls to:

AWS::AutoScaling::AutoScalingGroup,

AWS::AutoScaling::ScalingPolicy.

While with OpenStack Icehouse the following calls are supported:

OS::Heat::InstanceGroup,

OS::Heat::AutoScalingGroup,

OS::Heat::ScalingPolicy.

But regardless of the details, what is important is that it is possible to define a *Scaling-Group*, *i.e.* a group that can scale an arbitrary set of Heat resources, and a *ScalingPolicy*, which affects the number of scaling units in a group [71]. However, what is still missing is an easy and consistent way for users to express these policies. Heat is also still subject to numerous revisions and still depends a lot on the specifics of certain OpenStack versions (while OpenStack itself, due to its remarkable growth curve, undergoes frequent iterations in terms of functionalities and interfaces).

5˙**9.** *Portals.* – Scientific portals try to fill possible gaps between technology and users wishing to exploit the use of distributed resources. These gaps might be especially relevant for communities not fully committed, fluent or even interested in technological details.

As an example, such a gateway was developed in the context of the European FP7 DECIDE project (Diagnostic Enhancement of Confidence by an International Distributed Environment) [72]. The portal in that project [73] is a combination of layers involving research networks, Grid resources and domain-specific applications.

But valid questions would be: why does the development of such a gateway deserve a publication, or in general special funding? In other words, would it be possible to make this the norm rather than the exception? Or, with some more details:

– Would it be possible to structure this development around APIs that can be used by portals, desktop and mobile applications, and that can interconnect IaaS, PaaS and SaaS Clouds?

– And, how could one support big data workflows for science, easily integrating them into these portals?

This points to the fact that also in this area a number of developments for the effective use of Cloud Computing for science seem needed.

6. – Conclusions

This paper first described general features of Cloud Computing and of applications in the Cloud; it then proceeded to show that some technological gaps are still to be filled, if we want to use Clouds effectively for scientific applications. Before coming to a summary, there is still another point that needs to be mentioned, and it is a very important one: *how to evolve and sustain ourselves*, *i.e.* scientists trying to solve scientific problems using (or developing) state-of-the-art technologies?

Some current trends and open questions about this might be sketched:

– Use and extend what is available on the market, rather than "reinventing the wheel".

- Look for assistance to deploy and support your applications.

- Once we define which important or even essential features we are missing, will there be anybody interested in implementing and maintaining them for us?

- Watch out for the "I am capable of writing (or: I *must write*) everything myself, and be much more efficient than you / the rest of the world" syndrome.

- Are we ready and capable of adapting ourselves (our applications) to market offerings? Think of how an application would need to be adapted to really exploit Cloud Computing features, see sect. **4**.

- Sustainability might come through community support, but which community? Should we liaise with industry to entice them in supporting us? Is there a business case? Should we structurally assume to get some external (*e.g.* EC) funding to sort this out for us?

- Last but not least: is it fundamentally sustainable *not to rely* on externally funded e-infrastructures for science?

And now, let us try to draw some *conclusions*:

Currently, the reference platform for public Cloud computing, both technologically and marketwise, is still Amazon, offering and constantly introducing numerous advanced services and at a very large scale.

There are, however, several reasons justifying the existence of *private Clouds* or, in general, of Cloud infrastructures that are not Amazon's; in particular, the theme of how to support *hybrid Clouds* is and will be of great importance.

In terms of open source Cloud frameworks, *OpenStack*, which we did not really discuss in this paper, has at the time of this writing an absolutely remarkable popularity in terms of user base, developers and features; but this is indeed also one of the reasons why it is somewhat difficult to make sense of all its evolutions, that sometimes seem to just running after Amazon's. It is therefore important to understand its key features and limitations.

An essential point is that customers, be they scientists or not, wish to deploy applications *without being confined to technological limits imposed by single vendors*. This, together with the *strong evolution we observe from IaaS to PaaS and SaaS models* due to the added value given by the latter abstractions, is what will drive the evolution of Cloud frameworks, OpenStack included, in the coming months or years.

There are still *missing components* that are key to scientific communities wishing to "live in the Cloud". These should be developed, made available, exploited, and this from many viewpoints, involving technology, economics, vision, policy.

Last but not least, let us remind ourselves of the strategic and business importance, in particular for private and community Clouds linked to universities, research centers and public administrations, of *sharing methods and technological solutions through an effective federation of know-how and resources*.

* * *

This work was made possible also through contributions of the INFN CNAF SDDS (Software Development and Distributed Services) group.

REFERENCES

[1] FOSTER I., "What is the Grid? A Three Point Checklist", 2002, http://www.mcs.anl.gov/~itf/Articles/WhatIsTheGrid.pdf.

[2] The Worldwide LHC Computing Grid, http://wlcg.web.cern.ch.

[3] See the article "How grid computing helped CERN hunt the Higgs", available at http://www.isgtw.org/feature/how-grid-computing-helped-cern-hunt-higgs.

[4] OSG, the Open Science Grid, http://www.opensciencegrid.org.

[5] OGF, the Open Grid Forum, https://www.ogf.org.

[6] The DataTAG Project, http://datatag.web.cern.ch/datatag/project.html.

[7] The DataGrid Project, http://eu-datagrid.web.cern.ch/eu-datagrid/.

[8] The Globus Project, https://www.globus.org.

[9] The EGEE (Enabling Grid for E-SciencE) Project, http://eu-egee-org.web.cern.ch/eu-egee-org/index.html.

[10] SIENA, the Standards and Interoperability for eInfrastructure Implementation Initiative, http://www.sienainitiative.eu.

[11] EMI, the European Middleware Initiative, http://www.eu-emi.eu.

[12] EGI, The European Grid Infrastructure, http://www.egi.eu/.

[13] For the Virtual Organization Membership Service (VOMS), see http://www.eu-emi.eu/products/-/asset_publisher/1gkD/content/voms-2.

[14] For the Computing Resource Execution And Management (CREAM) software, see http://grid.pd.infn.it/cream/.

[15] For the ARC Compute Element, see http://www.nordugrid.org/arc/ce/.

[16] For the HTCondor software, see http://research.cs.wisc.edu/htcondor/.

[17] For the XRootD project, see http://xrootd.org.

[18] For the StoRM (Storage Resource Manager) software, see http://www.italiangrid.it/middleware/storm.

[19] For the dCache software, see https://www.dcache.org.

[20] For the WMS (Workload Management System), see http://www.italiangrid.it/middleware/wms.

[21] This quote by Darryl Zanuck can be found for example in http://www.techhive.com/article/155984/worst_tech_predictions.html, where one can also find several other bad tech predictions.

[22] These words were perhaps never said by Henry Ford but they illustrate the concept of discontinuous evolution of technology. See for example http://www.foolproof.co.uk/thinking/three-old-chestnuts-cracked/ for a discussion on the authorship of this quote.

[23] U.S. National Institute of Standards and Technology Definition of Cloud Computing, http://csrc.nist.gov/groups/SNS/cloud-computing/index.html.

[24] For some information on the extent of the Digital Divide in the European Union and possible corrective measures, see http://ec.europa.eu/digital-agenda/en/news/eu-digital-divide-infographic.

[25] This metaphor is taken from http://www.microsoft.com/en-us/government/blogs/cloud-computing-how-to-explain-it-to-others-in-your-organization/.

[26] Java Platform Enterprise Edition, see `http://www.oracle.com/technetwork/java/javaee/overview/index.html`.

[27] The picture is taken from `http://blogs.msdn.com/b/johnalioto/archive/2010/08/16/10050822.aspx`.

[28] Apache Hadoop, see `https://hadoop.apache.org`.

[29] The picture is taken from a Gartner report dated 1 August, 2012 and titled "Hype Cycle for Cloud Computing", available (subscription-based) at `https://www.gartner.com/doc/2102116`. An article commenting that report is available at `http://www.forbes.com/sites/louiscolumbus/2012/08/04/hype-cycle-for-cloud-computing-shows-enterprises-finding-value-in-big-data-virtualization/`.

[30] The Kernel Virtual Machine (KVM), see `http://www.linux-kvm.org/page/Main_Page`.

[31] The Xen Project, see `http://www.xenproject.org`.

[32] See, for example, the free VMware vSphere hypervisor, `http://www.vmware.com/products/vsphere-hypervisor`.

[33] QEMU is an open-source machine emulator, see `http://wiki.qemu.org/Main_Page`.

[34] See, for example, HAYDEN M., "Performance benchmarks: KVM *vs.* Xen", `https://major.io/2014/06/22/performance-benchmarks-kvm-vs-xen/`.

[35] CHIERICI A., SALOMONI D., *J. Phys.: Conf. Ser.*, **396** (2012) 032024.

[36] HUYNH K., THEURER A., HAJNOCZI S., "KVM Virtualized I/O Performance", February 2013, `ftp://public.dhe.ibm.com/linux/pdfs/KVM_Virtualized_IO_Performance_Paper_v2.pdf`.

[37] The OpenStack Security Guide, `http://docs.openstack.org/sec/`.

[38] See `http://virtualization.info/images/VMwarepreparestoentercloudcomputingmarke_D5AC/VMware_cloudcomputing.jpg`.

[39] "Cisco and Partners to Build World's Largest Global Intercloud", see `http://newsroom.cisco.com/release/1373639`, March 24, 2014.

[40] LLOYD R., "Introducing Cisco's Global Intercloud", `http://blogs.cisco.com/news/introducing-ciscos-global-intercloud`.

[41] An interesting article on Cloud differentiation is available at `https://www.linkedin.com/pulse/20140720153303-7142404-how-a-service-provider-can-monetize-openstack`.

[42] See the AWS Customer Agreement, `http://aws.amazon.com/agreement/`.

[43] The NSA story uncovered by Edward Snowden provides a good example here. Among the abundant available material, see for instance the article "NSA infiltrates links to Yahoo, Google data centers worldwide, Snowden documents say", The Washington Post, October 30, 2013, `http://www.washingtonpost.com/world/national-security/nsa-infiltrates-links-to-yahoo-google-data-centers-worldwide-snowden-documents-say/2013/10/30/e51d661e-4166-11e3-8b74-d89d714ca4dd_story.html`.

[44] See, for example, BIAS R., "Architectures for open and scalable clouds", February 2012, `http://www.slideshare.net/randybias/architectures-for-open-and-scalable-clouds/`.

[45] CACCO F., "Geoserver nel Cloud" (in Italian), Master Thesis in Computer Science, University of Padua, October 2013.

[46] For the eduGAIN service, see `http://www.geant.net/service/eduGAIN/Pages/home.aspx`.

[47] OpenStack, `https://www.openstack.org`.

[48] MAHESHWARI K. *et al.*, "Evaluating Storage Systems for Scientific Data in the Cloud", `http://datasys.cs.iit.edu/events/ScienceCloud2014/s05.pdf`.

[49] How OpenFlow-Based SDN Transform Private Cloud, `https://www.opennetworking.org/solution-brief-how-openflow-based-sdn-transform-private-cloud`.

[50] For a concise description of the OSI model, see for example https://en.wikipedia.org/wiki/OSI_model.

[51] RONCHIERI E., VERLATO M. *et al.*, PoS (ISGC 2013) 029, http://pos.sissa.it/archive/conferences/179/029/ISGC%202013_029.pdf.

[52] Open Cloud Computing Interface, http://occi-wg.org.

[53] Amazon Elastic Compute Cloud (EC2) API reference, http://docs.aws.amazon.com/AWSEC2/latest/APIReference/Welcome.html.

[54] The Glance project, http://docs.openstack.org/developer/glance/.

[55] The Nova project, http://docs.openstack.org/developer/nova/.

[56] The Slurm Workload Manager, http://slurm.schedmd.com.

[57] Docker, https://www.docker.com.

[58] FELTER W. *et al.*, "An Updated Performance Comparison of Virtual Machines and Linux Containers", IBM Research Division, RC25482 (AUS1407-001) July 21, 2014, http://domino.research.ibm.com/library/cyberdig.nsf/papers/0929052195DD819C85257D2300681E7B/$File/rc25482.pdf.

[59] For an introduction to Linux Control Groups (cgroups), see for example https://access.redhat.com/documentation/en-US/Red_Hat_Enterprise_Linux/6/html/Resource_Management_Guide/ch01.html.

[60] The Argus Authorization Service, http://argus-authz.github.io. Argus is based on the XACML 2 standard, renders consistent authorization decisions based on XACML policies, supports aggregation of policies from remote Argus endpoints (hierarchical policies composition) and as of the time of this writing is deployed on large-scale production infrastructures such as those provided by WLCG.

[61] Controlling Access to Amazon EC2 Resources, see http://docs.aws.amazon.com/AWSEC2/latest/UserGuide/UsingIAM.html.

[62] This unpublished picture was provided by courtesy of S. Bussolino (Santer Reply), and describes PaaS developments occurring in a Cloud-related project funded in Italy.

[63] Cloudify, http://getcloudify.org.

[64] Cloud Foundry, https://www.cloudfoundry.org/.

[65] WSO2, http://wso2.com.

[66] Open Shift, https://www.openshift.com.

[67] The Nimbus Project, http://www.nimbusproject.org.

[68] OpenStack Heat, https://wiki.openstack.org/wiki/Heat.

[69] Puppet, https://puppetlabs.com.

[70] AWS CloudFormation, http://aws.amazon.com/it/cloudformation/.

[71] See, for example, https://github.com/openstack/heat-templates/blob/master/hot/autoscaling.yaml for a Heat template creating an auto-scaling Wordpress cluster with load balancing, a scaling policy based on Ceilometer (metering) alarms and user data (which could be a Puppet template) used to install packages and customize VMs.

[72] DECIDE (Diagnostic Enhancement of Confidence by an International Distributed Environment), https://www.eu-decide.eu. The goal of the project was to exploit computer-aided extraction of diagnostic disease markers for Alzheimer disease and schizophrenia.

[73] ARDIZZONE V. *et al.*, *J. Grid Comput.*, **10** (2012) 689.

Proceedings of the International School of Physics "Enrico Fermi"
Course 192 "Grid and Cloud Computing: Concepts and Practical Applications",
edited by F. Carminati, L. Betev and A. Grigoras
(IOS, Amsterdam; SIF, Bologna) 2016
DOI 10.3254/978-1-61499-643-9-71

Clouds in biosciences: A journey to high-throughput computing in life sciences

V. Breton

CNRS-IN2P3, LPC Clermont-Ferrand - France
CNRS-IN2P3 Institut des Grilles et du Cloud - France

N. Lampe, L. Maigne and D. Sarramia

CNRS-IN2P3, LPC Clermont-Ferrand - France

B. T. Quang

CNRS-IN2P3 Institut des Grilles et du Cloud - France

Summary. — The journey towards high-throughput computing in life sciences is discussed in this paper. The earliest adopters of grid and cloud computing in the life sciences were molecular biology and medical imaging, later joined by drug discovery and neuroscience. Now that grid technology is mature and cloud technology is maturing, pilot agent platforms provide a powerful mechanism to hide technological evolution. The emergence of Big Data is also relevant to the life sciences where the growth in High-Throughput Sequencing machines in many laboratories around the world brings new challenges and opportunities.

1. – Introduction

This paper provides an overview of the usage of distributed computing infrastructures in life sciences. While the title "clouds in biosciences" may seem misleading, given a significant fraction of the content written here deals with grids, academic cloud computing remains a firm part of the journey. At least in the academic world, cloud computing is still

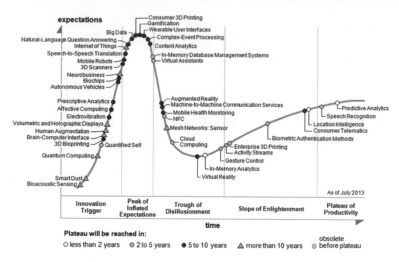

Fig. 1. – Gartner emerging technologies hype cycle in 2013 - Credit: [1].

a burgeoning technology, in relation to grids which have rapidly become quite popular in life sciences. Technologically speaking, grids are the ancestor of clouds and can be considered in many ways as a cloud platform. Indeed, the development of "Platform as a Service" cloud computing services provides cloud-based grid computing platforms and solution stacks "in the cloud".

The paper subtitle refers to high-throughput computing that is about analyzing large volumes of data. While supercomputers are best adapted to complex modeling; clusters, grids and clouds are best used in so-called embarrassingly parallel computations.

Grids, clouds and big data are technologies that have made or are still making bold promises. It is sometimes difficult to discern the hype from what is available. Gartner hype cycles have been invented by Gartner Inc., a leading information technology research and advisory company [1]. These Hype Cycles are a graphic representation of the maturity and adoption of technologies and applications, and how they are potentially relevant to solving real business problems and exploiting new opportunities. Gartner hype cycle methodology gives a view of how a technology or application will evolve over time, providing a source of insight to manage its deployment within the context of a specific business goal.

It is very interesting to look at Gartner emerging technologies hype cycle in 2013 (fig. 1 from [1]). Each hype cycle drills down into the five key phases of a technology's life cycle:

- Technology Trigger: A potential technology breakthrough kicks things off. Early proof-of-concept stories and media interest trigger significant publicity. Often no usable products exist and commercial viability is unproven.

- Peak of Inflated Expectations: Early publicity produces a number of success stories often accompanied by scores of failures. Some companies take action; many do not.

- Trough of Disillusionment: Interest wanes as experiments and implementations fail to deliver. Producers of the technology shake out or fail. Investments continue only if the surviving providers improve their products to the satisfaction of early adopters.

- Slope of Enlightenment: More instances of how the technology can benefit the enterprise start to crystallize and become more widely understood. Second- and third-generation products appear from technology providers. More enterprises fund pilots; conservative companies remain cautious.

- Plateau of Productivity: Mainstream adoption starts to take off. Criteria for assessing provider viability are more clearly defined. The technology's broad market applicability and relevance are clearly paying off.

From fig. 1, clouds are deep into the trough of disillusionment in 2013 while big data is at the highest on the peak of inflated expectation. Where are grids? In fact, they disappeared from Gartner emerging technologies hype cycle as early as 2009 but, in reality, they only reached production maturity in 2010 when CERN Large Hadron Collider started data taking.

If we compare fig. 1 to the experience of a scientist who needs to analyse data, the perception is clearly different in 2014: grids are operational, clouds in their infancy and big data a vague concept still far from any concrete outcome.

If we look back in history, life sciences were amongst the earliest adopters of grid technology, as early as 2000. In particular, the sub-disciplines of biochemistry, bioinformatics, genomics, medical imaging, molecular biology, neuroscience, pharmacogenomics, proteomics and structural biology make great use currently of high-throughput computing. Ecology and environmental sciences also produce growing volumes of data, and all of these require growing computational resources.

In this paper, we will not be able to visit all aspects of high-throughput computing in the life sciences. We will focus on four disciplines: molecular biology and bioinformatics, structural biology, biochemistry and medical imaging. the lecture is organized as follows:

- in the next section, we are going to introduce briefly these four disciplines and particularly their need for high-throughtput computing;

- after this introduction, we will present major results or initiatives achieved on grid infrastructures;

- we will then discuss the state of the art of the adoption and usage of clouds in life sciences;

- we will devote a section to the specific needs of medical applications;

- wo will finally introduce the new challenges related to the explosion of data.

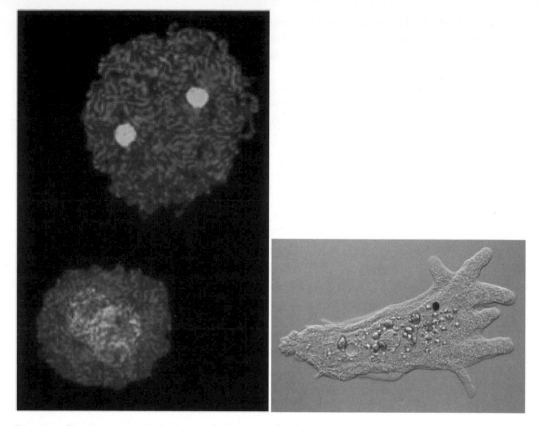

Fig. 2. – Smallest non-viral genome belongs to the bacteria *Carsonnella ruddii* with 0.16 Mbp pairs (left) while the longest is attributed to the freshwater amoeboid *Polychaos dubium* with 670 Gbp (right).

1˙1. *Short introduction to molecular biology*. – Molecular biology has experienced a change in scale in the last 10 years with the revolution of high-throughput sequencing. Now, it is possible to adopt an encyclopedic approach, to study all genes, all proteins, all interactions. As a consequence, biologists are flooded by an avalanche of heterogeneous data and spend today more time analyzing data than they spend collecting it.

The availability of massive volumes of data in molecular biology has completely changed the landscape of life sciences. In genomics, the development of High-Throughput Sequencing Technologies has allowed reducing the sequencing cost to 0.03 dollars per million sequenced nucleotids. One run on a next generation sequencer produces up to 3 billion fragments of 2×100 base pairs, corresponding to terabytes of raw data. To give a sense of scale, the smallest non-viral genome belongs to the bacteria *Carsonnella ruddii* with 0.16 Mbp pairs while the longest is that of *Polychaos dubium* with 670 Gbp (fig. 2)

In transcriptomics, the development of microarray technology provides a wealth of information on gene expression. In proteomics, hundred thousands of proteins are now fully sequenced. All these data are much harder to interpret than it was initially foreseen. As a result, human genome sequencing did not so much open an era of discoveries but rather highlighted the complexity of life. Modeling of living systems is just emerging with the onset of theoretical biology.

In front of the challenges raised by molecular biology, a new scientific discipline has emerged at the interface between computer and life sciences: bioinformatics. Bioinformatics aims at developing software tools to help biologists in the analysis of their data. Research in bioinformatics is therefore about new algorithms and new services with improved performances. Twenty years of research in bioinformatics has brought a wealth of new software tools, databases and portals. A major challenge specific to molecular biology is that a researcher needs to have constant access to the state of the art in order to compare his results to the existing information. Molecular biologists need on demand access to a constantly updated representation of all the knowledge accumulated in their field. This requirement is not as necessary in other field of sciences, such as physics or chemistry where the evolution of the body of knowledge is much slower.

There is therefore a need to offer to the biologist access to an up-to-date view of the molecular biology data relevant to his research. This requires integrating a large variety of databases filled with information relevant to the different expression levels of living systems. With the explosion of high-throughput data production systems, these databases are growing exponentially.

In summary, the main challenge for data analysis in life sciences is to offer to the molecular biologists an integrated and up-to-date view of an exponentially growing volume of data in a multiplicity of formats.

1˙2. *Short introduction to structural biology.* – Structural biology is a branch of molecular biology, biochemistry, and biophysics concerned with the molecular structure of biological macromolecules, especially proteins and nucleic acids. It describes how they acquire the structures they have and how alterations in these structures affect their function. Mass spectrometry, macromolecular crystallography and Nuclear Magnetic Resonance are among the methods that structural biologists use to determine the structure of macromolecules. They all generate large volumes of data to process. For instance, a human cell expresses typically from 5 to 6000 proteins. Analyzing these proteins on a mass spectrometer requires several hours in order to acquire the spectra of tens of thousands of peptide fragments [3]. This is equivalent to 10–15 GB of raw data that needs to be treated and transformed by identification and quantification algorithms.

Nuclear Magnetic Resonance allows the investigation of time-dependent chemical and conformational phenomena, including reaction and folding kinetics and intramolecular dynamics. For these reasons, NMR plays an important role within the life sciences. The principles underlying NMR are modulation of the natural magnetic moment of atomic nuclei, and measurements of how the system relaxes back to the initial state. The signal thus obtained is a fading wave consisting of many individual frequency contributions. Typically, up to 27000 different frequencies can be resolved at the highest magnetic fields that are nowadays available. To investigate the frequency contributions and their decays, such measurements have to be repeated many times, due to the low signal-to-noise ratio. To obtain structural information from NMR data, many more measurements have to be run, yielding substantial amounts of data that need processing [4].

Once the 3D-structure of biomolecules have been obtained, for instance by NMR spectroscopy or X-ray crystallography, there is a great interest to store them in public databases. The Protein Data Bank (PDB) [2] is a repository for the three-dimensional structural data of large biological molecules, such as proteins and nucleic acids. The PDB reached the symbolic milestone of 100.000 structures stored in 2014. The 3D structures stored in the PDB are very important as starting points for rational drug design and we are now going to shortly introduce the concepts relevant to *in silico* drug discovery.

1'3. *A short introduction to drug discovery.* – In silico drug discovery is one of the most promising strategies to speed-up the drug development process. Virtual screening is about selecting *in silico* the best candidate drugs acting on a given target protein [5]. Screening can be done *in vitro* but it is very expensive as they are now millions of chemicals that can be synthesized [6]. A reliable way of *in silico* screening could reduce the number of molecules required for *in vitro* and then *in vivo* testing from a few million to a few hundred [7].

In silico drug discovery should foster collaboration between public and private laboratories. It should also have an important societal impact by lowering the barrier to develop new drugs for rare and neglected diseases [8]. New drugs are needed for neglected diseases like malaria where parasites keep developing resistance to the existing drugs or sleeping sickness for which no new drug has been developed for years. New drugs against tuberculosis are also needed as treatment takes several months and is therefore hard to manage in poorly developing countries. However, *in silico* virtual screening requires intensive computing, on the order of a few teraflops per day to compute 1 million docking probabilities or for the molecular modeling of 1000 ligands on one target protein. Moreover, docking is only the first step of virtual screening since the docking output data has to be processed further [9].

1'4. *Introduction to medical imaging and neurosciences.* – Medical imaging is the technique and process of creating visual representations of the interior of a body for clinical analysis and medical intervention. Medical imaging seeks to reveal internal structures hidden by the skin and bones, as well as to diagnose and treat disease. Medical images can be simulated from digital models of the human body for a variety of applications in research and industry, including fast prototyping of new devices and the evaluation of image analysis algorithms [10]. Several image modalities are commonly simulated, including Magnetic Resonance Imaging (MRI), UltraSound imaging (US), Positron Emission Tomography (PET) and Computed Tomography (CT).

Progress in medical imaging is particularly important to the exploding field of neurosciences. Neurodegenerative diseases (NDD) such as Alzheimer's, grey matter, white matter and psychiatric diseases affect the brain and are responsible for a large share of disability in the population. For their early diagnosis, preventive and treatment therapies, effective disease-modifying drugs require accurate disease markers. Imaging can

TABLE I. – *Data requiring high-throughput computing.*

Scientific discipline	Massive data to be processed
Molecular Biology	Assembling of genomes from NGS data
Structural biology	Analysis of Nuclear Magnetic Resonance and Mass Spectrometry data
Neurosciences	Analysis of high-resolution brain images
Drug discovery	High-Throughput docking of molecular structures

detect the changes that take place in the brain of patients with Alzheimer's, multiple sclerosis and psychiatric diseases at the molecular, cellular, tissue and organ levels and therefore respond to the need for accurate disease markers. Recent advances in neuroimaging demonstrate subtle cognitive alterations that are detectable years prior to the development of objective memory deficit meaning that the disease can be diagnosed much earlier. Modern imaging techniques are essential not only for diagnosing but also for processing and sharing data all over the world [11]. Imaging techniques are computationally intensive, and as such, distributed computing is key to addressing the emerging need for user friendly access to data, analysis pipelines and computational resources, as imaging data of people with brain diseases are becoming increasingly available and accessible.

1‘5. *Summary.* – In this chapter, we have illustrated how life sciences have a growing need for high-throughput computing. Table I summarizes how the scientific disciplines we briefly introduced have growing needs to analyze massive amounts of data.

In addition, life sciences have a permanent need for comparative analysis between the data that are produced, like for instance new genomes or new protein structures, and the existing body of evidence collected over the years. They rely therefore extensively on the use of databases. Security is critical to protect these databases if they contain medical data, for privacy issues. Security is also a major concern for pharmaceutical laboratories in relation to intellectual property issues. Biological data is often open, except for that related to personalized medicine. It is worth noting that hundreds of bioinformatics algorithms and databases are now available everywhere on the web but only a handful of software programs are being used across the structural biology community.

If High-Throughput Computing is to become a major asset, High Performance Computing will be relevant to the life sciences, especially at the interface with computational chemistry, for applications such as Molecular Dynamics. Additionally, genome assembly also requires a large amount of memory (RAM) provided by Symmetric Multiprocessing (SMP).

When introduced by Ian Foster and David Kesselmann [12], grid technology promised to revolutionize many services already offered by the internet because it was deemed to offer rapid computation, large-scale data storage and flexible collaboration by harnessing

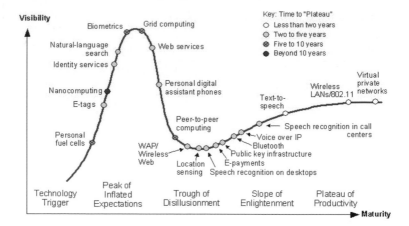

Fig. 3. – Gartner hype curve in 2002. Credit: [1].

together the power of a large number of commodity computers or clusters of other basic machines. The grid was devised for use in scientific fields, such as particle physics and bioinformatics, in which large volumes of data, or very rapid processing, or both, were necessary. Since 2002, we have been exploring how to use grids for life sciences. The next chapter speaks about our experience.

2. – Grid usage in life sciences

2`1. *Historical introduction*. – In Europe, the emergence of grid technology for users took mostly place from 2000 to 2005 in a number of projects funded by the European Commission, while grid technology was at the top of the hype curve (fig. 3).

Among the largest were the DataGrid and EGEE projects [13]. Of these pioneering efforts, the particle physics community laid the foundation of the LHC Computing Grid (LCG) in the following years while first successes were witnessed in the field of life sciences. Among them is the WISDOM initiative for drug discovery against neglected diseases that we will describe in the next section.

2`1.1. A pioneering application: WISDOM. The first large scale deployment of a scientific application in the field of life sciences on a grid infrastructure took place during the summer 2005 on the EGEE infrastructure [13]. Initiated and implemented by the Fraunhofer Institute for Algorithms and Scientific Computing (SCAI) in Germany and the Corpuscular Physics Laboratory (CNRS/IN2P3) of Clermont-Ferrand in France, its biological goal was to propose new inhibitors for a family of proteins produced by *Plasmodium falciparum*, a malaria parasite. This first large-scale docking experiment ran on the EGEE grid production service from 11 July 2005 until 19 August 2005. It saw over 46 million docked ligands, the equivalent of 80 years on a single PC, in about 6 weeks. Usually *in silico* docking was carried out on classical computer clusters resulting in around 100 000 docked ligands. This type of scientific challenge would not be possible without the grid infrastructure - 1700 computers were simultaneously used in 15 countries around the world.

Fraunhofer SCAI is known worldwide for developing one of the best docking algorithms, FlexX [15]. SCAI gave access to FlexX within the framework of this collaboration for a limited time. A server solution was studied to solve the license issue. As a consequence, the software was successfully deployed on more than 1000 machines at the same time.The SCAI group prepared 8 target scenarios for FlexX and 10 different target scenarios for AutoDock [16] based on the inclusion of water molecules in the proteins during the docking process. This first WISDOM data challenge demonstrated how grid computing could help drug discovery research by speeding up the whole process and reduce the cost to develop new drugs to treat diseases such as malaria.

The different parameter settings and target scenarios had a great influence on the virtual screening results. Although a high correlation could be found between the scores of the docked compounds under different conditions the differences were significant and partly different compounds were selected as the top-scoring ligands [18]. But the highest diversity was produced by the application of the different docking tools. There was almost no dependence between the docking scores calculated by AutoDock and FlexX: the docking tools preferred compounds with different properties. Both tools shared a preference for larger molecules with a high molecular mass which corresponds well to the reference ligands co-crystallized with the PDB structures. These findings clearly demonstrated that an application of several docking tools could enrich the candidate set and that parameters and target scenarios had to be carefully chosen in advance if it was not possible to perform several experiments.

Several strategies were employed to analyze the results including docking scores, ideal binding modes, and interactions to key residues of the protein. From the 500000 ligands screened a few hundred compounds having three different classes of structures were identified to be promising hits. To further address the parameters ignored during docking step like protein flexibility or solvation, an automatic procedure of refinement by molecular dynamics was applied on the best 5000 docked compounds using Amber software [17]. Indeed, it is generally agreed that docking results need to be post-processed with more accurate modeling tools before biological tests are undertaken. Molecular dynamics (MD) [13] has great potential at this stage: firstly, it enables a flexible treatment of the compound/target complexes at room temperature for a given simulation time, and therefore is able to refine compound orientations by finding more stable complexes; secondly, it partially solves conformation and orientation search deficiencies which might arise from docking; thirdly, it allows the re-ranking of molecules based on more accurate scoring functions.

Some 30 out of the 200 best compounds coming from this two-step *in silico* screening [19] were selected for *in vitro* testing in South Korea by Dr Doman Kim's team at Chonnam National University. Among the 30 compounds tested, six compounds confirmed *in vitro* the inhibitive action observed *in silico*. These results were extremely encouraging and suggested that the overall approach used to select the candidates was sensible for discovery of new malaria drugs.

During the fall of 2005, while we were analyzing the results coming from the first WISDOM deployment, the world was confronted with the growing concern that the influenza A virus (H5N1) could acquire the ability to be transmitted to humans. In March 2006, a collaboration of Asian and European laboratories was established to analyze 300000 possible drug compounds against the avian flu virus H5N1 using three Grid infrastructures: AuverGrid, EGEE and TWGrid [23]. The goal was to find potential compounds inhibiting the activities of an enzyme on the surface of the influenza virus, the so-called neuraminidase, subtype N1. This enzyme is a well-known biological target for drugs against influenza virus because its action is essential for virus proliferation and infectivity; therefore, blocking its activity generates antivirus effects. Two of the best drugs (oseltamivir and zanamivir) against the influenza A virus were discovered through structure-based drug design targeting neuraminidase.

The avian flu computing challenge resulted in the execution of more than 54000 jobs on 60 Grid Computing Elements to dock about 2 million pairs of target and chemical compound. The duration of the virtual screening process was successfully reduced from over 100 years to 6 weeks. High-throughput *in silico* docking was achieved with up to one docking every 2 seconds. Due to the fact that the Grid resources were used by other virtual organizations during the data challenge, a maximum of 2000 CPUs were concurrently running at the same time [24].

With the success achieved by these first projects both on the computation and biological sides, several scientific groups around the world proposed targets implicated in malaria, which led to a second assault on malaria, called WISDOM-II. Four different Plasmodial proteins from both *P. vivax* and *P. falciparum* were targeted [20]. Several grid infrastructures (EGEE, Auvergrid, EELA, EUChinaGrid, EUMedGrid) committed computing resources and FlexX was used to dock the whole ZINC database representing 4,3 million compounds into the four selected proteins. Re-docking against the co-crystallized compounds was performed to evaluate the docking parameters. During the 76 days duration of the project, nearly 140 million dockings were performed at a rate of almost 80 000 dockings per hour (equivalent to 413 years on a single PC). This second data challenge on malaria was followed by other large scale deployments targeting SARS [22] and diabetes [21], resulting again in the patenting of new promising molecules.

The outcome of these applications illustrates the power of virtual High-Throughput Screening in substantially reducing search time as well as providing a coarse filtering of large libraries of compounds. The use of grids as an initial screening tool should contribute significantly in the fight against neglected diseases as more resources become available. We will see in the next chapter how new ideas and tools have emerged to push further the use of distributed computing infrastructures for *in silico* drug discovery.

WISDOM was really the first initiative in the field of life sciences deploying large scale data challenges as early as 2005. Grid technology was already going down on Gartner hype curve (see fig. 4) but was gaining relevance and reliability for its users.

What made WISDOM successful were many factors:

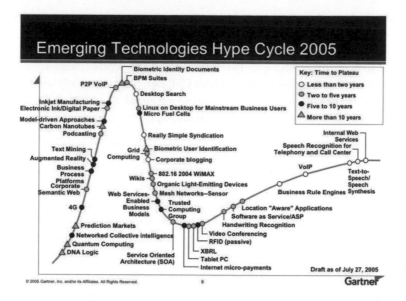

Fig. 4. – Gartner hype curve in 2005. Credit: [1].

– We received international support and all grid infrastructures were keen to contribute resources.

– We addressed a disease, malaria, that affects millions of people worldwide. There was a genuine motivation to achieve scientific progress and we succeeded as new bioactive molecules were patented.

– We were able to provide biological follow up, Professor Doman Kim (Chonnam and Seoul National Universities) took the most promising compounds selected *in silico* and tested them *in vitro*.

– Jean Salzemann developed a production environment that pushed automatically the docking jobs on the grid [25].

But WISDOM also highlighted a number of limitations

– 3D-structures of both compounds and biological targets were sent all around the world. This would have raised an obvious confidentiality issue if the compounds and targets were patented or owned by pharmaceutical laboratories.

– The grid had a high failure rate: over 30% of the jobs submitted failed for mostly unknown reasons.

WISDOM experience taught us that grid infrastructures were excellent environments for *in silico* drug discovery but pharmaceutical laboratories were too concerned by IP issues to ever use them. Nevertheless, researchers were beginning to recognize the power of grids.

2˙2. *Grid usage on the plateau of maturity*. – In 2010, grids reached their plateau of maturity with the kick-off of the Large Hadron Collider. They had left the yearly Gartner hype curve by 2009. In [14], we compared the situation at that time to a half empty, or half full glass: looking at the filled half, one could appreciate the capacity to access tens of thousands of cores on demand and have robust data management tools. Looking at the empty half, one could still complain about the lack of advanced data management service and the limited user friendliness. But everybody would agree that, at the time the paper was written (August 2010) the existing grid services were better than they had ever been. In other words, grids were offering more opportunities than ever to their users to do science differently. And indeed, the LHC Computing Grid worked extremely successfully and was instrumental to the early discovery of the Higgs Boson. If LHC kick-off had a very positive impact in terms of getting the grid to production quality, it also increased considerably the pressure on the resources.

The year 2010 marked also a major change in the organization of grid activities in Europe. Before, the grid infrastructure had developed within the framework of CERN led European projects: DataGrid from 2001 to 2004, then EGEE-I, EGEE-II and EGEE-III from 2004 to 2010. Besides constant technical progress, grid also caught the attention of the European Union to enable the vision of a European Research Area. On 30 May 2008, the EU Competitiveness Council promoted "the essential role of e-infrastructures as an integrating mechanism between Member States, regions as well as different scientific disciplines, also contributing to overcoming digital divides". By 2009, the grid governance model started to evolve towards a European Grid Initiative (EGI), building upon National Grid Initiatives (NGIs). In 2010, the EGI.eu organization was formed to sustain the services of the EGI. National Grid Initiatives (NGI) support scientific disciplines for computational resources within individual countries. The EGI is governed by a Council of representatives from each member NGI, which controls an executive that manages the international collaboration between NGI, so that individual researchers can share and combine computing resources in international collaborative research projects. The governance model of the EGI coordinating the collaboration of National Grid Initiatives uses general policies of co-operation and subsidiarity adopted in the European Research Area. A 32 million Euro project named the EGI-Integrated Sustainable Pan-European Infrastructure for Research in Europe (EGI.INSPIRE) was funded in September 2010 to pursue the deployment of EGI as an e-infrastructure offering services to the research communities in Europe and worldwide.

Two services were particularly important for the expansion of grids in the life sciences community: grid-enabled web portals and pilot agent platforms. The emergence of web portals was very important because it took away the need for users to ask for a certificate to access grid resources and it provided a mechanism to hide the complexity of the grid, granting seemingly transparent usage. Pilot agent platforms were able to hide grid limitations in terms of failure rate and information systems. Jobs having failed were automatically resubmitted to the most performing computing elements.

Two scientific disciplines within life sciences were particularly successful during this period in adopting the grid paradigm and making use of its services and resources: one of them is structural biology, under the leadership of Alexander J. Boivin, professor at University of Utrecht and coordinator of the eNMR and WeNMR European projects. The second community is medical imaging around the Virtual Imaging Platform at CREATIS. Both communities made their impact based on successful web portals and efficient strategies for exploiting grid resources.

2˙2.1. Structural biology on the grid. We spoke earlier about the importance for *in silico* drug discovery of the Protein Data Bank [2], repository for the three-dimensional structural data of large biological molecules, such as proteins and nucleic acids. 3D-structure data is typically obtained by X-ray crystallography or NMR spectroscopy. One of the early successes of grids for structural biology is the automated re-refinement of X-ray structure models in the PDB [26]. Homology modeling and rational drug design require accurate three-dimensional macromolecular coordinates. However, the coordinates in the Protein Data Bank (PDB) have not all been obtained using the latest experimental and computational methods. A method was developed at CMBI for automated re-refinement of existing structure models in the PDB. A large-scale benchmark with 16,807 PDB entries was deployed in 2008 on EGEE and showed that the PDB structures could be improved in terms of fit to the deposited experimental X-ray data as well as in terms of geometric quality.

Compared to other structural biology methods, NMR and X-ray cristallography provide the highest spatial resolution. They are, however, faced with many challenges, especially when the macromolecular systems under study become very large, comprise flexible or unstructured regions, exist in very tiny amounts, are membrane-associated, or when their constituents interact only transiently. In order to face these challenges, structural biologists often use different types of biochemical and biophysical experiments. Often, however, the collected data is rather sparse and/or of limited information content. As a consequence, researchers have to rely increasingly on multiple different experimental and computational techniques, share data of various natures and collaborate in order to solve a specific problem, which is at the core of integrative structural biology. The eNMR [27] and WeNMR [4] projects are two consecutive european projects that built a platform integrating services and streamlining the computational approaches necessary for Nuclear Magnetic Resonance (NMR) and Small-Angle X-ray Scattering data analysis. Small Angle X-Ray Scattering (SAXS) is a widely used method for the low-resolution structural analysis of biological macromolecules in solution.

To facilitate the use of NMR spectroscopy and SAXS in life sciences, the projects have established standard computational workflows and services through easy-to-use web interfaces. Thus far, a number of programs often used in structural biology have been made available through application portals (29 to date) that make efficient use of the European Grid Infrastructure (EGI). With over 650 registered VO users and a steady growth rate, WeNMR is currently the largest Virtual Organization in life sciences, gathering users from 44 countries worldwide (39% of users from outside Europe). The computational tools have been used so far mainly for NMR-based structural biology with SAXS portals recently been put into production. Since the beginning of the project, more than 110 peer-reviewed articles have been published by consortium members and external users in high-ranking journals for the field. It is mainly the user-friendly access to software solutions and the computational resources of the grid that attract users, together with the excellent support and training offered by the scientists of the project.

The success of application portals on top of grid resources is not limited to structural biology. Research communities in medical imaging and neurosciences have developed the same strategy as we are going to see in the next paragraph.

2˙3. *Virtual Imaging Platform*. – The Virtual Imaging Platform (VIP) [28] is a web platform for medical image processing and simulation on the European Grid Infrastructure. In a few years only, VIP has become a very successful tool used by more than 700 researchers based in 50+ countries, who consume 50 CPU years per month, and who published 23 peer-reviewed papers using VIP since 2011. In 2012, VIP's "robot" access keys were the most used of the whole European Grid Infrastructure. VIP is a science gateway accessible at `http://vip.creatis.insa-lyon.fr` to facilitate the sharing of object models and medical image simulators, and to provide access to distributed computing and storage resources.

Such a success was possible thanks to fundamental results on distributed systems giving birth to technological innovation:

– algorithms for dynamic load-balancing of Monte Carlo simulations [29] yield optimal task scheduling on the computing resources of the European Grid Infrastructure;

– self-administration methods [30] greatly reduce the human costs of platform operations;

– models of distributed systems [31] allow to simulate distributed executions and to easily identify performance bottlenecks;

– the MOTEUR workflow manager [32] efficiently exploits data parallelism;

– ontologies for the semantic annotation of input and output data [33] facilitate the organization and re-use of data in the long term.

A major innovation that changed user experience on the grid are pilot agent platforms. We are going to introduce their principle and illustrate their impact in the next section.

2˙4. *Pilot agent platforms*. – A pilot agent platform uses a pull model for efficient submission and controlling of user tasks: tasks are no longer pushed through the grid scheduler but are put in a master pool and pulled by pilot agents running on computing nodes. Scheduling a job is the process of ordering tasks in this pool. List scheduling is applied in it. The pilot agent itself is a regular grid job that is started through a grid

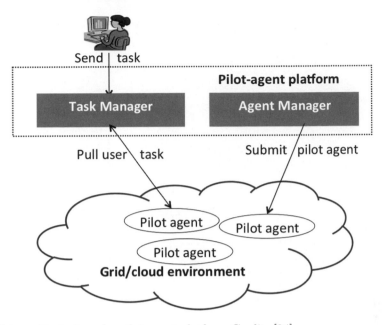

Fig. 5. – Schematic design of a pilot agent platform Credit: [34].

resource manager. It is automatically submitted by platform and run on a computing machine on grid. We can see a pilot agent as container of jobs. The pull model adapts to the heterogeneity of the grid (faster machines will pull more tasks than others), reduces faults (resubmission of failed tasks) and improves latency (the waiting time of a job in grid scheduler is reduced).

As shown in fig. 5, a pilot agent platform has two main modules, the Task Manager and the Agent Manager. The pilot agents are submitted automatically to the grid sites by an Agent Manager. Then each pilot agent communicates with the Task Manager and asks a user task to be executed. The Task Manager receives tasks from the users and controls the queue of user tasks. It also receives request from the pilot agents, choosing according to its scheduling policy the task within the queue to be sent to a pilot agent.

The most popular pilot agent platform on EGI is DIRAC [35]. Initially developed for the LHCb collaboration at CERN, DIRAC (Distributed Infrastructure with Remote Agent Control) is a software framework for distributed computing providing a complete solution to one (or more) user community requiring access to distributed resources. DIRAC builds a layer between the users and the resources offering a common interface to a number of heterogeneous providers, integrating them in a seamless manner, providing interoperability, at the same time as an optimized, transparent and reliable usage of the resources.

To reach out to the long tail of grid users, the French National Grid Initiative France Grilles has deployed a DIRAC service to provide a general solution to access resources,

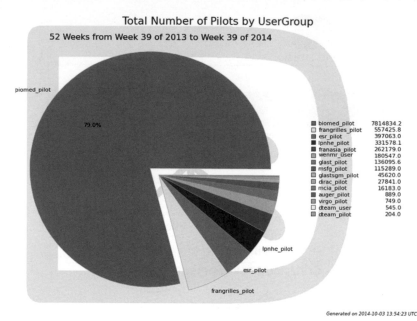

Fig. 6. – Number of jobs submitted to the EGI infrastructure by the different communities using the DIRAC service offered by the French National Grid Initiative France Grilles Credit: [36].

to manage computing and distributed data through a user friendly web interface [36]. In the last 2 years, the FG-DIRAC service has grown to serve today over 180 users in 17 virtual organizations. About 10 million pilot agents have been deployed from October 2013 to September 2014 on EGI resources, most of them through the Biomed virtual organization as shown on fig. 6. The Biomed virtual organization was created as early as 2001 within the framework of DataGrid for all life sciences. It has adopted from the beginning an opportunistic model for harvesting resources, asking support from all EGI sites willing to contribute computing power. The model has been very successful and the Biomed virtual organization was still representing about 80% of the total CPU-time consumed by life sciences on EGI in 2014. In the last few years, Virtual Organizations like We-NMR for structural biology or N4U for neurosciences have been trying to move away from this opportunistic usage and to progressively build an infrastructure within their own research community.

2˙5. *Conclusions*. – To conclude this chapter, the important messages are the following:

– Grids have reached the plateau of maturity, delivering yearly hundreds of millions of CPU hours to various scientific disciplines, including life sciences.

– Grids have reached this maturity because high-energy physics chose that technology to enable the analysis of LHC data. Production grids became operational when the

Large Hadron Collider started collecting data in 2010. The World LHC Computing Grid was immensely successful at analyzing LHC data, resulting in the discovery of the Higgs boson.

– Life sciences are intensely and increasingly using EGI infrastructure through pilot agent platforms and scientific gateways.

On this plateau of maturity, using a grid like EGI takes from 0 to 3 steps:

– Get a certificate from a national Certificate Authority. This step is not needed if you access the grid through a scientific gateway like VIP or We-NMR.

– Learn how to use a platform like DIRAC. Again, this step is not needed if you access the grid through a scientific gateway.

– Access services like FG-Dirac or EGI-DIRAC that are open to the "long tail" of science, namely any user from any academic laboratory in the world.

Adoption of grids is still hindered by a number of limitations:

– Operational cost of running a grid node is very high, of the order of one Full Time Equivalent engineer, because the middleware is very complex and needs to be regularly upgraded. As a consequence, most life sciences laboratories do not have the human resources to install and maintain a grid site. This is a clear issue for communities like structural biology or medical imaging that offer services on the grid but have difficulties to grow their own resources.

– Intellectual property issues have completely stopped the adoption of grids for *in silico* drug discovery. Large-scale deployment of docking computations is technically easy but is not a relevant option for pharmaceutical laboratories.

– Protection of medical data and the absence of a common legal framework at the European level are also a concern for the application of grids to health.

The reader may have noticed that molecular biology is not cited among the success stories for grid adoption by life sciences. There are several reasons for this. The first is technical: as pointed out earlier, molecular biology is characterized by a constantly growing multiplicity of software tools, databases and portals. Grid technology is quite rigid: for instance, the gLite middleware used on a large fraction of EGI resources only runs on a specific version of Scientific Linux. As a consequence, only algorithms running on this version of Scientific Linux can be deployed on EGI sites under gLite. But science is not only about technology but also culture. More than the technology itself, the grid computing model where resources are mutualized did not fit the organizational model of the molecular biology community. Despite success stories like for instance the analysis of genome wide haplotype of human complex diseases with EGEE [37], adoption of grids has remained marginal compared to the needs of molecular biologists and bioinformaticians.

Cloud computing offer exciting new opportunities to address the limitations we have listed earlier in terms of flexibility and operational cost. Pilot agent platforms and scientific gateways are also assets to enable a smooth transition from grids to clouds.

We are going to turn away now from grids and enter the world of clouds.

3. – Clouds in life sciences

The promises of cloud computing are very appealing to life sciences. On public clouds, users only pay for what they consume. No cost is involved to operate IT infrastructure, resources are unbound and there is the flexibility to upload one's favorite Operating System. Academic private clouds should have reduced operational costs compared to grids and also provide flexibility to upload one's favorite Operating System.

Cloud computing was at the top of Gartner hype curve as early as 2010. As a consequence, many infrastructures or initiatives providing cluster or grid resources were renamed with the new magic buzz word in the following years. Adoption of clouds in the life sciences community today is therefore hard to assess. Looking now at fig. 1, one could even think that cloud technology has delivered the services that it promised and is now being replaced by a new paradigm. No perception could be more wrong. Cloud technology is still under development, very far from having delivered to its potential users most of the promises that were made. Regarding technology adoption, three scenarios are to be considered:

– deployment of scientific applications on public clouds like Amazon,

– *de novo* deployment of scientific applications on academic clouds,

– migration to academic clouds using pilot agent platforms.

3˙1. *Deployment of life science applications on public clouds.* – Only a few research groups are using public clouds in France. Public clouds are perceived as expensive compared to academic clusters/grids. Moreover, the French funding model for academic research is hardly compatible with credit card payment for computing capacity. Even the few groups that used services like Amazon Web Service (AWS) do not have very positive feedback. For instance, [38] compares the experience porting the EOULSAN [39] analysis workflow of RNA-sequences on AMAZON and EGI. The workflow was deployed using Hadoop, an open-source implementation of the MapReduce framework introduced by Google. This framework makes it easy to deploy parallel computation, automatically handling duties such as job scheduling, fault tolerance and distributed aggregation. To compare AMAZON and EGI performances, Hadoop was deployed on an EGI cluster at Laboratoire Louis Leprince-Ringuet (Ecole Polytechnique). EOULSAN delivered quicker results on that cluster than using Amazon Web Services [38].

Additional considerations should be made on public cloud storage prices. In July 2014, Google Drive was offering external hard disk at a cost of about one dollar per byte per month, valid for 300 terabyte and above. Storage offers on commercial clouds

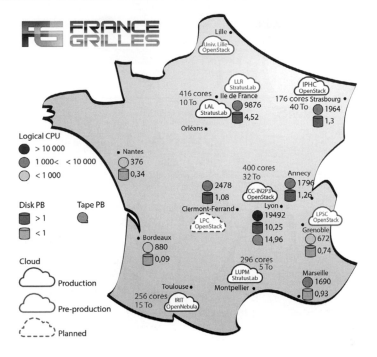

Fig. 7. – Geographical distribution, computing and storage resources provided by France-Grilles cloud and grid sites.

were typically of the order of 300K dollars per petabyte per year, Amazon S32 and Google3 having almost equivalent offers around 30 dollars per terabyte per month. But additional costs induced by the billing of requests and data transfers were significant: for instance, Amazon S3 [41] was charging 0.1 dollar per gigabyte of data transferred from S3 to internet (100K dollars per petabyte) while Google [42] was charging 0.2 dollar per gigabyte of data transferred from S3 to internet (200K dollars per petabyte).

These numbers show that the total cost for using public clouds must be understood in order to make fair comparisons with academic infrastructures. We are now going to discuss the recent emergence of private academic clouds and the services they provide.

3˙2. De novo deployment of scientific applications on academic clouds. – Under EGI initiative, an international federation of academic clouds is progressively emerging as a new IaaS (Infrastructure As A Service) resource for the research communities in Europe and worldwide. France has joined this initiative as early as 2012. After a slow start due to the economic crisis and the political choice of the French government to target only private companies for cloud computing investment, the France Grilles cloud federation has really moved up a gear in 2014. The federation now consists of eight sites (fig. 7), contributing up to 1800 cores and 100 terabytes. These clouds are operated using open

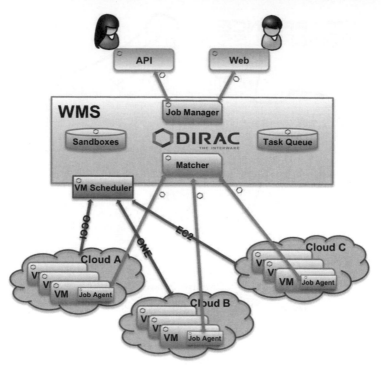

Fig. 8. – Deployment of DIRAC Virtual Machines running pilot jobs on clouds.

source middleware stacks such as Open Nebula, OpenStack and StratusLab. The first call for users was launched very recently (December 2014).

Beside the France-Grilles cloud federation, the French Institute of Bioinformatics (IFB) has put major efforts in a central resource for the management and analysis of biological data. As explained earlier, Grid middleware and computing resources do not optimally fit the core needs of molecular biology. For instance, genome assembly from Next Generation Sequencing raw data requires both RAM and large disk storage while bioinformatics analysis requires much more flexibility than current grid infrastructures provide. As a consequence, the central resource is a 10000 core and 1 PB academic cloud located at IDRIS, the CNRS national supercomputing center.

Another initiative at IDRIS is the E-Biothon project between CNRS, IBM, Institut Franais de Bioinformatique, INRIA and SysFera, that aims at exposing resources of a Blue Gene/P supercomputer through a cloud middleware [40]. The E-Biothon cloud aims at promoting access to computational resources to foster the development of large scale research programs in the field of biology, health and environmental projects.

These initiatives are gaining momentum but their users have to adapt to the cloud technology. One of the most attractive ways to ease a transparent migration from grids to clouds is through pilot agent platforms and scientific gateways. We are going to look at some examples in the next section.

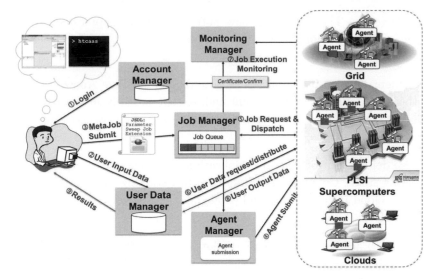

Fig. 9. – Job submission and execution steps in HTCaaS. Credit: [44].

3˙3. *Migration to academic clouds using pilot agent platforms.* – Pilot agent platforms such as DIRAC have been designed to enable the deployment of pilot agents on different architectures, including clouds. As shown on fig. 8, the VMDirac project within the DIRAC collaboration develops the virtual images relevant to the deployment of DIRAC on clouds running different middleware stacks (OpenNebula, OpenStack, Stratuslab). VMDirac is currently under deployment on some of the clouds of the France-Grilles federation.

Another example of a pilot agent platform running on cloud environments is HT-CaaS (High-Throughput Computing as a Service) (fig. 9) developed at KISTI [44]. HT-CaaS aims to facilitate exploring large-scale and complex High-Throughput Computing problems by leveraging various computing resources such as supercomputers, grids and clouds. It is able to hide heterogeneity and complexity of integrating different resources from users, and allow users to efficiently submit a large number of jobs at once. HTCaaS is currently running as a pilot service on top of PLSI (Partnership and Leadership for the nationwide Supercomputing Infrastructure) [43] which consists of distributed supercomputing clusters in Korea and supporting a number of scientific applications from pharmaceutical domain, high-energy physics, nuclear physics. HTCaaS employs agent-based multi-level scheduling and streamlined task dispatching where existing batch schedulers are utilized for submitting agents (pilot-jobs) and each agent bypasses the batch scheduler and directly pulls the tasks from the job queue.

Extensive experiments using real scientific applications on top of a dedicated production-level cluster have shown how HTCaaS can effectively support multiple users in a shared resource environment considering fairness and performance.

3˙4. *Conclusions*. – The reader may have noticed that the chapter dedicated to clouds for life sciences is much shorter than the chapter dedicated to grids. There are many reasons for this:

– Deployment of scientific applications on public clouds like Amazon is operational but the costs induced are significant and, except possibly in the UK, the funding model for science in Europe does not provide scientists with access to a credit card on which they can buy IT resources.

– *De novo* deployment of scientific applications on academic IaaS clouds is still at a pioneering stage. Countries like France are just starting to offer a proper federated academic cloud infrastructure and deploying the relevant services on top of these clouds will take time.

– Migration to academic clouds using pilot agent platforms is certainly a powerful way to hide the technical complexity to the user. Existing tools such as DIRAC or HTCaaS should help gaining time and reduce the cost for users to make the transition between the two infrastructures. They also grant access to new resources like supercomputers for High-Throughput Computing.

4. – Grids and clouds for e-Health

4˙1. *Introduction*. – The grid was devised for use in scientific fields, such as particle physics and bioinformatics, in which large volumes of data, or very rapid processing, or both, are necessary. Unsurprisingly, the grid was also used early on in a number of ambitious medical and healthcare applications. While these initial examples have been mainly restricted to the research domain, there was a great deal of interest in real world applications. However, there is some tension between the spirit of the grid paradigm and the requirements of medical or healthcare applications. The grid maximises its flexibility and minimises its overheads by requesting computations to be carried out at the most appropriate node in the network; it stores or replicates data at the most convenient storage node according to performance criteria. On the other hand, a hospital or other healthcare organisation is required to maintain control of its confidential patient data and to remain accountable for its use at all times. The very basis of grid computing therefore appears to threaten certain inviolable principles, from the confidentiality of medical data through the accountability of healthcare professionals to the precise attribution of "duty of care" [47]. Despite these hurdles, pioneer projects have not been discouraged from exploring and demonstrating the potential impact and relevance of grids to such outstanding healthcare issues as early diagnosis of breast cancer or improved radiotherapy treatment planning.

The European community working on applications of grid computing to health and biomedicine joined forces in the HealthGrid initiative, subsequently incorporated as a charitable organisation in France. Through its annual conferences and a White Paper published in 2005 [46], HealthGrid has defined a vision of grids as the infrastructure of choice for biomedical research in the first place and healthcare delivery in the longer term. Nevertheless, adoption of grids for healthcare encountered many obstacles. A obvious first obstacle was that grid technology was still immature in 2005 and neither robust nor secure enough to offer the quality of service required for routine clinical use. Another important reason is that all grid infrastructures are deployed on national research and education networks which are both separate from the networks used by healthcare structures and very much less secure than they would need to be. Another potential obstacle is the legal framework in the EC member states which has to evolve to allow the transfer of medical data on a European healthgrid.

To address these issues, two strategies were adopted: some communities like neurosciences [11] only handle anonymous data such as medical images on the grid, using platforms similar to VIP (see earlier) for image analysis. Another strategy is to set up dedicated grid infrastructures with authentication and data encryption ensured by healthcare professional smartcards. We are going to briefly present such an infrastructure deployed in the GINSENG project.

4˙2. *GINSENG*. – Emerging challenge concerning public health statistics is the ability to provide real time information on population health. It is especially relevant in case of emergency scenarios: pollution through toxic gas emission or radioactivity, heat waves, pandemic flu viruses. The daily improvement in care practice can also benefit from any real time information on patients hosted in medical structures. To face this problematic, the French GINSENG project uses European Grid Technology to create a sentinel network for e-health and epidemiology [45]. This distributed network architecture offers many advantages:

- medical data banks from each hospital or lab can be interrogated directly without centralizing any information,

- such architecture is cost effective,

- statistical studies are available in real time through a web interface accessible by the medical staff.

While patient data consistency can mainly be achieved by working on medical databases standardization, patient identification and medical data linkage mechanisms are performed dynamically through the grid network. Ontologies and semantic annotations are used to strengthen the usage of the network and to ease epidemiologists work. Authentication and data encryption are ensured by healthcare professional smartcards containing an X509 grid-compatible certificate delivered by a trusted certification authority. The GINSENG project focuses on two fields: cancer surveillance and perinatal health. Regarding cancer surveillance, its goals are to improve screening characteristics and effectiveness for breast and colon cancer and to produce indicators on cancer impact. Regarding perinatal health, it aims at producing indicators on mortality and morbidity during pregnancy, birth defects, very low birthweight and gestational age babies. Another goal is to assess characteristics and longitudinal changes in professional practices

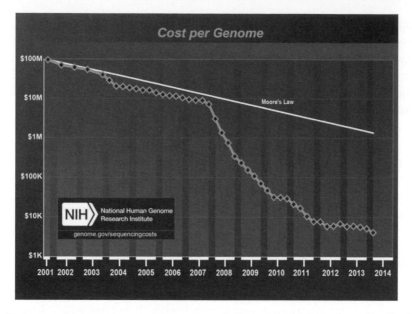

Fig. 10. – Decrease of sequencing cost per genome is faster than Moore law. Credit: [50].

towards specific care (*e.g.* some viral screening procedure and possible consequent management, maternal serum screening of Down syndrome, *in utero* transfers, Caesarean sections, epidurals and spinal anesthesia).

The GINSENG project aims at building a distributed network infrastructure for public health. Currently, ten medical structures are part of the network producing daily updated indicators on cancer and perinatal health.

5. – Entering a new world

5˙1. *Introduction.* – Since the discovery of the Higgs boson, high-energy physics has entered a new world. For three decades, the Standard Model has guided its path. The model has successfully described electroweak physics at LEP, predicted the discovery of the top quark at Fermilab and the Higgs boson at LHC in 2012. After the 2013 Nobel prize, the community must now turn the page and go beyond the model into new physics, without the theoretical guidance it has enjoyed in the last decades.

In this new world, Moore's law does not apply any more to the cost of computer memory and storage. Memory prices in 2014 are comparable to 2011. At the same time, the cost to sequence a genome is decreasing faster than Moore's law (fig. 10). As a consequence of the constant drop of genome sequencing, more than 2500 high-throughput sequencing machines located in more than 900 research centers in the world will produce about 60 PB of data in 2014, comparable to the LHC [48]. This exponential growth of the data volume is not observed only in life sciences and is at the heart of the concept of *big data*.

5˙2. *Big Data*. – "Big data" is a very dynamic market sector at the heart of science most exciting frontiers. The multiplication of sensors, mobile equipments and data intensive programs in all scientific fields together with the explosion of Internet and social networks has driven the emergence of the "big data" phenomenon. The unprecedented growth in data volume, complexity, acquisition rate and variability brings new challenges for their capture, storage, mining, sharing, analysis and representation. The Big Data phenomenon is often described using four Vs (Volume, Velocity, Variety and Veracity):

- Volume refers to the vast amounts of data generated every second.

- Velocity refers to the speed at which new data is generated and the speed at which data moves around.

- Variety refers to the different types of data we can now use.

- Veracity refers to the messiness or trustworthiness of the data.

The challenges of big data can be illustrated through an important episode of the history of England: the edition and compilation of the Domesday book, a manuscript record of the great survey, completed in 1086 on orders of William the Conqueror. According to the Anglo-Saxon chronicle, "While spending the Christmas time of 1085 in Gloucester, William had deep speech with his counsellors and sent men all over England to each shire to find out what or how much each landholder had in land and livestock, and what it was worth".

The Domesday book had absolute authority to define property rights since Middle Age till last century in England. As written in [49]: "for as the sentence of that strict and terrible last account cannot be evaded by any skilful subterfuge, so when this book is appealed to ... its sentence cannot be quashed or set aside with impunity. That is why we have called the book 'the Book of Judgement' ... because its decisions, like those of the Last Judgement, are unalterable".

To achieve the survey, a number of issues had to be tackled that are still relevant to present day massive data analysis:

- In terms of data collection: every shire was visited by a group of royal officers (1085-1086). The unit of inquiry was the Hundred (a subdivision of the county).

- In terms of data veracity: return for each Hundred was sworn to by twelve local jurors, half of them English and half of them Normans.

- In terms of data analysis: names of the new holders and the assessments on which their tax was to be paid were listed to produce the annual value of all the land in the country.

– In terms of data presentation: properties were listed by fiefs, by owner categories (king's holdings, holdings of churchmen and religious houses, aristocrats, lay men, etc.).

– In terms of data preservation: the book was kept in the Royal Treasury in Westminster till the 19th century and later on stored at UK National Archives in Kew. In 1986, a digital version was produced but due to the obsolescence of the software to read it, it was no longer usable from 2002 onwards.

The story of the Domesday Book beautifully illustrates the challenges of Big Data and its preservation.

6. – Conclusions

The goal of this lecture was to give an overview of the achievements in using grid and cloud infrastructures over the last 15 years.

Grid computing has allowed building a truly multidisciplinary distributed IT infrastructure. This infrastructure is built upon a human network of engineers and scientists that have worked together to make it functional and reliable. Life sciences were among the first disciplines to explore the relevance of the grid paradigm, to deploy large-scale computations and they contribute today the second largest user community after physics. Grids are not just infrastructures: they open new avenues to search for new drugs or to build health surveillance networks. They also build upon human networks of engineers and scientists that may very well be their most precious asset.

Life sciences, and particularly molecular biology and bioinformatics, will benefit even more of cloud computing that allows extending the grid functionalities. Today, public cloud prices and performances are not so appealing but there is still a long way to the plateau of maturity for academic clouds. Pilot agent platforms allow a smooth transition from grids to clouds for users. They also grant access to HPC resources for High-Throughput Computing.

Big Data is the next frontier where volume will not necessarily be the most difficult challenge. We will conclude this contribution by a question: what data produced today will still be used in 900 years?

* * *

The authors gratefully acknowledge Alexander Bonvin, Vanessa Hamar, Martin Hofmann, Vinod Kasam, Jik-Soo Kim and Tristan Glatard for providing supporting material on DIRAC, HTCaaS, VIP, WeNMR and WISDOM. Vincent Breton acknowledges the support of France Grilles management team, especially Geneviève Romier, Gilles Mathieu, Jérome Pansanel and Géraldine Fettahi.

REFERENCES

[1] http://www.gartner.com/technology/home.jsp.
[2] BERMAN H., HENRICK K. and NAKAMURA H., *Nat. Struct. Mol. Biol.*, **10** (2003) 980.
[3] CARAPITO CHRISTINE, BUREL ALEXANDRE, GUTERL PATRICK, WALTER ALEXANDRE, VARRIER FABRICE, BERTILE FABRICE and VAN DORSSELAER ALAIN, *Proteomics*, **14** (2014) 1014.
[4] WASSENAAR TSJERK A., VAN DIJK MARC, LOUREIRO-FERREIRA NUNO, VAN DER SCHOT GIJS, DE VRIES SJOERD J., SCHMITZ CHRISTOPHE, VAN DER ZWAN JOHAN, BOELENS ROLF, GIACHETTI ANDREA, FERELLA LUCIO, ROSATO ANTONIO, BERTINI IVANO, HERRMANN TORSTEN, JONKER HENDRIK R. A., BAGARIA ANURAG, JARAVINE VICTOR, GNTERT PETER, SCHWALBE HARALD, VRANKEN WIM F., DORELEIJERS JURGEN F., VRIEND GERT, VUISTER GEERTEN W., FRANKE DANIEL, KIKHNEY ALEXEY, SVERGUN DMITRI I., FOGH RASMUS H., IONIDES JOHN, LAUE ERNEST D., SPRONK CHRIS, JURKŠA SIMONAS, VERLATO MARCO, BADOER SIMONE, DAL PRA STEFANO, MAZZUCATO MIRCO, FRIZZIERO ERIC and BONVIN ALEXANDRE M. J. J., *J. Grid. Comput.*, **10** (2012) 743.
[5] LYNE P. D., *Drug Discov. Today*, **7** (2002) 1047.
[6] CONGREVE M. *et al.*, *Drug Discov. Today*, **10** (2005) 895.
[7] SPENCER R. W., *Biotechnol. Bioeng.*, **61** (1998) 61.
[8] NWAKA S. and RIDLEY R. G., *Nat. Rev. Drug Discov.*, **2** (2003) 919.
[9] GHOSH S. *et al.*, *Curr. Opin. Chem. Biol.*, **10** (2006) 194.
[10] GLATARD T., LARTIZIEN C., GIBAUD B., FERREIRA DA SILVA R., FORESTIER G., CERVENANSKY F., ALESSANDRINI M., BENOIT-CATTIN H., BERNARD O., CAMARASU-POP S. *et al.*, *IEEE Trans. Med. Imaging*, **32** (2013) 110.
[11] HAITAS NIOBE, ROMIER GENEVIÈVE, GRENIER BAPTISTE, FRISONI GIOVANNI, MANSET DAVID, MCCLATCHEY RICHARD, MUNIR KAMRAN, REVILLARD JÉRÔME, COVER KEITH, SPULBER GABRIELLA, GLATARD TRISTAN, OIS MANGIN JEAN-FRAN, TOGA ARTHUR, EVANS ALAN, *Distributed Computing for Neurosciences: the N4U Example*, in *Proceedings of the Workshop "Journées scientifiques mésocentres et France Grilles"*, Paris, October 1-3, 2012, available at http://mesogrilles2012.sciencesconf.org/.
[12] FOSTER IAN and KESSELMANN KARL, *The Grid 2: Blueprint for a New Computing Infrastructure* (Morgan Kaufmann) 2003.
[13] GAGLIARDI F., JONES B., GREY F. *et al.*, *Philos. Trans. R. Soc. A: Math., Phys. Eng. Sci.*, **363** (2005) 1729.
[14] BRETON V., MAIGNE L., SARRAMIA D. and HILL D., *Eight Years Using Grids for Life Sciences*, in *Collaborative Computational Technologies for Biomedical Research*, edited by EKINS SEAN, HUPCEY MAGGIE A. and WILLIAMS ANTONY J. (John Wiley & Sons, Hoboken) DOI: 10.1002/9781118026038.ch15.
[15] RAREY M., KRAMER B., LENGAUER T. and KLEBE G., *J. Mol. Biol.*, **261** (1996) 470.
[16] MORRIS G. M., GOODSELL D. S., HUEY R., HART W. E., HALLIDAY R. S., BELEW R. K. and OLSON A. J., *J. Comput. Chem.*, **19** (1998) 1639.
[17] FERRARI A. M., DEGLIESPOSTI G., SGOBBA M. and RASTELLI G., *Bioorg. Med. Chem.*, **15** (2007) 7865.
[18] KASAM V., MAA A., SCHWICHTENBERG H., ZIMMERMANN M., WOLF A., JACQ N., BRETON V. and HOFMANN M., *J. Chem. Inf. Model.*, **47** (2007) 1818.
[19] DEGLIESPOSTI G., KASAM V., DA COSTA A., KANG H. K., KIM N., KIM D. W., BRETON V., KIM D. and RASTELLI G., *Chem. Med. Chem.*, **4** (2009) 1164.
[20] KASAM V., SALZEMAN J., BOTHA M., DACOSTA A., DEGLIESPOSTI G., ISEA R., KIM D., MAASS A., KENYON C., RASTELLI G., HOFMANN-APITIUS M. and BRETON V., *Malaria J.*, **8** (2009) 88.

[21] Nguyen Thi Thanh Hanh, Ryu Hwa-Ja, Lee Se-Hoon, Hwang Soonwook, Cha Jaeho, Breton Vincent and Kim Doman, *Biotechnol. Lett.*, **33** (2011) 2185.

[22] Nguyen T. T. H., Ryu H.-J., Lee S.-H., Hwang S., Breton V., Rhee J.-H. and Kim D., *Bioorg. Med. Chem. Lett.*, **21** (2011) 3088.

[23] Jacq N., Breton V., Chen H.-Y., Ho L.-Y., Hofmann M., Lee H.-C., Legr Y., Lin S. C., Maa A., Medernach E., Merelli I., Milanesi L., Rastelli G., Reichstadt M., Salzemann J., Schwichtenberg H., Sridhar M., Kasam V., Wu Y.-T. and Zimmermann M., *Lect. Notes Comput. Sci.*, **4360** (2007) 45.

[24] Lee H.-C., Salzemann J., Jacq N., Chen H.-Y., Ho L.-Y., Merelli I., Milanesi L., Breton V., Lin S. C. and Wu Y.-T., *IEEE Trans. Nanobiosci.*, **5** (2006) 288.

[25] Jacq N., Breton V., Chen H.-Y., Ho L.-Y., Hofmann M., Kasam V., Lee H.-C., Legr Y., Lin S. C., Maa A., Medernach E., Merelli I., Milanesi L., Rastelli G., Reichstadt M., Salzemann J., Schwichtenberg H., Sridhar M., Wu Y.-T. and Zimmermann M., *Parallel Comput.*, **33** (2007) 289.

[26] Joosten R. P., Salzemann J., Bloch V., Stockinger H., Berglund A.-C., Blanchet C., Bongcam-Rudloff E., Combet C., Da Costa A., Deleage G., Diarena M., Fabbretti R., Fettahi G., Flegel V., Gisel A., Kasam V., Kervinen T., Korpelainen E., Mattila K., Pagni M., Reichstadt M., Breton V., Tickle I. and Vriend G., *J. Appl. Cristallogr.*, **42** (2009) 1.

[27] Bonvin A. M. J. J., Rosato A. and Wassenaar T. A., *J. Struct. Funct. Genomics*, **11** (2010) 1.

[28] Glatard T., Lartizien C., Gibaud B., Ferreira da Silva R., Forestier G., Cervenansky F., Alessandrini M., Benoit-Cattin H., Bernard O., Camarasu-Pop S. *et al.*, *IEEE Trans. Med. Imaging*, **32** (2013) 110.

[29] Camarasu-Pop S., Glatard T., Ferreira da Silva R., Gueth P., Sarrut D. and Benoit-Cattin H., *Future Gener. Comput. Syst.*, **29** (2013) 728.

[30] Ferreira da Silva R., Glatard T. and Desprez F., *Future Gener. Comput. Syst.*, **29** (2013) 2284.

[31] Glatard T. and Camarasu-Pop S., *Parallel Comput.*, **37** (2011) 684.

[32] Glatard T., Montagnat J., Lingrand D. and Pennec X., *J. High Perform. Comput. Appl.*, **22** (2008) 347.

[33] Gibaud B., Forestier G., Benoit-Cattin H., Cervenansky F., Clarysse P., Friboulet D., Gaignard A., Hugonnard P., Lartizien C., Liebgott H. *et al.*, *J. Biomed. Inform.*, **52** (2014) 279.

[34] Quang B. T., Nguyen H. Q., Medernach E. and Breton Vincent, *Multi-level queue-based scheduling for virtual screening application on pilot-agent platforms on grid/cloud to optimize the stretch*, in *Proceedings of the Sixth International Conference on Future Computational Technologies and Applications, Venice, Italy, May 2014*.

[35] Tsaregorodtsev A., Bargiotti M., Brook N., Ramo A. C., Castellani G., Charpentier P. *et al.*, *J. Phys. Conf. Ser.*, **119** (2009) 62048.

[36] https://dirac.france-grilles.fr/DIRAC/.

[37] Trégouët D. *et al.*, *Nat. Genet.*, **41** (2009) 283.

[38] Le Crom S. *et al.*, *Proceedings of Journées SUCCES 2013, Paris, November 2013*, http://succes2013.sciencesconf.org/.

[39] http:/transcriptome.ens.fr/eoulsan/.

[40] Bard N., Boin S., Bothorel F., Chaumeil P., Collinet P., Dayde M., Depardon B., Desprez F., Fie M., Franc A. *et al.*, *Proceedings of Journées SUCCES 2013, Paris, November 2013*, https://hal.archives-ouvertes.fr/hal-00927495/document.

[41] http://aws.amazon.com/fr/s3/pricing/.

[42] https://cloud.google.com/products/cloud-storage.

[43] http://www.plsi.or.kr/.

[44] THE QUANG BUI, KIM JIK-SOO, RHO SEUNGWOO, KIM SEOYOUNG, KIM SANGWAN, HWANG SOONWOOK, MEDERNACH EMMANUEL and BRETON VINCENT, *A Comparative Analysis of Scheduling Mechanisms for Virtual Screening Workflow in a Shared Resource Environment*, to be published in *Proceedings of the CCGrid Conference, 2015*.

[45] CIPIERE SÉBASTIEN, ERETEO GUILLAUME, GAIGNARD ALBAN, BOUJELBEN NOUHA, GASPARD SÉBASTIEN, BRETON VINCENT, CERVENANSKY FRÉDÉRIC, HILL DAVID, GLATARD TRISTAN, MANSET DAVID, MONTAGNAT JOHAN, REVILLARD JÉROME and MAIGNE LYDIA, *Global Initiative for Sentinel e-Health Network on Grid (GINSENG), Medical data integration and semantic developments for epidemiology*, in *Proceedings of the CCGRID Conference, 2014*.

[46] BRETON V., DEAN K. and SOLOMONIDES T. (EDITORS ON BEHALF OF THE HEALTHGRID WHITE PAPER COLLABORATION), *The Healthgrid White Paper*, in *From Grid to Healthgrid, Proceedings of the Healthgrid Conference 2005, Studies in Health Technology and Informatics Series*, Vol. **112** (IOS Press) 2005.

[47] OLIVE MARK, RAHMOUNI HANENE, SOLOMONIDES TONY, BRETON VINCENT, LEGRÉ YANNICK, BLANQUER IGNACIO, HERNANDEZ VICENTE, *Int. J. Med. Inform.*, **78**, Suppl. **1** (2009) S3.

[48] http://omicspmaps.com.

[49] FITZNEAL RICHARD, *Dialogus de Scaccario* (1179).

[50] http://www.genome.gov/SequencingCosts/.

Proceedings of the International School of Physics "Enrico Fermi"
Course 192 "Grid and Cloud Computing: Concepts and Practical Applications",
edited by F. Carminati, L. Betev and A. Grigoras
(IOS, Amsterdam; SIF, Bologna) 2016
DOI 10.3254/978-1-61499-643-9-101

Monitoring and control of large-scale distributed systems

I. C. LEGRAND

California Institute of Technology - Pasadena, CA, USA

CERN, European Organization for Nuclear Research - Geneva, Switzerland

Summary. — An important part of managing large-scale, distributed computing systems is a monitoring service that is able to monitor and track in real-time many site facilities, networks, and tasks in progress. The monitoring information gathered is essential for developing the required higher level services, the components that provide decision support and some degree of automated decisions and for maintaining and optimizing workflow in large-scale distributed systems. Our strategy in trying to satisfy the demands of data intensive applications was to move to more synergetic relationships between the applications, computing and storage facilities and the network infrastructure. These orchestration and global optimization functions are performed by higher-level agent-based services which are able to collaborate and cooperate in performing a wide range of distributed information-gathering and processing tasks.

1. – Introduction

In this paper we present the experience in developing and deploying the MonALISA (Monitoring Agents in A Large Integrated Services Architecture) [1] framework to monitor large-scale distributed systems and how it is used to control and manage complex workflows. The aim of the MonALISA project was to provide a distributed service system capable to control and optimize large-scale, data-intensive applications. Its initial target field of applications is the "Grid Systems" and the networks supporting data processing and analysis for high-energy physics (HEP) collaborations. The MonALISA framework provides a set of distributed services for monitoring, control, management and global optimization for large-scale distributed systems. It is based on an ensemble of autonomous, multithreaded, agent-based subsystems which are registered as dynamic services. They can be automatically discovered and used by other services or clients. The distributed agents can collaborate and cooperate in performing a wide range of management, control and global optimization tasks using real-time monitoring information. Current applications of MonALISA's services include optimized dynamic routing, control and optimization for large-scale data transfers on dedicated circuits, data transfers scheduling, distributed job scheduling and automated management of remote services among a large set of grid facilities. MonALISA is currently used around the clock in several major projects and has proven to be both highly scalable and reliable. More than 350 services are running at sites around the world, collecting information about computing facilities, local and wide-area network traffic, and the state and progress of the many thousands of concurrently running jobs.

2. – The system design

The MonALISA system [1,2] is designed as an ensemble of autonomous self-describing agent-based subsystems which are registered as dynamic services. These services are able to collaborate and cooperate in performing a wide range of distributed information-gathering and processing tasks.

An agent-based architecture [3] of this kind is well-adapted to the operation and management of large-scale distributed systems, by providing global optimization services capable of orchestrating computing, storage and network resources to support complex workflows. By monitoring the state of the grid-sites and their network connections end-to-end in real time, the MonALISA services are able to rapidly detect, help diagnose and in many cases mitigate problem conditions, thereby increasing the overall reliability and manageability of the distributed computing systems [4]. The MonALISA architecture, presented in fig. 1, is based on four layers of global services. The entire system is developed based on the Java [5] technology.

The network of Lookup Discovery Services (LUS) provides dynamic registration and discovery for all other services and agents. MonALISA services are able to discover each other in the distributed environment and to be discovered by the interested clients. The registration uses a lease mechanism. If a service fails to renew its lease, it is removed from the LUSs and a notification is sent to all the services or other application that subscribed for such events. Remote event notification is used in this way to get a real overview of this dynamic system.

The second layer, represents the network of MonALISA service that host many monitoring tasks through the use of a multithreaded execution engine and to host a variety of loosely coupled agents that analyze the collected information in real time. The collected information can be stored locally in databases. Agents are able to process

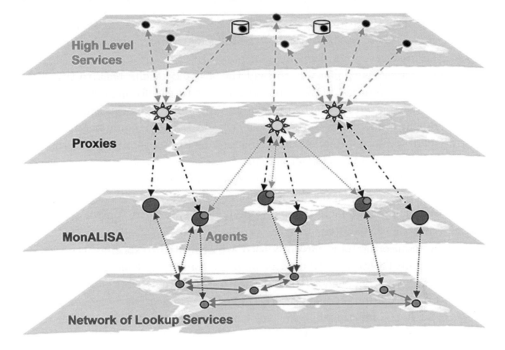

Fig. 1. – The four layers, main services and components of the MonALISA framework.

information locally and to communicate with other services or agents to perform global optimization tasks.

A service in the MonALISA framework is a component that interacts autonomously with other services either through dynamic proxies or via agents that use self-describing protocols. By using the network of lookup services, a distributed services registry, and the discovery and notification mechanisms, the services are able to access each other seamlessly. The use of dynamic remote event subscription allows a service to register an interest in a selected set of event types, even in the absence of a notification provider at registration time.

The third layer of Proxy services, shown in the figure, provides an intelligent multiplexing of the information requested by the clients or other services and is used for reliable communication between agents. It can also be used as an Access Control Enforcement layer to provide secures access to the collected information.

Higher level services and client access the collected information using the proxy layer of services. A load balancing mechanism is used to allocate these services dynamically to the best proxy service. The clients, other services or agents can get any real-time or historical data by using a predicate mechanism for requesting or subscribing to selected measured values. These predicates are based on regular expressions to match the attribute description of the measured values a client is interested in. They may also be used to impose additional conditions or constraints for selecting the values. The subscription requests create a dedicated priority queue for messages. The communication with the clients is served by a pool of threads. The allocated thread performs the matching tests for all the predicates submitted by a client with the monitoring values in the data flow. The same thread is responsible to send the selected results back to the client as compressed serialized objects. Having an independent thread for clients allows sending the information they need, in a fast and reliable way, and it is not affected by communication errors which may occur with other clients. In case of communication problems these threads will try to re-establish the connection or to clean-up the subscriptions for a client or a service which is no longer active.

The main aim for developing the MonALISA system was to provide a flexible framework capable to use in near real time the complete monitoring information from large number of jobs, computing facilities and wide-area networks to control and optimize complex workflows in distributed systems.

Most of the monitoring tools currently used are dedicated to specific activities. Ganglia [6], and Lemon [7] are mainly used to monitor computing clusters while tools like MRTG [8], perfSONAR [9], Nagios [10] and Spectrum [11] are network oriented tools providing monitor information on the network traffic, and connectivity. In the MonALISA system we provide the functionality to collect any type of information and in this way to offer a more synergetic approach, necessary to control and optimize the execution of data intensive applications on large-scale distributed systems [12]. The framework provides integrated mechanisms to access the monitoring information from all the other MonALISA services or third party applications interfaced with the system.

Most of the monitoring tools use a set of procedures to collect the information from computing nodes or network equipment which is stored locally using XML format, the Round Robin Database (RRD) [13] or relational databases. The stored information is than accessed using specific queries procedures by other applications to generate monitoring reports or plots. In the MonALISA system it is possible to dynamically subscribe to any class of information, to filter or generate aggregated values on the fly or to take actions based on certain values using modules that are dynamically deployed. The mechanism to select and construct the information requested by other remote services is done in memory by each MonALISA service and in this way is possible to handle significantly more information (tens of thousands of monitoring messages per second) in near real time.

2˙1. *Registration and discovery.* – MonALISA services are able to discover each other in the distributed environment and to be discovered by the interested clients. This functionality is implemented in the MonALISA system based the JAVA/JINI technology [14]. Each MonALISA service registers itself with a set of Lookup Services (LUSs) as part of one or more groups and it publishes a set of dynamic attributes that describe it. In this way any interested application can request MonALISA services based on a set of matching attributes. JINI can use both multicast and unicast to bootstrap the discovery of LUSs. We use at least two LUSs (one in Europe and one in US) for redundancy, to bootstrap the discovery. The registration information as well as the time dependent attributes for services are replicated in near real time in the LUSs. The registration uses a lease mechanism. If a service fails to renew its lease, it is removed from the LUSs and a notification is sent to all the services or other application that subscribed for such events. Remote event notification is used in this way to get a real overview of this dynamic system. The registration of services into the LUSs can be open or protected by X509 certificates.

2˙2. *The MonALISA service.* – The basic component of the monitoring framework is the MonALISA service. This is an ensemble of multithreaded subsystems, which carry out several functions in an independent fashion, being able to operate autonomously. Here are some of the most important functions it performs:

- *monitoring* of a large number of entities (hosts, services, applications, network) using simultaneously several modules which interact actively with the entities or passively listen for information, or interface with other existing monitoring tools;

- *filtering and aggregation* of the monitoring data, providing additional information based on several data series;

- *storage* for short period of time of the monitoring information, in memory or in a local database. This way, clients can get also history for the monitoring information they are interested in, not only the real-time monitored values;

- *web services* for direct access to the monitored data, from the monitoring service. This way, local clients can get the information directly, without following the whole chain;

- *triggers, alerts and actions* based on the monitored information, being able to react immediately when abnormal behavior is detected;

- *controlling* using dedicated modules allow performing more complicated actions, that cannot be taken only to the local flow of information. This way, the service can act based on monitoring information from several services at the command of a controlling client, or direct or indirect users request.

The communication between clients and the selected services is performed through a set of proxy services. The proxy services also register their existence in the lookup services and are dynamically discovered. The usage of proxies for the communication has multiple advantages. First, the data from a service can be sent only once and is multiplexed to all the interested clients connected to the same proxy. This reduces the load on the service and on the network, in case of many clients. It also provides a natural way of scaling the system, to support a large number of clients. Second, this has an extremely valuable practical advantage: the services do not require incoming network connectivity when clients running outside service's domain connect to the service. This distributed architecture is fault tolerant because it does not have a single point of failure. All the core services (lookup and proxy services) are replicated in different locations worldwide.

2˙3. *Monitoring modules and information gathering.* – The system monitors and tracks site computing clusters, applications and network links, routers and switches and it dynamically loads modules that make it capable of interfacing existing monitoring applications and tools. The core of the monitoring service is based on a multithreaded system used to perform the many data collection tasks in parallel, independently. The modules used for collecting different sets of information, or interfacing with other monitoring tools, are dynamically loaded and executed in independent threads. In order to reduce the load on systems running MonALISA, a dynamic pool of threads is created once, and the threads are then reused when a task assigned to a thread is completed. This allows one to run concurrently and independently a large number of monitoring modules, and to dynamically adapt to the load and the response time of the components in the system. If a monitoring task fails or hangs due to I/O errors, the other tasks are not delayed or disrupted, since they are executing in other, independent threads. A dedicated control thread is used to stop properly the threads in case of I/O errors, and to reschedule those tasks that have not been successfully completed. A priority queue is used for the tasks that need to be performed periodically. This approach makes it relatively easy to monitor a large number of heterogeneous nodes with different response times, and at the same time to handle monitored units which are down or not responding, without affecting the other measurements.

A Monitoring Module is a dynamic loadable unit which executes a procedure (or runs a script / program or performs a SNMP or TL1 request) to collect a set of parameters (monitored values) by properly parsing the output of the procedure. In general a monitoring module is a simple class, which is using a certain procedure to obtain a set of parameters and report them in a simple, standard format. Monitoring Modules can be used for pulling data and in this case it is necessary to execute them with a predefined frequency or pushing programs (scripts) which are sending the monitoring results (via SNMP, UDP or TCP/IP) periodically back to the Monitoring Service.

We developed a dedicated client API, named ApMon that allows sending any type of customized information into the MonALISA system. ApMon is using UDP datagram to transport the information (XDR encoded) and is using a sequence number to verify the integrity for all the monitoring reports. In addition, it provides complete system monitoring of the host that runs the application instrumented with ApMon. It can be dynamically configured from remote services: which parameters to report, at which frequently and to which MonALISA services and sent the information. ApMon implementations are provided for five programming languages (C, C++, Java, Perl and Python) and it can easily be used by any program or script to report into the MonALISA system. ApMon is currently used by the CMS [15] and ALICE [16] experiments at CERN to monitor tens of thousands of running jobs distributed in computing centres all over the word. It is used to collect and transport more than 50 million monitoring parameters per day.

In the MonALISA framework we developed dedicated modules to easily integrate monitor information collected from monitoring tools like Ganglia [6], Lemon [7], MRTG [8], Nagios [10] and Spectrum [11].

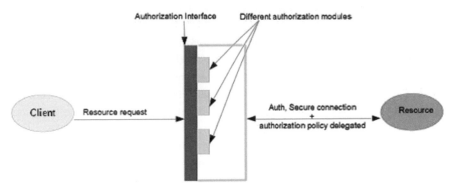

Fig. 2. – The secure Client Server Communication for the MonALISA services.

To monitor the execution of jobs in different clusters we developed dedicated modules to collect such information from several batch systems: LSF [17], Condor [18], PBS [19], Sun Grid Engine [20].

Any monitoring module can be dynamically loaded from the local system or from a (few) central repositories in a secure way. The functionality to dynamically load these modules from centralized sites when they are needed makes much easier to keep large monitoring systems updated and to provide new functionalities dynamically. Users can implement easily any new dedicated modules and use it the MonALISA framework.

2`4. Security infrastructure. – Monitoring modules in a MonALISA service may collect sensitive data from the regional centre it runs on. In this case, cluster's administrators have the possibility to define access policies in order to control the access. The confidentiality of data flow between services and clients must be assured too.

The security infrastructure implemented, relies on standardized X.509v3 certificates for mutual authentication, on access control lists (ACLs) for authorization and also on Secure Sockets Layer (SSL) communication protocol. The Public Key Infrastructure (PKI) supporting this security sub-system can be configured to use existing root Grid CAs certificates (when deployed in Grid environments) or custom CAs certificates (when deployed in intranets).

The security infrastructure must also support different types of authorization (*e.g.* push model, pull model, end entity certificate, GSI proxy certificates). Access control lists have to be manageable and maintainable (adding, removing and modifying user privilege need to be kept easy and intuitive).

In the actual architecture clients interact with MonALISA services via the proxy service. Figure 2 describes clients-services communication. The architecture provides a proxy service which is used by clients to connect to different services. In our service design we use the mutual discovery between services and proxies to detect when a certain service runs run behind a firewall or NAT.

In this case the service initiates a connection to all the available proxies for a community and registers itself with the LUSs. Any client can interact now with such services via the proxy services. Since clients do not directly connect to MonALISA services, a proper place for authorization enforcement is the proxy itself. In order to achieve this, the MonALISA service must delegate the authorization actions to proxy service. But, first of all, the proxy service must be trusted to do this on behalf of MonALISA service. This can be assured by establishing a trust relationship with the proxy it connects to, using a public-key cryptography mechanism based on X509 certificates. Whenever the MonALISA service connects to a proxy it authenticates the proxy service (*i.e.* verify that it received a trusted host identity certificate).

Any further data request from a client is managed by the proxy service. It authorizes this request based on authorization policy received from monitoring service and the credentials presented by the client.

MonALISA security infrastructure implementation is based on existing standards: TLS, PKIX and GSS-API. A client accessing monitoring data follows the following scheme:

User authenticates to the proxy service using his/her identity certificate. Users operating in a Grid environment can also use their proxy certificate. Upon the final of this step the client proved his identity.

Based on client identity (Distinguished Name —DN— from approved certificate) the proxy service retrieves the access control list (rights granted) for this client from the AAA services. The integrity of the connection between the authorization server and the proxy service checking the authorization information is assured. Further requests from this client will be filtered based on these ACLs (*i.e.* proxy service acts as a Policy Enforcement Point). Also the communication between client and MonALISA services is protected, assuring integrity and confidentiality of the messages exchanged. The security infrastructure described eliminates the problems with single-points of failure by distributing the security gateways and it offers a high level of availability and scalability.

2˙5. *Data storage.* – The system is able to store data in almost real time and to quickly retrieve it on demand and transparently handle management operations on the stored data.

A MonALISA API provides an abstract interface to data storage. The two main functions are adding new values and querying the storage for data matching a given predicate. Particular implementations are available for different purposes: plain text files logging or database backend storages, values averaged in time or keeping original data as it was produced. All database-backed storage structures have the option to re-sample the values on the fly, to provide a uniform time distribution of values. New storage implementations that fit particular needs can be easily added.

The default database backend for all MonALISA services is PostgreSQL [21]. Both the service and the repository come with a precompiled PostgreSQL package that is used by default, but the configuration parameters allow using a different backend.

In addition to any permanent storage for the monitoring values a volatile memory buffer is kept internally, serving as cache for recent data. The size of this memory buffer is dynamically adjusted function of how much memory was allocated to the Java Virtual

Machine and how much of it is free. This volatile storage is enough for running a light monitoring service, being able to serve history requests in the limit of how much data the service was able to keep in memory.

This storage layer is shared by both the service and the repository, allowing services to keep long term archives of the monitoring data if necessary.

All structures are used in parallel. Data is written in the database only at the end of an aggregation interval, using asynchronous operations, to minimize the impact of IO over the main monitoring tasks. Upon request the code will automatically select the most appropriate storage structure, depending on the time interval and the number of data points that are requested.

2˙6. *Wavelets data compression.* – Wavelets transforms are among the most frequently used transformations for image and time series compression. Unlike Fourier Transform, the Wavelets transform provide time and frequency information, offering good compression rates, and are able to describe signals exhibiting sharp variations. The wavelet analysis is appropriate for both stationary and non-stationary signals and can be used to describe the signal trends, discontinuities and self-similarity.

The Discrete Wavelet Transform (DWT) is implemented as a digital filter technique. It analyzes the signal at different frequency bands with different resolutions by decomposing the signal into a coarse approximation and detail information. DWT uses two sets of functions, called scaling functions and wavelet functions, which are associated with low-pass and high-pass filters. A single level decomposition puts a signal through two complementary low-pass and high-pass filters. The output of the low-pass filter gives the approximation coefficients, while the high pass filter gives the detail coefficients. The decomposition of the signal into different frequency bands is done by using successive high-pass and low-pass filtering on the time representation for the signal.

Compression for time series data can be done by keeping only a set of significant coefficients from the DWT. The amount of monitoring data collected for LHC experiments is continuously increasing and we need to store and analyze tens of TB of data. In fig. 3 is presented the total number of persistent monitoring values collected and stored in MonALISA system for CMS and ALICE experiments.

Developing effective procedures to compress these large sets of time series data is becoming and important part in managing monitoring information. We developed a prototype storage and compression system using the wavelets decomposition.

In fig. 4 is presented the efficiency of compression using Daubechies Discrete Wavelets Transform for data traffic data on one major LHC network links. The wavelet based analysis for these time series data can also be used to cluster and classify components in the grid systems (see sect. 4˙3.).

When the original time series signal is decomposed by time-frequency wavelets transformation into coefficients representing different scales for each time window. Keeping only the coefficients with higher absolute values is the general technique, named "Thresholding" and is used to compress time series data or images. It is important to select appropriate thresholding scheme to obtain good compression while preserving the signal energy.

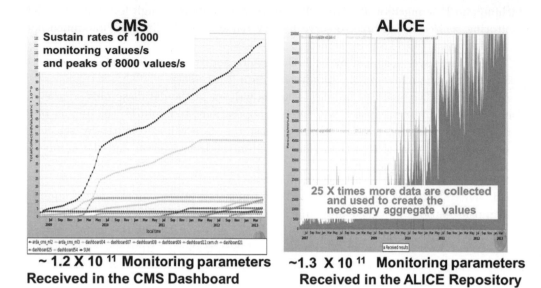

Fig. 3. – The total number of persistent parameters collected by the MonALISA system for the CMS and ALICE experiments.

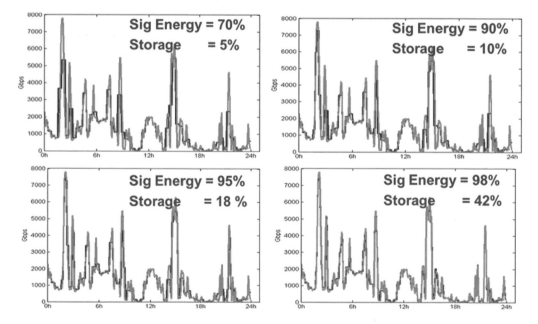

Fig. 4. – Wavelet compression with different thresholds for the transformed coefficients used for data traffic on a major LHC network segment.

Based on these results, for long-term storage we can for example reduce the data volume to $\sim 10\%$ while keeping the signal accuracy to $\sim 90\%$.

2˙7. *Monitoring clients and optimization services*. – The clients of this monitoring framework use the LUSs to find all the active MonALISA services running as part of one or several groups. Once the connection is established through one of the proxies, clients can get any real-time or historical data by using the predicate mechanism.

There are three types of clients that can use the MonALISA framework to display the gathered monitoring information from all the distributed services:

– *Graphical clients*, who provide dedicated panels for some of the common monitored parameters. They also allow the user to interactively choose what parameters he wants to observe and in what format (real-time chart/histogram, history plot, pie charts, stacked bars etc.) and get immediately the result from one or several services. This provides great flexibility in investigating the monitored entities (detailed, correlated, multisite plots);

– *Repository clients*, that offer long history for a few, preconfigured parameters. The time series for these parameters are stored in a database for long-term viewing purposes. Due to the large amount of data (from all the services in community), the typical usage is for storing aggregated and summary values. For those, it offers a set of predefined charts in a web application format that allow selecting among the set of time series and the time interval to plot. The repository client has been extended to support actions and alerts. The two clients complement each other in the support they offer to the community administrator;

– *Stub clients*, which represent the shared core among the first two clients and is the platform that can be used to build custom clients capable to take local and global action in the MonALISA framework.

Clients can also send back to the monitoring services predicates to select the monitoring information they are interested in and commands, based on security infrastructure previously described, that allow changing the configuration of the service or controlling the available modules. Users can issue these commands directly from the graphical client or as a result of the configured actions in the repository or other dedicated clients.

The *stub client* represents the platform for developing high level services that consider the optimization of a large distributed system that they can monitor and control through the help of the distributed services.

2˙8. *Fast data transfer*. – To satisfy the demands of data intensive applications we developed the Fast Data Transfer (FDT) [22] an efficient data transfer program, which is well integrated in the MonALISA framework. FDT is being developed to support efficient large-scale data transfer services and also to help in the active monitoring of the available bandwidth between sites. FDT is capable of reading and writing at disk speed over Wide-Area Networks, with standard TCP. Compared with other high-performance data transfer applications GridFTP [23] and BBCP [24], FDT can be dynamically controlled by the

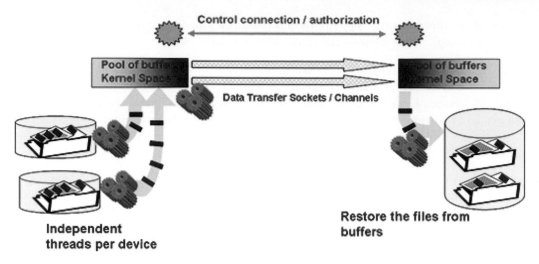

Fig. 5. – The Fast Data Transfer architecture.

MonALISA system. The bandwidth used to transfer data can be dynamically adjusted for large-scale data transfer services that support priorities and have real-time information on network topology. FDT is written in Java [5], runs an all major platforms and it is easy to use. FDT can be used as an independent application but it can also be controlled and managed by the MonALISA system to provide effective data transfer services.

FDT is based on an asynchronous, flexible multithreaded system and is using the capabilities of the Java NIO libraries. Its main features are:

- Streams a dataset (list of files) continuously, using a managed pool of buffers through one or more TCP sockets.

- Uses independent threads to read and write on each physical device

- Transfers data in parallel on multiple TCP streams, when necessary

- Uses appropriate-sized buffers for disk I/O and for the network

- Restores the files from buffers asynchronously

- Resumes a file transfer session without loss, when needed

A schematic view of the FDT design is presented in fig. 5. FDT can be used to stream a large set of files across the network, so that a large dataset composed of thousands of files can be sent or received at full speed, without the network transfer restarting between files. The FDT architecture allows to "plug-in" external security APIs and to use them for client authentication and authorization. FDT supports several security schemes: IP filtering, SSH, GSI-SSH, Globus-GSI, and SSL.

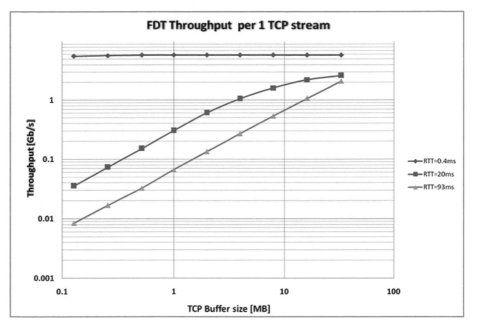

Fig. 6. – The FDT throughput (logarithmic scale) for one TCP stream for different RTT and buffer sizes.

The TCP throughput per stream depends on the Round Trip Time (RTT) and the buffer size (fig. 6).

On connections with large RTT is really necessary to use parallel streams for high speed data transfers. FDT architecture was design to correctly handle concurrent TCP streams and in this way to offer high performance data transfers on long RTT connections.

FDT memory to memory performance tests: These first tests were done on USL-HCNet network using the segment between CERN and New York (Round Trip Time (RTT) = 93 ms).

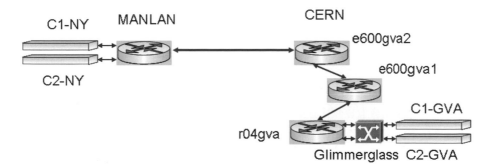

Fig. 7. – The topology used for FDT memory to memory tests.

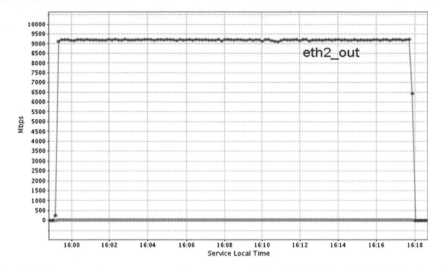

Fig. 8. – FDT memory-to-memory performance tests in WAN; The CPU utilization for the sender and receiver.

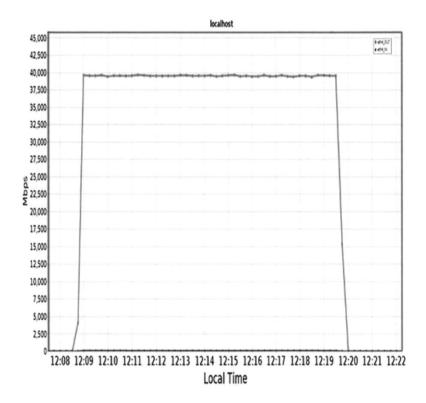

Fig. 9. – FTD performance tests with 40 Gbps Mellanox network cards.

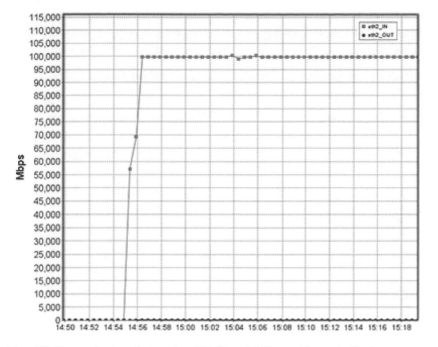

Fig. 10. – FDT transferring data using 100 Gbps Mellanox Network Card.

The systems (Cx-NY and Cx-GVA, $x = 1, 2$) used for these tests are:

2 CPUs Dual Core Intel Xenon @ 3.00 GHz, 4 GB RAM, 4×320 GB SATA Disks

Connected with 10 Gb/s Myricom cards in the routers at CERN and MANLAN. The topology used is presented in fig. 7.

One pair (C1-NY and C1-GVA) was used to test the maximum throughput we can get from one system. We used 2 MB for the TCP buffer size and 35 streams.

The throughput in each direction was very stable at $\sim$ 9.4 GB/s (fig. 8). The CPU utilization for the sender and receiver is also presented.

The results of memory to memory transfers using FDT with 40 Gbps Mellanox network cards are presented on fig. 9. The two computers were locally connected and we used two TCP streams to reach 40 Gbps data transfer rate.

In recent tests done at Caltech using the new Intel Haswell processors and 100 GE NICs from Mellanox using FTD to transfer data between two data server nodes show that the strategy to handle serval concurrent TCP streams scale very well and we can move data at $\sim$ 99.00 Gbps (see fig. 10). To achieve this performance FDT is using the processing power of $\sim$ 4 CPU cores (one data server has 28 cores).

FDT disk to disk performance tests: For a first test we used two 1U servers with four hard disks between CERN and MANLAN (New York) (RTT $\sim$ 93 ms). Each system used a 10 Gb/s network card and we used the USLHCNET. The results are presented in fig. 11, left. FDT was used to read and write on all four disks in parallel. FDT is capable

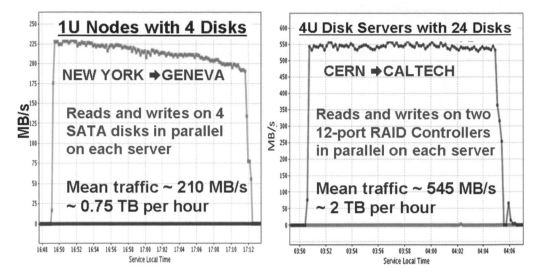

Fig. 11. – FDT disk to disk results in transferring large data sets from CERN to Caltech.

to transfer data over WAN at the limit of the disks IO rate. The rate decreases in time as the write speed on normal disks decreases as the disks are filled.

A second performance test was done using two disk servers between CERN and Caltech (RTT $\sim$ 170 ms). Each system used a 10 Gb/s network card (Myricom). The connection between the two systems used the USLHCNET for the transatlantic part and Internet2 in US. The disk servers used: 4U - 2 CPUs Dual Core Intel Woodcrest @ 3.00 GHz, 6 GB RAM, 2 ARECA RAID controllers and 24 SATA HDDs. The results presented in fig. 11, right, show that the transfer runs practically at the IO limit of the disk servers we used.

3. – Network monitoring and management

Network monitoring is vital to ensure proper network operation over time, and is tightly integrated with all the data intensive processing tasks used by the LHC experiments. In order to build a coherent set of network management services it is very important to collect in near real-time information about the network traffic volume and its quality, and analyze the major flows and the topology of connectivity. Access to both real-time and historical data, as provided by MonALISA, also is important for developing services able to predict the usage pattern, to aid in efficiently allocating resources "globally" across a set of network links. A large set of MonALISA monitoring modules has been developed to collect specific network information (SNMP, TL1, ICMP) or to interface it with existing monitoring tools (NetFlow [25], sFlow [26] MRTG [8] and Nagios [10]). These modules have been field-proven to function with a very high level of reliability over the last few years.

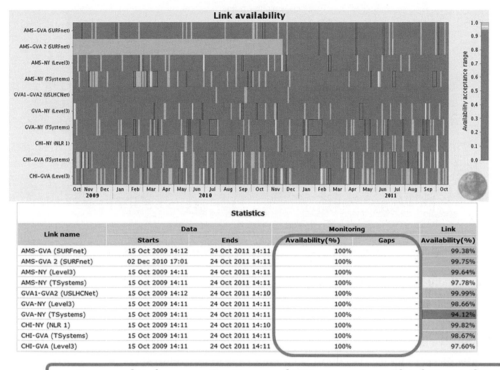

| Link name | Data | | Monitoring | | Link |
	Starts	Ends	Availability(%)	Gaps	Availability(%)
AMS-GVA (SURFnet)	15 Oct 2009 14:12	24 Oct 2011 14:11	100%	-	99.38%
AMS-GVA 2 (SURFnet)	02 Dec 2010 17:01	24 Oct 2011 14:11	100%	-	99.75%
AMS-NY (Level3)	15 Oct 2009 14:11	24 Oct 2011 14:11	100%	-	99.64%
AMS-NY (TSystems)	15 Oct 2009 14:11	24 Oct 2011 14:11	100%	-	97.78%
GVA1-GVA2 (USLHCNet)	15 Oct 2009 14:12	24 Oct 2011 14:10	100%	-	99.99%
GVA-NY (Level3)	15 Oct 2009 14:11	24 Oct 2011 14:11	100%	-	98.66%
GVA-NY (TSystems)	15 Oct 2009 14:11	24 Oct 2011 14:11	100%	-	94.12%
CHI-NY (NLR 1)	15 Oct 2009 14:11	24 Oct 2011 14:10	100%	-	99.82%
CHI-GVA (TSystems)	15 Oct 2009 14:11	24 Oct 2011 14:11	100%	-	98.67%
CHI-GVA (Level3)	15 Oct 2009 14:11	24 Oct 2011 14:11	100%		97.60%

No monitoring gaps for 2 years (~30 seconds polling interval)

Fig. 12. – Monitoring the status of major WAN links in USLHCNet. MonALISA system was able to offer reliable monitoring for the entire network infrastructure. With 30 s polling interval there are no monitoring gasps for the two years interval presented in the plot. The second link from the top, AMS-GVA 2 was commissioned at the beginning of December 2010 and has no previous history.

3˙1. *The Network Monitoring the USLHCnet.* – MonALISA is used to provide reliable, real-time monitoring of the USLHCNet [27] infrastructure. In each point of presence (GVA, AMS, CHI, NYC) we run a MonALISA service to monitor the links, the network equipment and the peering with other networks. Each major link is monitored at both ends from two independent MonALISA services (the local one and one from a remote site). MonALISA services keep locally the history of all the measurements and a global aggregation, for long term history, is kept in a MonALISA repository. Dedicated TL1 modules for the Ciena CD/CI [28] were developed to collect specific information on topology, dynamic circuits and operational status. We monitor the status for all WAN links and peering connections. For the Force10 switches [29] we use SNMP and for the Ciena CD/CI the TL1 interface.

The repository analyzes the status information from all the distributed measurements, for each segment, to generate reliable status information. Measurements are done every ~ 45 s and the full history is kept in the repository database. The system allows one to

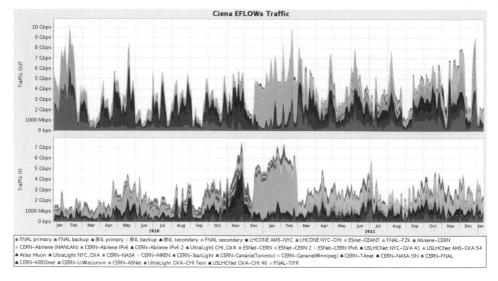

Fig. 13. – Traffic history for the major links in USLHCNet.

transparently change the way a WAN is operated (via Force10 or Ciena CD/CI) and keeps consistent history. Figure 12 shows the panel that allows analyzing the links availability for any time interval.

The MonALISA framework is used to monitor the total traffic on all the Force 10 ports and on the Ethernet ports on the Ciena CD/CIs. Different aggregated views are presented: total traffic (an example is shown in fig. 13), total trans-Atlantic traffic, peering at each point of presence as well as integrated traffic over any time interval (fig. 14).

The operational status for the Force10 ports and all the Ciena CD/CI alarms are recorded by the MonALISA services. They are analyzed and email notification is generated based on different error conditions. We also "monitor" the services used to collect monitoring information. A global repository for all these alarms is available on the MonALISA servers, which allows one to select and sort the alarms based on different conditions.

3·2. Network topology. – The MonALISA framework is used to construct in near real time the network topology for different types of technologies currently used in the High Energy Physics infrastructure. For the routed networks, MonALISA is able to construct the overall topology of a complex wide-area network, based on the delay on each network segment determined by tracepath-like measurements from each site to all other sites, as it is illustrated in fig. 15.

The combined information from all the sites allows one to detect asymmetric routing or links with performance problems. For global applications, such as distributing large data files to many grid sites, this information is used to define the set of optimized replication paths.

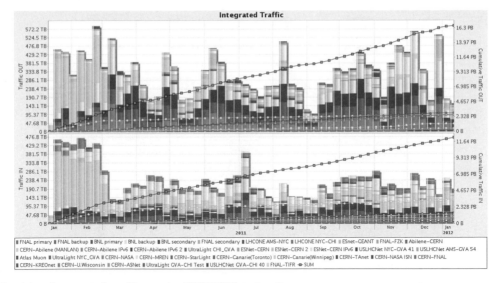

Fig. 14. – Integrated traffic on the USLHCNet circuits.

Specialized TL1 modules are used to monitor the power on Optical Switches (Glimmerglass [30] and Calient [31]) and to present the topology. The MonALISA framework allows one to securely configure many such devices from a single GUI, to see the state of each link in real time, and to have historical plots for the state and activity on each link. In fig. 16 we show the MonALISA GUI that is used to monitor the topology on Layer 1 connections and the state and optical power of the links.

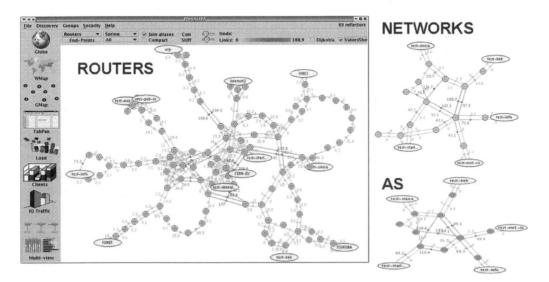

Fig. 15. – MonALISA real-time view of the topology of WANs used by HEP. A view of all the routers, or just the network or "autonomous system" identifiers can be shown.

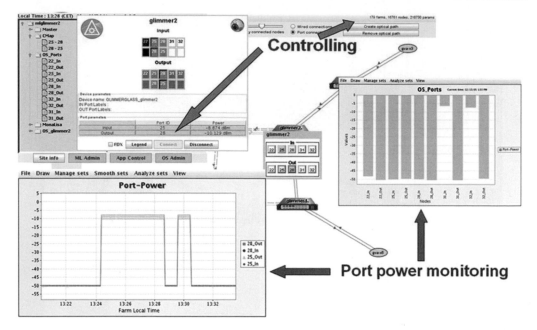

Fig. 16. – Monitoring and autonomous control for optical switches and optical links.

For the Ciena CD/CI nodes we provide real-time information for the OSRP connections with all the attributes for the SONET links. The topology of all the circuits created in the entire network is presented in real time in the MonALISA interactive client. This panel allows one to select any set of circuits, and it presents how they are mapped onto the physical network, with all their attributes.

4. – Monitoring ALICE distributed computing environment

The ALICE [16] collaboration, consisting now of 86 institutes, is strongly dependent on a distributed computing environment to perform its physics program. The computing centers around the world provide many different computing platforms, operating systems flavors and storage solutions. The software and operating conditions are rapidly changing and evolving. In these conditions, a system to monitor the global state of the Grid down to the individual building blocks, both hardware and software, is needed. The monitoring system should trace the resource usage, software performance, and in fact any event of interest for the developers, operators and users. At the same time, the monitoring system should be non-intrusive and use a minimal amount of computational resources. Based on these requirements, MonALISA framework was chosen as a monitoring framework for the entire AliEn Grid System [4].

According to the ALICE Computing Model, each site member of the collaboration provides a machine dedicated to running VO-specific services, frequently called *VoBox*.

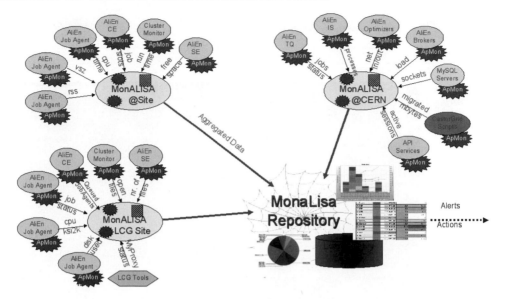

Fig. 17. – ALICE distributed environment monitoring architecture.

The distributed computing infrastructure is controlled by AliEn [32] (ALIce Environ-ment), a software package that has two main sets of services: central services that deal with job submission, file catalogue, scheduled transfers, users, authentication and so on, and site services that manage local site resources (jobs, storage and software packages).

A MonALISA service instance is installed on each VoBox (fig. 17) and on each of the machines running central services. These services are used to collect monitoring information from each active job, transfer or service and make available to any client the information in raw or aggregated form. For example the full information about each job is available on demand, but values like number of jobs in each state or total CPU power consumed by all the jobs running on that site are also available.

4˙1. *Services monitoring*. – AliEn components, consisting of central services, such as the Task Queue, Information Service, Optimizers and APIService; site services, such as Cluster Monitor, Computing and Storage Elements and Job Agents which wrap all the jobs that are actually executed are all instrumented with ApMon and send monitoring information to the MonALISA service at the site. The AliEn Job Agents send information about their status (such as requesting job, running job, finishing). Other, non-AliEn services are also monitored using a small external ApMon-based script. Such services include the MySQL [33] database for AliEn TaskQueue and File Catalogue, xrootd [34] servers and staging and migration to the CASTOR [35] mass storage system. The overall status page from the MonALISA repository shown in fig. 18 presents the status of all services running on a site. It is also the starting point for expert debugging of a problem. The experts can immediately see which component is not working properly and what

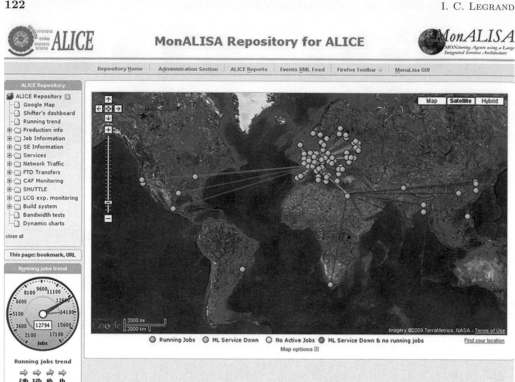

Fig. 18. – The MonALISA repository for the ALICE experiment.

the cause of the failure is. In addition, automatic e-mail notification is sent to a pre-configured list of people (individual for every site) when a service failure is detected. Another monitoring module is used to perform simple tests that check the status and availability of the grid middleware services and authorization credentials (Grid proxies), needed to interact with these services.

4˙2. *Jobs and resource monitoring.* – In the ALICE system, jobs are executed within Job Agents which are also enabled to send monitoring information to the configured MonALISA service. They send data about the current job status (such as started, running, saving etc.) and about the resource usage of the job itself (how much memory, disk space, CPU time, CPU SpecInt units the job consumes). Nodes where critical AliEn services are running are also monitored to assure an immediate detection of a service failure or other critical events.

AliEn Job Agents, like all the other AliEn services read their configuration from a central LDAP directory. In the site service configuration there is an entry for the MonALISA service that should receive the monitoring information from all the services and the jobs running in that site. The MonALISA services running on each site comprise several monitoring modules that receive the local monitoring data and an Agent Filter

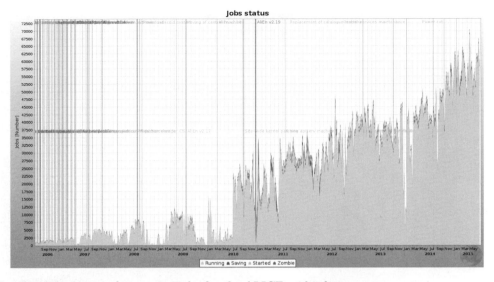

Fig. 19. – The history for running jobs for the ALICE grid infrastructure.

that aggregates it. The Agent Filter, an AliEnFilter instance in this case, receives and aggregates the information collected by the monitoring modules, for example how many jobs are running in each of the possible states, what is the total CPU usage on this site, which is the average memory usage of the jobs, how many job agents are currently waiting to receive a job, how many queued job agents were submitted in the batch queuing system.

Following the model for the possible status for AliEn jobs, the monitoring system provides various views of these job categories: site views, user views and task queue. In site views, one can plot summary retrospective and near real-time job or job agent information for each site. Visualizations at various aggregation levels of the usage for the set of resources available to members are also available: consumed CPU time for ALICE jobs, total CPU SPECint2000 units, Wall time, jobs efficiency in time (CPU time / Wall time) and SPECint2000 units (CPU SI2K / Wall SI2K). The used CPU power in SI2K is normalized taking into account each node's parameters (processor type, cache size, core frequency). Network traffic is also monitored (incoming / outgoing) as well as key system parameters: memory usage by the jobs at each site, virtual memory usage, system memory usage, opened files, sizes of the working directories, disk and CPU usage. An example for long history of jobs executed on ALICE grid system is presented in fig. 19.

The chart presents the total number running jobs for the last 9 years. The system also allows adding operational annotations for specific events relevant to the currently plot data sets.

Figure 20 shows the distribution of how long a job waits in the queue before it is picked up by the site (red) *versus* the execution time of the job (blue). The conclusion

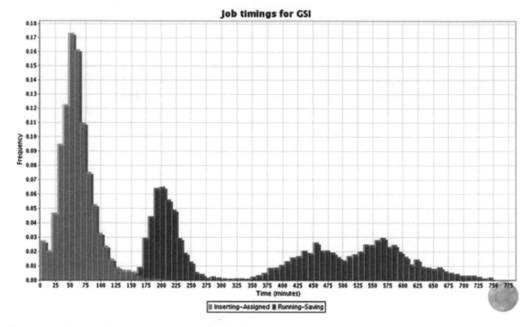

Fig. 20. – Site performance analysis for different types of jobs.

is that jobs are waiting in average one hour in the central queue to be picked up by the sites, while the two peaks in the blue series show the shorter user jobs and the longer MonteCarlo "production" jobs. The chart is based on the derived values produced by the AliEnFilter that tracks individual job state changes and reports the timings in a job-independent data stream. The user views detail jobs status, error types and cumulative parameters for each user. The Task Queue view presents AliEn Task Queue jobs status, parameters and errors summaries; tables containing extended details of the jobs in the Task Queue can also be dynamically generated as well as complete job information tables.

Another important aspect for such a large-scale computing system is monitoring and understanding the performance of the storage systems. The ALICE experiment is using xrootd application to server data for the computing nodes in a distributed architecture. The aggregated traffic for all these data servers is presented in fig. 21.

In fig. 22 is presented the throughput *vs.* the xrootd servers' load for all data storage systems (358 distributed among all regional centers) used in the ALICE experiment.

Sometimes the performance of storage system is affected by either large number of concurrent clients (overload) or by problems related with the hardware. In these cases the load can increase a lot on these computers while to total throughput they provide is small. This can significantly affect the efficiency of CPU utilization for the data processing jobs that use these data servers.

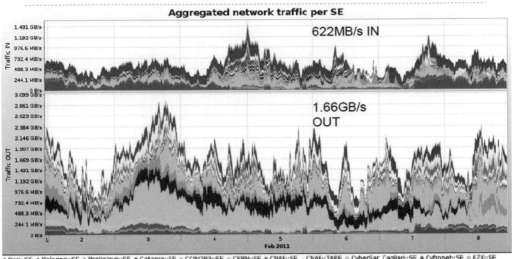

Fig. 21. – The aggregated and long term average traffic for the storage systems used in the ALICE experiment.

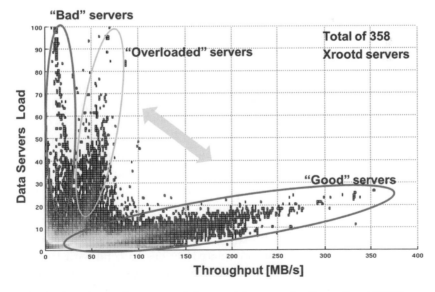

Fig. 22. – Monitoring the performance of the xrootd servers for the entire ALICE experiment.

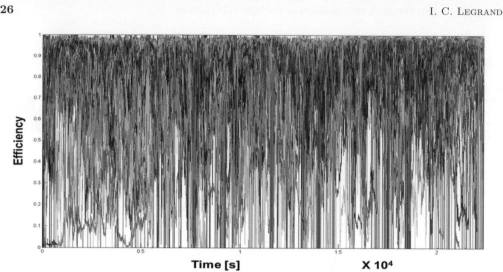

Fig. 23. – Efficiency for job processing tasks at the grid ALICE sites for a period of two months. These values are collected with one measurement per minute so that the efficiency time series per each site has ∼ 86000 points.

4˙3. *Analyzing multiple time series data.* – The amount of monitoring information collected for an experiment like ALICE is quite large and presenting and analyzing this information is a challenging tasks. As an example in fig. 23 we present the efficiency plot for all the grid sites in ALICE using high-resolution data for a period of two months. Understating such plots is not easy.

We tried to analyze such information using the wavelet approach [36] to this multi-dimensional grid structure in order to cluster and organize the information. By using wavelet transform into the feature space will create dense regions for the patters with similar time behavior. Apply the wavelet transform multiple times will result in clusters at different scales from fine to coarse. The results for such a clustering approach is presented in fig. 24. We can see that time dependent efficiency at the ALICE grid sites can be classified in several similar groups. Drops in the efficiency to process data are correlated among several sites and in general are due to problems or overland of major data storage systems. There also a few sites which have configuration problems and are less efficient in processing jobs. The strategy to find clusters in the transformed space allows detecting arbitrary cluster shapes at different scales, it is robust to noise or missing data and can be done fast as the computation time is linear with the number of points.

4˙4. *Automated management.* – Based on the monitoring information received from sites, the repository can take various automated actions to cope with the events. The simplest action is sending an alert (by email or instant messenger) when something has stopped working (an AliEn site or central service, storage element, critical machines and so on). From the web interface anybody can subscribe to receive notifications in each category and (in some cases) for each particular site or for all sites. In addition to sending

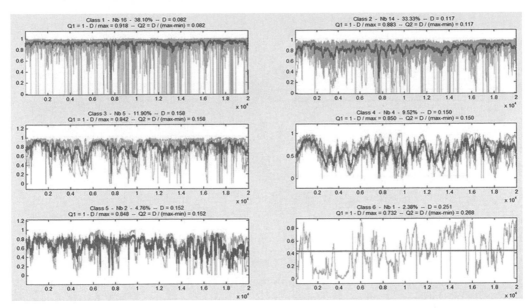

Fig. 24. – Classification or clustering for the grid sites in 6 groups with similar time dependence behavior for the efficiency in job processing.

emails to the subscribed email addresses, an event is also made available as RSS/Atom feed and history charts are automatically annotated with these events (where it makes sense), so correlations between peaks or lows of activity and events for example can be easily made.

Another kind of automated action is maintenance of central services load balancing. The load balancing is DNS-based, with the repository updating the CERN DNS servers with the list of IP addresses where various central services are available to service remote site services/jobs/users etc. The lists are dynamically generated, so newly added services that pass the functional tests are automatically added to the load balancing, while non-responding or overloaded services are immediately removed. So this function not only maintains the load-balancing but also protects the central services from a flood of requests.

The repository is also responsible for the MonteCarlo data production. By continuously monitoring the number of queued jobs in the system and reacting when the number goes below a threshold, new production jobs are automatically submitted in AliEn and jobs finishing in various error states are resubmitted for execution (fig. 25, left). The jobs to be executed are taken from a list of production requests made by physics working groups, according to the relative priority between the requests and keeping track of the number of events that were produced for a given job type (fig. 25, right).

From this central point the site services are also controlled. By an SSL channel established between the repository and each remote service, failing AliEn services are automatically restarted, but with additional constraints like verifying that all the central

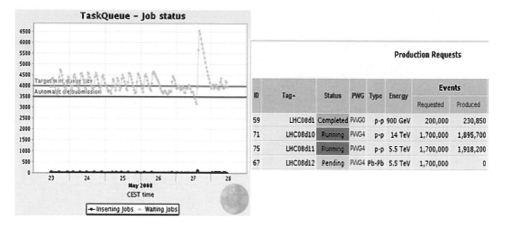

Fig. 25. – Running MC data production jobs according to physics requests.

services are functional. This feature, combined with email alerts sent to site administrators and Grid operators when problems cannot be automatically solved, has improved a lot the overall availability of the system.

5. – Data transfer services

In order to support large-scale data-driven applications, as those specific to HEP community, particularly as the amount of data becomes more prevalent, a large set of subsystems have to be configured and tuned simultaneously. Performing these operations manually, not only demands expensive human expertise, but also limits the maximum practical size of such a system. Also, it becomes difficult to deal with dynamically changing demands and to coordinate the resource requirements of different applications.

To provide the desired quality of service, we developed in the MonALISA framework a set of agents able to coordinate and optimize large-scale data transfers in the WAN. The problem of data management has to be tackled at all the layers, in an integrated approach:

- physical layer has to provide the means to move packets in an efficient way, and scalable to the speeds of the next-generation networks;

- hosts have to be properly configured, taking into account the necessities for wide-area network transfers (proper network buffer settings and appropriate TCP stacks);

- data transfer applications have to know the environment in which they run, and use the proper resources when they are available, in an optimal manner.

The data transfer service we are developing has two main parts:

- *optimizing the network topology* (*i.e.* choosing different paths to use for certain data transfers, temporary activation of network paths that guarantee the bandwidth

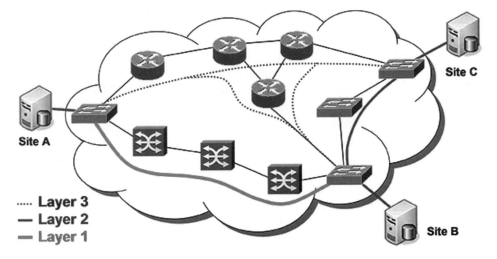

Fig. 26. – Multiple paths in the network core available at different OSI layers.

requirements, or changing the entire set of overlay channels that a distributed application uses in order to improve the global efficiency);

– *optimizing the handling of data-related requests* (*i.e.* the process of ordering and executing the received requests in order to satisfy the priority requirements and avoid overloading certain network paths or end-point storage devices).

Considering a distributed environment, with multiple sites, interconnected through different types of services (fig. 26), we build the system and the necessary components that optimize the inter-site data transfers.

The requirements for quality of service specific to data intensive applications can be assured only by dedicated virtual circuits at level 1 or 2 in the ISO/OSI stack. The cost of these equipments is much lower than for devices achieving similar speeds at layer 3 and therefore this approach is of great interest currently. However, dedicated circuits are an expensive resource and their usage must be maximized. This implies that the exploited dedicated virtual circuits are setup when needed and then freed when the requests finish. This objective is pursued in order to keep the underlying network segments free for other alternative usage.

The connectivity between sites can be assured by a set of possible paths with different characteristics in regard to bandwidth, delay, quality of service or cost. By default, if no administration privileges are available on the end hosts, routing to various destinations is determined by the default site network configuration. However, if end system's parameters, can be changed, alternate but predefined paths, can be used instead the default. When paths can be dynamically setup by sending commands to various network devices, the flexibility of the system can be increased by providing more alternative paths.

Setting up an alternative path is a process that could require activating each individual link on the path, by sending specific commands to the corresponding optical switch.

Moreover, different administrative domains typically employ different technologies for this purpose and may be reluctant to allow a global system co control parts of their network. A system such as the one presented here should be able to take advantage of network segments which are managed through other technologies and provide the interfaces required for inter-operability with them. Therefore, it should be able to both get the topology (even in a very generic form, *i.e.* possible interconnections and bandwidth) and send the necessary commands to reserve paths from other systems, and to provide these features to other systems.

5˙1. *Abstracted network topology.* – The real network topology is abstracted as a graph within the *optimizer*, based on the available network segments reported by all the distributed services. This graph includes a set of nodes, interconnected through a number of links with additional information. The algorithms implemented in the *optimizer* will run over this abstracted topology.

Some of these nodes represent real network devices or end-points. Likewise, some of the links are the representation of the actual underlying connections, others are only logical connections. However, due to the restrictions present in existent networks (*i.e.* firewalls), some of these nodes might not be visible to conventional network monitoring tools. Moreover, it could be impossible or unfeasible to add the complexity of the underlying network of various network domains. Therefore, we consider two types of network elements: real and virtual. For each of those, we can distinguish between manageable and fixed configuration network elements. An example of manageable virtual element would be another service that configures a set of links on the computed path.

On the real network, we can distinguish between two types of paths:

– *concrete network paths* – consists of the existing network links, which do not need any additional setup in order to be used, typically at layer 3 in the OSI hierarchy;

– *configurable paths* – end-to-end virtual circuits that already exist or that can be setup dynamically.

Figure 27 shows an environment supporting multiple path types, with the features and the commands suitable for each of them in the process of executing a request.

Among the parameters specific for each link we should find at least:

– *Name* – Each link in the system must have a name. Between two nodes there can be several links. If they share the same underlying supporting network link, they can have the same name, but different IDs (see below). If not, they must have different names. This kind of grouping allows sharing the other link parameters among the IDs in the group. Also, if a request is designated to a certain link ID, its load (traffic) will contribute to the load of the entire group, *i.e.* the entire underlying physical link.

– *Source and destination nodes* – the bounding nodes for a link. Out of these, the source node is of particular interest since it can designate also the local node from

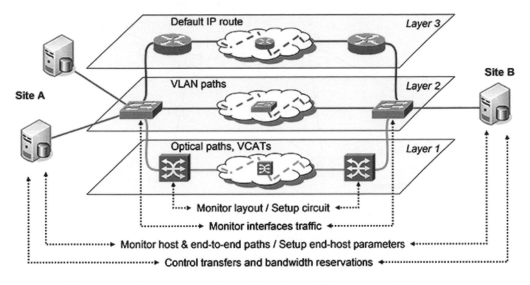

Fig. 27. – Choosing and setting-up end-to-end paths at different network layers.

the perspective of the monitoring and controlling service, which can provide monitoring information and accepts commands to setup the link. Source node can have a *physical interface* attached and an *IP address* which can be used as parameters for the execution process of the request.

– *Bandwidth, delay* and *cost* – the "classic" parameters for the links, used in the process of taking the scheduling decisions. They also offer the possibility of idealizing the network, or segments of the network, like infinite bandwidth, zero delay or no administrative cost.

– *Enabled* and *active* flags – they reflect the administrative status of the link and the current operational status, respectively. For example, the source node of an inactive link might not have a defined IP address, but will receive one once a set of commands is executed and the link is activated.

– *ID* – represents the circuit ID for which this link can be used. For example, it could be the same as the VLAN ID which this link describes. There can be several links with the same name

5˙2. Network graph model. – The underlying topology, consisting of end points, intermediary devices or virtual nodes and links, can be abstracted as a graph. In order to support the paradigm of virtual circuits, there can be multiple links between two nodes and some of the links may be tagged with a certain path ID. This tagging is needed because not all possible paths in this graph can be followed in reality.

With this convention, describing the virtual circuits at levels 1 and 2 would mean adding links between the intermediary nodes, with a certain ID. Supporting paths at

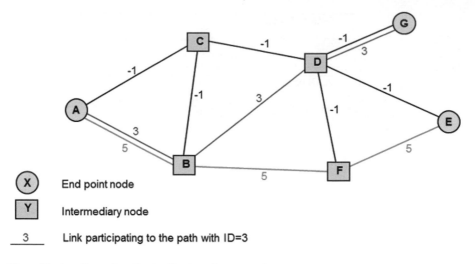

Fig. 28. – Abstraction of paths in the topology graph.

layer 3 would mean tagging all these links with a default tag (for example -1). Now, finding a path from a source to a destination node is reduced to exploring this graph (based on a certain cost criteria) with the restriction that all the links in the path must have the same ID (fig. 28).

For example, in the figure above, from node A to node E there are two possible paths:

– A, C, D, E – following the default Internet path;

– A, B, F, E – following the virtual circuit with ID 5.

Besides the regular monitoring information, the links in this graph should have associated a queue holding the current and future requests to be executed. This information should be used by the *scheduling algorithm*, so that once a path is chosen, it can decide the time interval when a new request can be allocated to the links in this path.

5`3. *Path allocation and data transfer scheduling.* – The process of handling users' requests, either bandwidth reservations or data transfers can be seen as a two-step procedure, requiring the solution for two problems: a) the *path discovery problem* —finding possible paths between the two end-points involved in the request; b) the *path allocation problem* —allocating the request to one of the available paths.

The *path discovery problem* (PDP) is a variant of the *breadth-first search* (BFS) algorithm [37] that we have developed for exploring graphs. The similitude comes from the constraint of finding shortest paths from source to destination. The difference of PDP from BFS stems from the possibility of having multiple edges between the same two nodes and their tagging. Another difference is the stopping condition: the algorithm will stop as soon as it finds the destination, instead of exploring the entire graph.

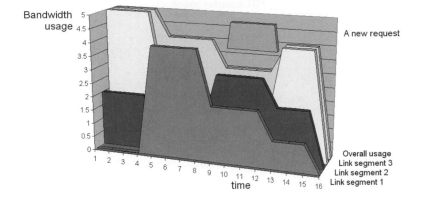

Fig. 29. – Bandwidth usage over the links in a path.

In the following two subsections we define and present the design details for two policies we have implemented for handling the path allocation problem: a) *time-based path scheduling* —the requests are scheduled in time over the existing links; b) *dynamic bandwidth allocation* —priority based, immediate execution with dynamic bandwidth allocation for the existing requests.

5˙4. *Time-based path scheduling.* – The *path allocation problem (PAP)* concerns the allocation of all the network segments on the path associated with users' requests. The requests arrival in the system is *on-line*. Due to the fact that the capacity of the network is limited, the requests cannot be executed immediately, as they are received. System's goal is to execute all of them eventually, optimizing the resources usage. In our case, the allocated resources consist in the network segments, defined for the underlying physical network.

With a running system, when a new request is received, the scheduling process means finding the starting time for this request based on the estimated processing time (from the *prediction* module), the path (from the *PDP* algorithm) and the used bandwidth (as specified by user, in the path's limits).

There are two constraints, which differentiate this scheduling process from a classic job scheduling problem: a) the request requires not a single, but a set of resources in order to be executed successfully —all the network link segments, are needed in order to perform a transfer, end-to-end; b) a resource can be only partially used by a request —on the same network link segment several data transfers can be performed simultaneously, provided that the link's bandwidth is sufficient.

A visual representation of the constraints is depicted in fig. 29. When scheduling a new request, we have to make sure that there is sufficient available bandwidth on all the link segments in the path, for at least an interval equal to the request's processing time.

The complexity of the time based path scheduling algorithms can vary from simple greedy approaches to complex algorithms and data structures for handling optimally

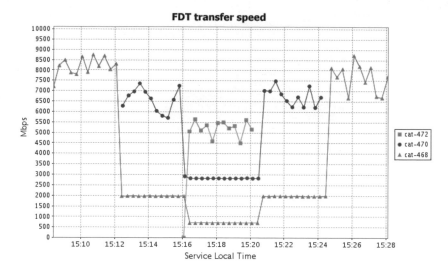

Fig. 30. – FDT transfer speed for dynamic priorities: 1, 4, 9.

all the needed details. However, in the current work we focus on the infrastructure itself, being concerned with its generality and flexibility to accommodate any scheduling algorithm.

5˙5. *Dynamic bandwidth allocation*. – The *time-based scheduling* policy works fine especially for batch-style requests. Regardless of the quality of the schedule and the efficiency of the scheduling algorithm, the handling of *high-priority requests* is not very good.

Typically, there are two basic approaches: a) *non preemptive* scheduling, when the higher priority request is executed only after the end of the currently running requests (that affect the requested links) —which could mean an arbitrary long delay for the high priority request; b) *preemptive* scheduling, when the currently running requests are interrupted and they are restarted (possibly from the beginning) when the higher priority request ends —which could mean the arbitrary delay of low-priority requests.

Another, novel policy is to start the high-priority request immediately and reduce the bandwidth of the ongoing requests dynamically, without stopping them. This way, the two problems of classic time-based scheduling are solved. For this approach to work, it is needed that the underlying transfer protocol supports changing dynamically the bandwidth limitation.

The two policies are not exclusive and can be used simultaneously. In fact, in practice, dynamic bandwidth allocation should be supported by a time-scheduling mechanism, since the requests duration can vary in time, compared to the initially estimated interval.

5˙6. *Priority-based dynamic bandwidth allocation for data transfers*. – In the following experiment we present another feature of the *Transfer Scheduler Optimizer* —the ability to dynamically adjust the bandwidth of running requests, based on the priority of the requests received by the system.

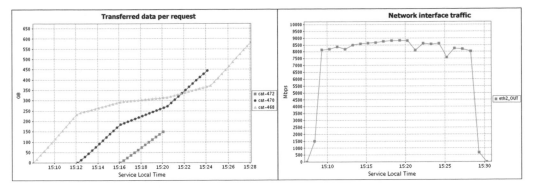

Fig. 31. – Transferred data during dynamic bandwidth allocation with priorities: 1, 4, 9.

Consider the following scenario: on a 10GE path between two nodes in the network there is a running transfer request, with priority 1. At some point, another request arrives in the system, requiring the same path, with priority 4. After a while, a third request arrives, with priority 9. The system tries to accommodate the requests based on their priority (fig. 30).

Figure 31 shows the transferred amounts for each of the three requests and the total bandwidth usage, on the network interface. It can be seen that the bandwidth does not fluctuate much during the start/end (implying bandwidth adjust commands) phases.

5˙7. *Bandwidth measurements for the ALICE Grid.* – For this purpose, we have updated the configuration scripts for the MonALISA services that run in ALICE to start the FDT monitoring modules, the AppTransfer control modules and include the public key of the *Optimizer*, in order to be allowed to issue the remote commands for this purpose. The data transfer service is used by the ALICE experiment to perform bandwidth measurements between all sites, by instructing pairs of site MonALISA instances to perform FDT memory-to-memory data transfers with one or more TCP streams.

The results are used for detecting network or configuration problems, since with each test the relevant system configuration and the *tracepath* between the two hosts are recorded as well. The MonALISA services are also used to monitor the end system configuration and automatically notify the user when these systems are not properly configured to support effective data transfers in WAN (see fig. 32).

The results of performing continuously transfer measurements using FDT (with one TCP stream) between all the grid sites in ALICE ($\sim$ 80 sites) are presented in fig. 33. The measurements are scheduled by the Data Transfer Service and executed using the local MonALISA service that starts and monitor the FDT transfer. Measurements are done in both directions for each peer of sites using the local VoBox as a testing host. In this case FDT was adopted for its ease of use and the seamless integration within the MonALISA framework for both monitoring and controlling.

The MonALISA management modules can easily control the desired bandwidth leveraging the advanced capabilities inside FDT like number of TCP streams and dynamic

Aalborg ▼ »

‹Aalborg›

Chart view »

IN from

No.	ID	Site	Speed (Mbps)	Hops	RTT (ms)	Streams
1.	126976	NDGF	685.81	11	6.87	1
2.	131876	DCSC_KU	430.88	6	6.61	1

OUT to

No.	ID	Site	Speed (Mbps)	Hops	RTT (ms)	Streams
1.	127538	UiB	679.24	16	33.91	1
2.	128970	IPNO	662.03	17	36.19	1
3.	129355	NDGF	627.51	11	6.78	1
4.	127195	DCSC_KU	564.75	7	6.38	1
5.	126998	LUNARC	314.01	14	31.54	1
6.	130490	ISS	162.100	19	49.94	1
7.	129827	CSC				
8.	130994	CNAF				
9.	128512	CNAF-CR				
10.	130365	OSC				
11.	126963	SARA				
12.	130267	NIHAM				
13.	127450	Kolkata-(				
14.	129399	RAL				
15.	128153	CERN-L				
16.	131295	Prague				
17.	131055	Kolkata				
18.	127177	PNPI				
19.	130170	GSI				
20.	129558	Grenoble				
21.	129903	Catania				
22.	127138	SINP				
23.	131236	Trujillo				
24.	92520	UPB				
25.	131713	Madrid				
26.	126729	TriGrid				
27.	129296	Legnaro				
28.	131748	ITEP				
29.	129381	KPI				

Nodes configuration for test 128970

‹Aalborg›	Source
IP	130.225.192.122
OS	Ubuntu 8.04.1
Kernel	2.6.24-17-server
TCP algo	reno
Write buffers	8388608 (4096 1875000 8388608)
Suggestions	

‹IPNO›	Target
IP	134.158.78.52
OS	Scientific Linux SL release 4.6 (Beryllium)
Kernel	2.6.9-67.0.4.ELlargesmp
TCP algo	
Receive buffers	8388608 (4096 87380 8388608)
Suggestions	

Tests from Aalborg to IPNO

No.	ID	Speed (Mbps)	Hops	RTT (ms)	Streams
1.	128970	662.03	17	36.19	1
2.	123260	523.89	19	36.23	1
3.	117348	324.43	19	36.17	1
4.	112041	445.69	16	36.19	1
5.	107523	384.84	17	36.04	1

Tracepath for test 128970

Tracepath from **Aalborg** to **IPNO**

Hop	IP	RTT (ms)	Domain
0	130.225.192.122	0	aau.dk
1	130.225.192.126	0.57	aau.dk
2	130.225.192.126	0.47	aau.dk
3	192.38.59.54	0.59	
4	192.38.59.213	6.33	
5	130.225.242.34	6.28	fsknet.dk
6	130.225.244.145	6.93	fsknet.dk
7	130.225.244.218	6.72	fsknet.dk
8	193.10.68.121	6.68	nordu.net
9	62.40.124.45	6.68	geant2.net
10	62.40.112.78	19.66	geant2.net
11	62.40.112.138	27.71	geant2.net
12	62.40.112.105	35.11	geant2.net
13	62.40.124.78	35.73	geant2.net
14	193.51.179.90	35.74	
15	193.51.188.161	35.98	
16		no_reply	
17	193.51.188.161	36.19	

Target was not reached

Fig. 32. – Inter-site bandwidth test results. For each measurement between any two sites, we also monitor the path, the end systems configuration.

bandwidth adjustments. Various types of problems like asymmetric routing, incorrect buffer size, underperforming TCP congestion control algorithms were easily identified (fig. 33) combining the advanced network monitoring capabilities inside the MonALISA framework with the reported bandwidth utilization of the FDT software.

6. – On demand, end-to-end optical circuits

The MonALISA framework has been applied to develop an integrated Optical Control Plane system (OCPS) that controls and creates end-to-end optical paths on demand, using optical switches. As part of the development of end-to-end circuit-oriented network management services, we developed dedicated modules and agents to monitor, administer and control Optical Switches; specifically the purely photonic switches from Glimmer-

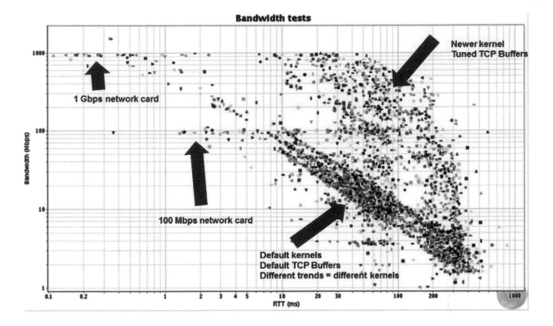

Fig. 33. – The bandwidth measurements results between all the ALICE sites *vs.* the RTT. These measurements are done with FDT using one TCP stream.

glass [30] and Calient [31]. The modules use TL1 commands to monitor the connectivity matrix of each switch, as well as the optical power on each port. Any change in the state of any link is reported to dedicated agents. If a switch is connected to the network, or if it ceases to operate, or if a port's light level changes, these state changes are detected immediately and are reflected in the topology presented by the MonALISA Graphical User Interface (GUI).

The distributed set of MonALISA agents was used to control the optical switches, and to create an optical path on demand. The agents use MonALISA's discovery layer to "discover" each other, and then communicate among themselves autonomously, using the Proxy services. Each proxy service can handle more than 15000 messages per second, and several such services are typically used in parallel. This ensures that the communications among the agents is highly reliable, even at very high message-passing rates.

The set of agents also is used to create a global path or tree, as it knows the state and performance of each local area and wide-area network link, and the state of the cross connections in each switch. The routing algorithm provides global optimization by considering the "cost" of each link or cross-connect. This makes the optimization algorithm capable of being adapted to handle various policies on priorities, and pre-reservation schemes. The time to determine and construct an optical path (or a multicast tree) end-to-end is typically less than one second, independent of the number of links along the path and overall the length of the path. A schematic view of how the MonALISA

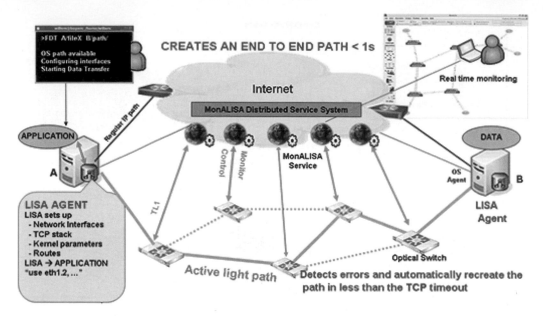

Fig. 34. – MonALISA agents are used to monitor and control optical switches. The agents interact with end-user applications to provision an optical path on demand.

agents are used to create an optical path for an (authorized, authenticated) end-user application is presented in fig. 34.

If network errors are detected, an alternative path is set up rapidly enough to avoid a TCP timeout, so that data transfers will continue uninterrupted. This functionality is important in the construction of the virtual circuit-oriented network services.

Figure 35 shows an example of how MonALISA is used to create dynamically, on demand, a path between two end-systems at CERN and Caltech. The topology, the cross-connections, the ports and the segments where light is detected and the end-to-end path created by the system all are displayed in real time. The end to end path is created in approximately 0.5 seconds, and then disk-to-disk data transfer using Fast Data Transfer is started. We simulated 4 consecutive "fiber cuts" in the circuits over the Atlantic. The agents controlling the optical switches detect the optical power lost and they created another complete path in less than 1 second. The alternative path was set up rapidly enough to avoid a TCP timeout, so that data transfers continue uninterrupted (fig. 35, right). As soon as the transfer initiated by the end-user application was completed, the path was released.

7. – Optimizing the global connectivity for the EVO videoconferencing system

EVO [38] is a videoconferencing system, based on a distributed architecture, which was created to provide support for the High Energy Physics community. In this section we

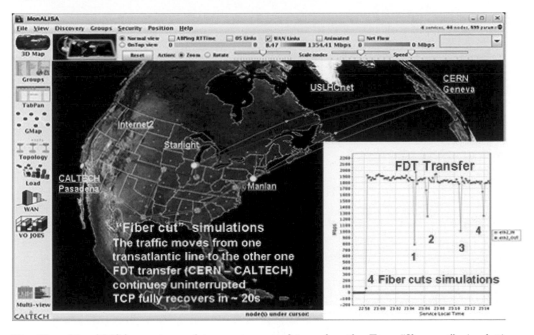

Fig. 35. – MonALISA agents used to create an end-to-end path. Four "fiber cut" simulations were done for the transatlantic circuits. The alternative path was created rapidly enough to avoid TCP timeout and the FDT traffic continued uninterrupted.

present how MonALISA is used as a *Global Connectivity Optimizer* in the EVO system, to achieve the goals of adaptability and flexibility required in such a large distributed system.

The optimization of the entire connectivity in this videoconferencing system is based on near real-time end-to-end monitoring, including the end-user's computer as well as the network infrastructure. This way, the user is informed of any potential or arising problems (*e.g.* excessive CPU load or packet loss) and when possible, the problems are resolved automatically and transparently on user's behalf (*e.g.* switching to another server node in the network, reducing the number of received video streams etc.).

EVO includes a Client (named Koala) that runs on the end-user's client machine and provides the videoconferencing experience, and a Server (named Panda) that is used to provide an intelligent, secure and reliable communication channel between the different entities in the system, and some other services (scheduler, directory services, etc.). Together they provide support for both pre-booked and immediate (ad-hoc) point-to-point and multipoint collaborative sessions initiated through Instant Messaging. The videoconferencing is "adaptive" in that the resolution and the refresh rate of windows are varied automatically if the CPU load on the end-system exceeds a pre-set limit, or if the bandwidth required to sustain the video stream exceeds what is measured to be available.

The Servers communicate with each other through a set of channels —secure TCP connections— which form an overlay network over the actual network topology. The data, video and audio packets that travel from one user to all the other users participating to

Fig. 36. – Monitoring the Internet links quality.

the same conference are routed over this overlay network. To keep this protocol simple, the layout of this topology has to be that of a tree.

Maintaining this overlaid topology in an optimum state, in the conditions of the permanent and dynamic evolution of the underlying network parameters, can be achieved only by proper monitoring and prompt control of the system when required.

7˙1. *The monitoring and controlling architecture.* – The end-to-end monitoring support is performed by employing the MonALISA framework. On each videoconference server there is also a MonALISA service running. It receives monitoring information concerning the local server and all the clients that are connected to it. From that Mon-ALISA service, the information is further available to all the interested clients, through the MonALISA communication platform. Clustering the information in this way proved to be very effective towards reaching the goals of a globally distributed, dynamic and autonomous system. The EVO system uses ~ 40 servers distributed worldwide. In fig. 36 we show the quality of the possible interconnecting links among the Servers, information which is based on the monABPing monitoring.

7˙2. *Connectivity monitoring.* – Connectivity monitoring is the basic network information we can monitor. It includes *round trip time (RTT)*, *packet loss* and *jitter*. These are the factors that determine the quality of a link or path between two network entities.

We have developed a MonALISA module, monABPing, which performs these measurements and provides the interested clients the values and a quality for the respective link. The module sends UDP packets to the other peer MonALISA services which have

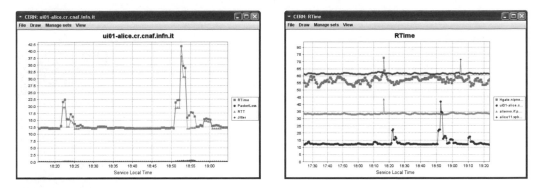

Fig. 37. – Left: ABPing parameters evolution. Right: Links' quality comparison.

this module running. The receiving peer responds by sending back the packet immediately. Based on the parameters directly measurable this way (RTT and PacketLoss) we have arrived at the following formula:

$$RTimeQuality = OVERALL\_COEF + RTT\_COEF * RTT$$
$$+ PKT\_LOSS\_COEF * loss\% + JITTER\_COEF * jitter,$$

where Jitter is the time variation of RTT: for last k probes, Jitter = sum(abs(RTT – Avg(RTT)))/k.

While other, more complete formulas exist [39,40], we have kept this one as we cannot find the number of hops reliably (as needed in [14]) and we do not have to couple the link status with the videoconferencing application as in [15]. This formula is simple and flexible enough to allow calculating any kind of quality, based on RTT, Packet Loss and Jitter (fig. 37, left).

The list of available peers for each service and the *_COEF coefficients is configurable, to allow for dynamic reconfiguration The configuration file is the same for all services, each one knowing to extract only the information that is needed. The coefficients must be the same for all services in order to obtain comparable RTime qualities (fig. 37, right).

In our setups, the coefficients for calculating the quality were chosen in such a way that, the lower the RTime, the better the quality. We have refined these coefficients along several years of running the system and observing the behavior during network breakdowns. Particularly, PKT_LOSS_COEF is very high (500), in order to penalize severely the loss of packets on a link. A large jitter is not very good for videoconferencing, so this is 10, while a high RTT just denotes that the peer is far, so the chosen coefficient was 0.5. In order to remove noise, the values are averaged over a short period ($k = 5$ probes), with the removal of extremes.

The configuration file is loaded at start, and then it is periodically checked, from a URL set when starting MonALISA service. If a new peer is found in the configuration for a reflector, it is added to the list of peers in the monABPing module. Similarly,

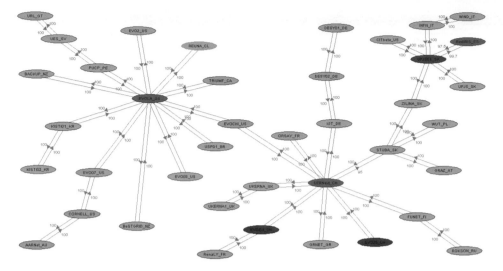

Fig. 38. – Overlay topology for connecting the servers —Minimum Spanning Tree.

if a known peer is not found anymore in the configuration file, it is deleted from the peer list. If at least one of the coefficients modify, all measurements are reset and the new values are computed using the formula presented above. For the EVO system, this configuration is a plain file, updated manually by system administrators when a reflector is added or removed, in order to limit the peer nodes for a reflector to a known, fixed set. However, in the other use-cases presented earlier (Network Topology or ALICE Bandwidth measurements) this configuration is generated on the fly, by one or more services registered in LUSs, based on the currently active peers.

7˙3. *The optimization of the overlay topology*. – We have adapted the *Global Connectivity Optimizer* to run in the context of the EVO system. It receives monitoring information about the quality of the links (both available and selected in the current topology) and computes the minimum spanning tree that connects all the servers (the reflector nodes). The generated commands are sent through the communication platform and then they are forwarded to the servers. These act on them, by changing the active communicating peers. In fig. 38 we show the generated tree topology.

The cost of this tree is based on the monitored quality of the selected links. This quality varies in time according to the changes in the network. In fig. 39 we present the evolution of the MST cost as it is computed by the *Global Connectivity Optimizers*. In this case, there were no major events —*i.e.* the network was stable enough and there were no changes in the topology.

After several experiments, we have been able to set up proper thresholds to be used in the process of triggering the sending of the generated commands. This process takes the cost of the links to activate and compares it to the cost of links to deactivate. If this cost is both twice as good (relative threshold) and is 75 better (absolute threshold) then the

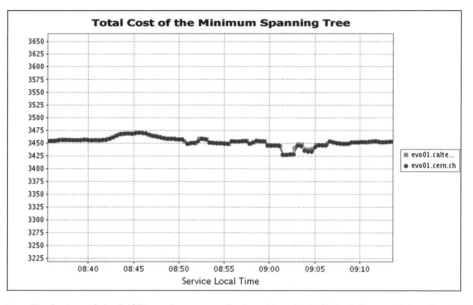

Fig. 39. – Evolution of the MST total cost as calculated by the 2 Global Connectivity Optimizers.

commands are being sent. The number 75 was chosen to trigger a change in topology if a server in US that was connected to another one in Europe now can be safely connected to another peer in US. The cost of a transatlantic link is around 90 and we have to set these thresholds to a value lower than this, but not very low, in order to prevent useless oscillations.

When a node is unstable, all its connections will be penalized with high cost. This way, we can keep the nodes that misbehave outside of the computed tree's core. Higher peaks represent a larger instability in the network (either of essential core nodes, that have many peers, or multiple leaf nodes). Based on this approach, the system quickly restores the tree and brings the topology to a stable status.

We note that this system is in production since 2007, being actively used by the community. In fig. 40 we present a view with the servers' topology and the clients connected to the system. We have deployed two *Connectivity Optimizer* services, one running at Caltech and another at CERN. Anytime one of them is the master while the other slave. This provides the system with flexibility for the administrators by allowing transparent updates and large degree of fault tolerance, being able to resist to failures in any of the points.

In the whole system there is no single point of failure, each of the core services being replicated: there are at least two lookup services, two proxies and two services for connectivity optimization. The tolerance to failures has proved its effectiveness several times since the system is in production, being able to survive to major network breakdowns both at CERN and Caltech, while the rest of the topology was kept properly connected, avoiding the affected areas.

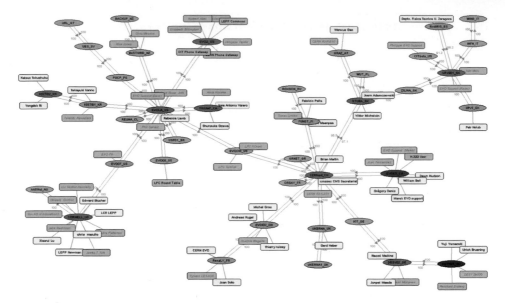

Fig. 40. – EVO connectivity overview: reflectors and currently active and inactive users.

8. – Implementation challenges

This subchapter presents key challenges which arouse during the implementation of the framework. The author had a major contribution in addressing communication related aspects of the framework and concurrency and scalability issues.

8'1. *Network-related challenges*. – During the development of the framework one of the challenging aspects was the network communication between the components of the system. A concise summary of anti-patterns for network communication in distributed systems is represented by the "*The Eight Fallacies of Distributed Computing*" [41, 42]:

1. The network is reliable

2. Latency is zero

3. Bandwidth is infinite

4. The network is secure

5. Topology does not change

6. There is one administrator

7. Transport cost is zero

8. The network is homogeneous

The initial communication between the MonALISA monitoring service and the clients was based on RMI. It proved to be an elegant solution, which was very handy as it was embedded in the Java platform and was very well suited for a fast development cycle, when new features and interfaces are added at fast-pace. As soon as the monitoring service had to be deployed over a more heterogeneous environment, different security policies in different locations started to arise. Most of them were related with the issue of opening incoming ports in firewalls at the sites. Another one was the fact that the client had also a remote handle which could be called by the service, which means that the client had an opened port for remote notifications sent over RMI.

Most common issues, which may impede the normal communication between two peers and were encounter during the development and deployment, are: network unavailability (most likely at the end sites; usually in the core the redundancy of the links address the problem), firewall and router ACLs which may change, local network reconfigurations, bugs in the underlying TCP implementation (we had a few a long time ago with kernel 2.4), and the list may continue.

From the plethora of problems which may affect communication the most challenging is the one when the reachability "silently" drops. In these cases usually the remote call over the RMI call gets blocked. There is not too much control one could get, at least not at the time the MonALISA was started, so one thing become more and more clear: RMI had to be replaced by plain TCP sockets, and all the remote methods which are called over RMI had to be multiplexed using a messaging mechanism. Java helped again in the respect to this change; the serialized information exchanged between the client and the monitoring service remaining the same, so backward compatibility was easily achieved. For a transition period both RMI-enabled and the new clients continued to interact with new deployed services. Once all the services were updated the RMI support for data communication was dropped.

The same connection implementation is used now in both the client-to-proxy and proxy-to-service communication. A keep-alive mechanism at the application level is used to guard the connection of possible reachability issues which may arise. The most appropriate approach was a "fail-fast" mechanism, in which eventual problems are detected in ordered of tens of seconds (instead of minutes or tens of minutes for usual TCP keep-alive mechanism). Once any of the involved peers detects an issue the connection is teardown, followed by a clean-up of all allocated I/O resources. A separate watchdog thread guards all the activity on each connection, in terms of last activity (send or receive) and closes the underlying socket. This is the one and only reliable way to "interrupt" a thread blocked in I/O over the socket.

The communication wrapper supports different strategies. In the client, the simplest component from the network I/O perspective, there is one thread per read and another one per write, as it connects to a single proxy service. In the service and the proxy the writing is realized using a pool of threads for all the connection. The reading still uses one thread, as there is no event-based approach possible with standard blocking I/O in Java. A priority based mechanism is used for messages (e.g. the agent messages have the highest priority in the system).

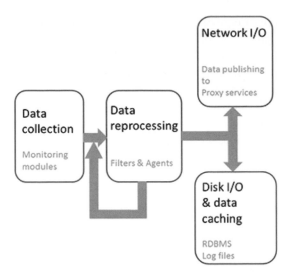

Fig. 41. – Schematic view of major components and data flow in the MonALISA monitoring service.

In time the network I/O approach described here proved reliable and with no major drawbacks. All the components in the system can easily handle tens of thousands of messages per second without problems.

8˙2. *Scalability and concurrency aspects*. – Current CPU trend is shaping a future of multicore hardware, even for commodity systems. Concurrency and parallelism usually go hand in hand and are very frequently associated with the execution of tasks in parallel to solve a goal faster. In the case of CPU-intensive applications the strategy is usually a "divide & conquer" approach in which the problem is split in subtask executed in parallel. Nonetheless, not all applications are only CPU-intensive and they can still benefit from employing parallelism even on single CPU systems (arguably that there will be any such systems any time rather soon).

An important challenge which has a strong, arguably even the strongest, influence on application responsiveness is constituted by the I/O-related operations. Both, the disk and the network I/O, may introduce delays which may vary from seconds to minutes. The delay is influenced not only by the speed of the underlying storage or network, but also the fact that usually any blocking I/O-related operation suspends the calling thread, or process, until data is available for reading or until the device is ready for writing. Another important aspect is that any I/O operation (disk or network) may fail. The optimistic approach here is that the failure is signaled and does not block the operation.

The reliable approach to deal with any I/O failures is to use asynchronous calls for I/O operations with a handle which can signal the completion or the error. If this is not possible at least the I/O call should be made with a timeout. A schematic view of the major components inside the monitoring service is presented in fig. 41.

The monitoring data is initially produced by the monitoring modules (both passive and active; push and pull strategies) in the "*Data collection*" component. It is passed then to the "*Data reprocessing*" component. This is where the monitoring filters and agents are residing. After reprocessing they may re-inject other monitoring data back into the data flow. For the data reprocessing each of the filters and agents are run in a separate thread. Finally data is pushed in parallel into the two main I/O subsystems: towards the disk and/or storage and towards the network. In each of the subcomponents the data flow is using again a set of threads to push data in parallel to different storage types and different proxies. The filtering, based on predicates, happens at the very end of the chain.

All these I/O-related challenges are reliably addressed in different parts of the Mon-ALISA framework. The component most exposed to the environment in which was deployed is the MonALISA monitoring service. The application is currently installed and runs around the clock on a large variety of commodity hardware, file systems and networks, all of them with different performance characteristics and different degrees of reliability. The only robust solution to address the challenges of I/O in such a heterogeneous environment was to design and employ a proficient multithreading system.

Another important aspect is that each and every one of these components is separated by bounded lock-free queues. If an I/O subsystem (disk or network) is unable to sustain the load, the handover (or rendezvous) queues will start dropping data. Different strategies are adopted (*e.g.* if the database is not able to cope, first thing will be to try to write the SQL INSERT-s in a different file, if this fails as well data will be dropped). It is very important to have the subsystems separated by these queues. In this way the whole system will continue to gathered and process data in other subsystems if one of them gets stuck. We have encountered situations for disk related tasks which may get stuck in write, especially if the underlying storage is a network file system, which, for example, is very common in the HEP Grid environment. Another point where the I/O may block is towards the network if silent drops appear. Although a fail-fast mechanism is embedded in the connection, it may be the case that the remote end may not be fast enough to sink the data. As a conclusion, employing concurrency in all the important components helped to address not only the response time of the application but also the reliability.

8˙3. *Automatic updates publishing mechanism.* – A key feature of the platform is the automatic update mechanism of the MonALISA monitoring service, the component which has the widest proliferation throughout the world. The initial implementation was based on the Java Web Start mechanism. Due to the fact that the service runs on headless systems the default implementation bundled in the Java platform was not suitable. An open-source library, NetX [43], currently used by the OpenJDK project [44], was tailored to download the jar files.

Two issues were the prerequisite to develop a new custom update mechanism from the scratch: the first one was that the library had a concurrency problem when multiple TCP streams were used to download the necessary resources, and the second one was related with the JNLP and the Web Start mechanism itself. The former was easily addressed (but not so easily discovered) by enforcing a single download flow/thread. The later was related once again with the I/O and the heterogeneity of the environment. The JNLP has no checksum mechanism specified. It relies on the fact that the jar files may be signed to enforce the security and consistency in the same time. The problem was that the verification is done at runtime when the jar files are loaded by the JVM with no possibility to verify them in advance, *e.g.* once they are downloaded. For some network file systems, even though the timestamp and size presented to the library appeared to be fine the content was altered. This can be detected only at runtime, which may crash the service if the main jar file is broken. The solution was a new update mechanism which uses a cryptographic checksum [45] (MD5, SHA1, SHA512, etc.) mechanism to verify the necessary libraries, before the service is started. For the moment SHA1 is used, but this can be easily changed to SHA2 variants like SHA-256 or SHA-512.

The update mechanism is integrated with the MonALISA build system, but is generic enough to be used with any application. It was designed to support both stable and development releases. It uses a simple web based approach in which the necessary files are published on a web server, along with two extra files which describe the update. It has more or less the similar strategy with the Web Start approach but it has the extra added value of multistream downloads and cryptographic checksum validation of the downloaded files. In the first phase, right after the build it, all the necessary jars are copied in a temporary area. A checksum is computed and, along with the timestamp and the size of the libraries, a manifest file is build. It consists of two parts:

- A header which contains the application name, version, a build identifier, the digest algorithm used to compute the cryptographic hash, the timestamp of the build.

- A "payload" which consists of the list of ManifestEntry with the details, in a <key,value> tuple, of each library which needed to be downloaded. The name represents the relative path of the library, the size, timestamp and the digest of the file.

To speed-up the checking for possible update a new file is created based on the information in the header of the manifest, named "cookie file". This is the file which is requested from remote sites to check if a new version is available.

Once the building phase is finished the files are copied on the update web server in using the same directory structure used in the application. The name of the application is the root directory followed by the version number. On the web server a soft link is created with the latest version. In this way the update mechanism provides the possibility to roll-back to any previous version of the application.

When a new update is available, the updater builds the list of properties for locally installed files, including the checksum, size and last modification timestamp and cross checks this list with the manifest file. Then, as soon as it determines any new files which have to be downloaded it passes the URLs to a download manager component.

The download manager component throws each download in a pool of threads which can be configurable in the respect to the number of streams which can be used. Once a resource is downloaded in the temporary area a new checksum is computed in parallel while the others are still downloaded. It may sound redundant to do the checksum computation again, but "silent" write errors may appear while writing to the disk. At the time of this writing the only file systems which use a checksum validation at the block level are ZFS [46] and BTRFS [47], and things may not change in the near future. As soon as this checksum is finished the files can be updated locally.

The local update employs a transaction based approach towards the persistent storage. It consists in copying the files in temporary files in their destination directories, making a backup of the current files, and then using the rename file system command to rename the new files into their destination files. In case any of these operations fails a rollback is forced. This extra transaction towards the file system and the underlying storage at the application level eliminates the problem which may arise if a power-cut happens during the local update or the disk gets full. For increased reliability and availability the current setup for MonALISA monitoring service uses two web servers, one at CERN and one at Caltech. If any of the servers are down, the other one is used. Once again the single point of failure is avoided and is augmented using replication.

9. – Summary

During the past twelve years we have been developing a monitoring platform that provides the functionality to acquire process, analyze and create hierarchical structures for information on the fly, in a large distributed environment. The system is based on principles that allow for scalability and reliability together with easing the communication among the distributed entities. This approach in collecting any type of monitoring information, in such a flexile distributed framework can be used for further developments to help operate and efficiently use distributed computing facilities.

It is fair to say that at the beginning of this project we underestimated some of the potential problems in developing a large distributed system in WAN and the practical experience in deploy it to many grid sites. The distributed architecture we used, without single points of failure, proved to offer a reliable distributed service system. In round-the-clock operation over the last five years we never had a breakdown of the entire system. Replicated major services in several academic centers successfully handled major network breakdowns and outages in our environment.

The MonALISA services currently deployed are used by the HEP community to monitor computing resources, running jobs and applications, different Grid services and network traffic. The system is used to monitors detailed information on how the jobs are submitted to different systems, the resources consumed, and how the execution is progressing in real-time. It also records errors or component failures during this entire process. As of this writing, more than 350 MonALISA services are running throughout the world. These services monitor more than 60000 compute servers, and tens of thousands of concurrent jobs for which it collects more than 100 million "volatile" monitoring parameters per day. More than 6 million "persistent" monitoring parameters are currently monitored in near real time with an aggregate update rate of approximately 35000 parameters per second.

This information also is used in a variety of higher-level services that provide optimized grid job-scheduling services, dynamically optimized connectivity among the video streaming reflectors, and the best available end-to-end network path for large file transfers. Global MonALISA repositories are used by many communities to aggregate information from many sites, to properly organize them for the users and to keep long term histories. During the last year, the entire repository system served more than 15 million user's requests.

As a conclusion, employing concurrency in a distributed architecture in all the important components helped us to build a scalable and reliable system capable to collect large amounts of complex monitoring information and to use it in near real time to control and optimize complex systems.

REFERENCES

[1] Legrand I., Newman H., Voicu R., Cirstoiu C., Grigoras C., Dobre C., Muraru A., Costan A., Dediu M. and Stratan C., *Comput. Phys. Commun.*, **180** (2009) 2472.
[2] MonALISA project web page: web site http://monalisa.caltech.edu.
[3] Legrand I. C., Newman H. B., Voicu R., Cirstoiu C., Grigoras C. and Toarta M. C., *DobreMonALISA: An Agent based, Dynamic Service System to Monitor, Control and Optimize Grid based Applications*, in *Proceedings of CHEP04*, edited by Aimar A., Harvey J. and Knoors N. (CERN) 2004.
[4] Legrand Iosif, Voicu Ramiro, Cirstoiu Catalin, Grigoras Costin, Betev Latchezar and Costan Alexandru, *ACM Queue*, **7** (2009) 40.
[5] Java web page: http://java.sun.com.
[6] Ganglia web page: http://ganglia.info/.
[7] CERN cluster monitoring project LEMON, http://lemon.web.cern.ch/lemon/index.shtml.
[8] MRTG web page: http://oss.oetiker.ch/mrtg.
[9] perfSONAR web page: http://www.perfsonar.net/.
[10] Nagios web page: http://www.nagios.org/.
[11] Spectrum monitoring system: http://www.ca.com/us/root-cause-analysis.aspx.
[12] Voicu R., PhD Thesis, https://ramiro.web.cern.ch/ramiro/thesis/RamiroVoicu_PhD_FINAL.pdf.
[13] RRDtool web page: http://oss.oetiker.ch/rrdtool/.
[14] JINI web page: http://www.jini.org/.
[15] The CMS experiment at CERN: http://cms.web.cern.ch/.
[16] The ALICE experiment at CERN: http://aliceinfo.cern.ch.
[17] Platofrm's LSF web page: http://www.platform.com/Products/platform-lsf.
[18] Condorproject web page: http://www.cs.wisc.edu/condor/.
[19] PBS web page: http://www.pbsgridworks.com/.
[20] Sun Grid Engine web page: http://gridengine.sunsource.net/.
[21] PostgreSQL web page: http://www.postgresql.org/.
[22] Fast Data Transfer web page: http://monalisa.cern.ch/FDT/.
[23] GridFTP web page: http://dev.globus.org/wiki/GridFTP.
[24] BBCP web page: http://www.slac.stanford.edu/~abh/bbcp/.
[25] Cisco's NetFlow web page: http://www.cisco.com/en/US/products/ps6645/products_ios_protocol_option_home.html.

[26] sFlow web page: `http://www.inmon.com/technology/index.php`.

[27] The web page for the USLHCnet project: `http://uslhcnet.org`.

[28] CIENA web page: `http://www.ciena.com`.

[29] Force10 Networks web page: `http://www.force10networks.com/`.

[30] GlimmerGlass web page: `http://www.glimmerglass.com`.

[31] Calient web page: `http://www.calient.com`.

[32] The web page for the software toolkit ALIEN: `http://alien.cern.ch`.

[33] MySQL web page: `http://www.mysql.com`.

[34] SCALA web page: `http://xrootd.slac.stanford.edu/`.

[35] CASTOR web page: `http://castor.web.cern.ch/castor/`.

[36] Matlab wavelets toolbox: `http://www.mathworks.com/products/wavelet/index.html`.

[37] CORMEN THOMAS H. *et al.*, *Introduction to Algorithms*, second edition (McGraw-Hill) 2001.

[38] EVO web page: `http://evo.caltech.edu`.

[39] COUTO DSJD, AGUAYO D., BICKET J. and MORRIS R., *A High-throughput Path Metric for Multi-hop Wireless Routing Wireless Networks* (Springer) 2005.

[40] VENKATASUBRAMANIAN N. and NAHRSTEDT K., *An integrated metric for video QoS*, in *Proceedings of the Fifth ACM International Conference on Multimedia, 1997* (ACM, New York) 1997.

[41] DEUTSCH PETER and GOSLING JAMES, *The Eight Fallacies of Distributed Computing* (online), available at: `http://blogs.oracle.com/jag/resource/Fallacies.html`.

[42] ROTEM-GAL-OZ ARNON, *Fallacies of Distributed Computing Explained* (online), available at: `http://www.rgoarchitects.com/Files/fallacies.pdf`.

[43] *Netx - NETwork eXecute* (online), available at: `http://jnlp.sourceforge.net`.

[44] *OpenJDK project* (online), available at: `http://openjdk.java.net`.

[45] ROGAWAY P. and SHRIMPTON T., *Cryptographic Hash-Function Basics: Definitions, Implications, and Separations for Preimage Resistance, Second-Preimage Resistance, and Collision Resistance*, in *Fast Software Encription*, edited by ROY B. and MEYER W., *Lect. Notes Phys.*, Vol. **3017** (Springer) 2004.

[46] BONWICK, JEFF and MOORE BILL, *ZFS: The last word in file systems* (online), available at: `https://blogs.oracle.com/video/entry/zfs_the_last_word_in`.

[47] MASON C., *The Btrfs File system* (The Oracle Corporation) 2007.

Proceedings of the International School of Physics "Enrico Fermi"
Course 192 "Grid and Cloud Computing: Concepts and Practical Applications",
edited by F. Carminati, L. Betev and A. Grigoras
(IOS, Amsterdam; SIF, Bologna) 2016
DOI 10.3254/978-1-61499-643-9-153

Big data: Challenges and perspectives

D. DUELLMANN

CERN - European Organization for Nuclear Research
Information Technology Department
1211 Geneva 23, Switzerland

Summary. — In this paper, we give an introduction to the basic data storage and access techniques which have been used and evolved over several decades in High Energy Physics. We further relate the science data handling workflow to more recent "Big Data" trends outside of science. The paper concludes with an outlook on upcoming technology changes and their potential impact on scientific data systems.

1. – Introduction

The High Energy Physics (HEP) community builds since several decades electronic detectors to collect and analyse large volumes of measurements in an automated fashion. The goal of fully exploiting powerful accelerators and high precision detectors has naturally resulted in today's large and distributed collaborations: Thousands of scientists from hundreds of institutes word-wide participate in experiment design, construction and scientific analysis. As a result, an enormous amount of data needs to be managed over a long project lifetime (several decades) and made available to a large world-wide community.

Given this challenge, the area of storage and data management has consistently taken a crucial position in HEP computing environments. Computing in large distributed grid environments (*e.g.* the World-wide LHC Computing Grid WLCG) is today an established science tool complementing particle accelerators and detectors.

The detectors at the Large Hadron Collider (LHC) are highly segmented and consist of hundreds of millions of active sensors. During data taking they record measurements for 40 millions particle collisions per second. If all produced data would be retained, then one would need to store and manage a data stream of some petabyte per second, which is not feasible. Even after the complex process of hierarchical filtering for further storage and processing the remaining data rates are of the order of several $GB s^{-1}$. Together with data copies for redundancy, derived data and simulated data a total volume of some 25 PB is currently added per year of LHC operation.

Storage managements and data mangement. – While some publications use the terms data management and storage management interchangeably, we will here use *storage management* to refer to the basic activity of maintaining the integrity of an opaque sequence of bytes. This includes the support of storing, retrieving the sequence as well as internal operations to repair and replace storage media. These functions imply that the *storage system* maintains storage-level meta-data (*e.g.* user file names, directory structures, access and creation time stamps, access control data). Apart from this, most storage systems are largely unaware of user specific datatypes or workflow semantics. Storage management can hence be seen as a generic infrastructure service that is provided by scientific computer centers in a standardised fashion to a variety of different scientific projects and workflows.

In contrast, the term *data management* is used to refer to the higher-level activity of orchestrating the creation and distribution of large, coherent data collections to support a specific scientific analysis goal. This activity is performed by experiment responsible, who implement a specific scientific strategy using the generic services pledged by contributing sites. The concrete workflow systems used by the larger experiments can be quite complex and differ in concepts, user level meta-data (*e.g.* provenance tracking) and data distribution policies.

Still, both storage and data management need to take place in close coordination to achieve an effective use of storage resources and to plan the integration of upcoming technologies without disruption for a potentially large community of science users. This coordination and collaboration is indeed one of the main challenges in large scale projects like LHC and one of the significant achievements of the WLCG Collaboration.

2. – Storage media and organisation

Scientific research is today usually based on statistical data analysis of large ensembles of measurements, often comparing measured quantities with predictions from simulations of several proposed theoretical models. The statistical nature of this comparison implies that often *more processed data volume* directly translates into *higher precision*

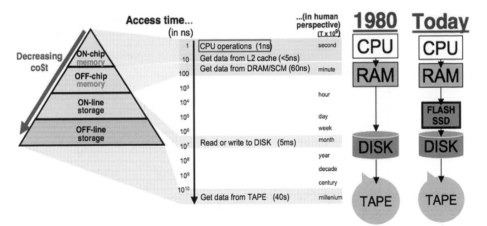

Fig. 1. – Storage media hierarchy evolution over three decades.

model comparisons —hence more concrete scientific results. As a consequence, scientific computing systems are —unlike many commercial setups— operated continuously in resource-limited mode. Storage systems for example, are usually kept filled with data which may be reused in the future. To achieve a good resource (price-) efficiency in this environment, a hierarchy of storage media has been deployed from early on (see fig. 1). This hierarchy allows to exploit different key media properties such as price-per-volume, access speed and reliability.

In the following we briefly recall these properties for magnetic disks, flash memory and magnetic tape.

2'1. *Magnetic disk*.

"I think Silicon Valley was misnamed. If you look back at the dollars shipped in products in the last decade, there has been more revenue from magnetic disks than from silicon. They ought to rename the place Iron Oxide Valley."
— Al Hoagland

During the last few decades magnetic disk has been the dominating storage medium for supporting scientific analysis. Disk technology and its constraints are well understood and technologic advances in disk storage density have outperformed the evolution in processor complexity: CPU complexity increased roughly according to Moore's "law" [1] —*e.g.* doubling the circuit complexity (transistor count) every 18 to 24 months. On the storage side, the density on disk media evolved according to Kryder's law —doubling roughly every 13 months (see fig. 2).

Magnetic disks organise their magnetised surface as concentric *tracks* of equally sized byte-*blocks* (see fig. 3), which can be read or written to with a few ms latency. This direct positioning is an important capability, in particular for the use case of data analysis, since

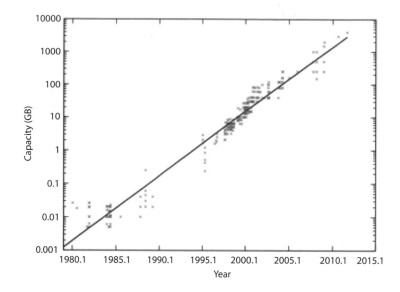

Fig. 2. – Storage volume of consumer hard disk drives (source: wikipedia).

many workflows profit from sparse access to selected data from a larger, often shared, input sequence.

The access latency properties of magnetic disk can be estimated by taking into account the rotational speed of the disk platter (rotational delay) and the time to position and stabilise the read/write head on a new track (seek time). Since both latencies are tightly coupled to the mechanical movement of macroscopic objects (disk platters and heads), the room for technological improvement in this area has been limited.

As a result, magnetic disks have become over the last decades many orders larger

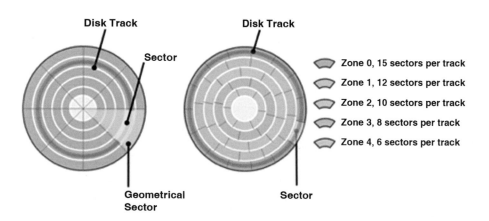

Fig. 3. – Disk organisation in sectors and tracks (source: wikipedia).

in capacity and consequently also faster in transfer speed. At the same time, magnetic disks have seen only much smaller changes in access latency.

The impact of this evolution on different disk access modes can be seen from a simplified model for read access:

$$(1) \qquad \text{read time} = \text{seek time} + \text{rotational latency} + \text{transfer time}.$$

Depending on the science application, sematics storage systems need to provide a mix of:

– Sequential access

   This access pattern will require only few seek operations and rotational waits and is dominated by long periods of data transfers. Hence sequential access workloads profit directly from density related improvements.

– Random access

   This access pattern with one seek and rotational wait per accessed block will often result in $\mathcal{O}(10\text{--}100)$ lower data access rates than sequential access. This performance gap between sequential and random access is growing with increasing storage density.

The above observation has been put into famous quotes:

   "The secret to making disks fast is to treat them like tape." — John Ousterhout

   "Tape is Dead, Disk is Tape, Flash is Disk, RAM Locality is King." — Jim Gray

2˙1.1. Storage tuning *versus* data spreading. Since the performance gap between random access and sequential access is widening with increasing storage density, it is increasingly important to design, plan and provision storarge systems according to the *specific* required operations mix of their main application —often not storage volume or data throughput. While sequential processing in an organised fashion may in some cases reach the sequential throughput, it is increasing common that large deployments are instead constrained by their aggregate rate of I/O operations per second (IOPS). Storage systems in environments with a larger fraction of random access, like databases, are therefore sized for IOPS rather than volume. The limiting resource here is the number of disk heads that can move independently. One will instead choose either a larger number of smaller disks or to use only part of the available magnetised surface.

One technique in this area is the so-called "short-stroking", which deliberately uses only the external, higher density tracks of a disk. This constrains the average distance for head movements and hence decreases the average seek time.

The resulting storage cost per volume with higher IOPS capability is usually significantly higher (by a factors of 5–10) than the corresponding raw media volume cost. This price difference together with the support costs is one of the limiting factors for a larger scale use of database systems in HEP.

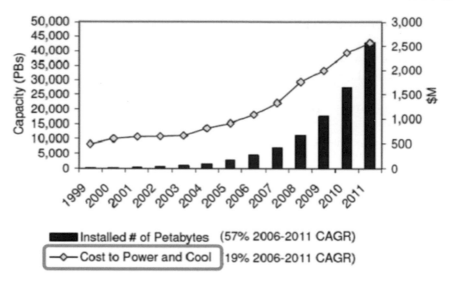

Fig. 4. – The Real Cost to Power and Cool the world's external storage (source: SNIA IDC, June 2008).

An alternative approach used by many modern storage systems (including CEPH, HDFS, EOS, Huawei UDS, Seagate Kinetic) is to spread user data onto a larger number of different disks. This approach is based on the observation that in larger systems usually only a small subset of the volume is frequently accessed at a given time. Placing all data widely spread-out therefore enhances the chances to later spread also the data access load on many disk spindles.

2˙1.2. *Power and cooling.* A significant factor and constraint in larger setups is the cost to power (and cool) storage systems. As fig. 4 shows, this cost has been increasing faster than the installed volume and can account for 40% or more of the total computing power consumption.

The power consumption of magnetic disks can empirically be approximated as [2]

$$(2) \qquad\qquad \text{power} \propto \text{diameter}^{4.6} \times \text{RPM}^{2.8} \times N_{\text{platters}},$$

which shows why disks can neither significantly grow in physical dimensions nor increase in rotational speed without violating power constraints.

2˙2. *Aggregation and redundancy.* – From early on storage system had to cope with several closely related requirements when building larger scale setups from many individual components.

It is desirable to provide

– more access performance than available from a single storage device

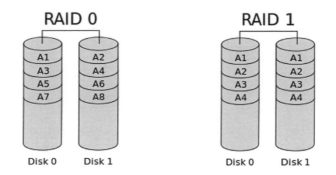

Fig. 5. – Mirroring and striping using two disks (source: wikipedia).

- larger data availability and reliability than a single storage device
- an user abstraction from individual storage devices to allow storage reorganisation without affecting end users

These goals are conceptually quite different, but their implementation overlaps and requires to make trade-offs between the above goals. Typical compromise scenarios have been categorised under the term Redundant Array of Inexpensive/Independent Disks (RAID) and are briefly described here.

2˙2.1. Basic approaches: mirroring and striping. The most trivial aggregations across multiple disk are called data striping and data mirroring and are shown schematically in fig. 5.

- Striping or RAID 0 refers to the process of distributing the data in an alternating sequence of blocks on each disk. This process does not imply any storage overhead, but also does not provide any availability benefit. If any of the involved disks fails, then the data of the aggregate become unavailable. Striping does provide though several parallel access paths to the data, which means that the data can be accessed in parallel from several disk platterns and that access latencies (rotational/head positioning) may not be accumulated, assuming suitable application software.

- Mirroring or RAID 1 is referring to storing one exact copy of each data block on each disk device. This implies a significant storage overhead: N times the storage volume (with N being the number of disks in a mirror aggregate), but also provides higher data availability as only one remaining functional disk is required to access the data. The impact of this approach on the access performance side is that all tranfers are performed with the speed of the slowest involved disk.

2˙2.2. RAID and erasure encoding. While the basic RAID levels (0 and 1) are indeed used in many deployed systems, they only provide limited options to compromise between the main system parameters: access speed, availability and price. To achieve a more fine-grained balance, more complex redundancy procedures are available involving erasure

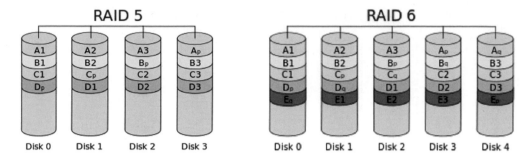

Fig. 6. – Data and parity block layout in RAID 5 and RAID 6 (source: wikipedia).

encoding (*e.g.* single or multiple parity codes, Reed-Solomon encoding). Examples for RAID 5 and RAID 6 are shown in fig. 6.

As the schema shows, additional parity blocks (*e.g.* A_p and A_q) are calculated from the original data (A_n). This allows, depending on the chosen encoding parameters, to lose one of more disk drives without losing access to the data.

2˙2.3. RAID scalability issues. The RAID concepts described above provide a successful methodology to construct storage systems with a given balance between reliability and performance. The RAID implementation as hardware disk controller or software module in a single machine though has failed to demonstrate scalability in larger systems for several reasons:

– The assumption of independent drive errors does not hold for example during the RAID recovery phase and due to common failure sources such as power supplies, fans and networking components.

– the total capacity of individual disk drives has increased faster than the recovery speed. As a consequence, the RAID recovery times increased and also the probability for additional failures during recovery, which would cause in data loss.

Many larger scale storage systems therefore abandoned the RAID approach on the device level, but instead apply similar concepts either on on-file or sub-file level. The capabilities of modern CPU allows to implement even complex erasure encoding methods in software rather than utilising a hardware disk controller. This opens up the possibility to aggregate —now via the network— devices from within a larger cluster. This increased flexibility to choose participating storage devices (disks) from all over the cluster enables to run recovery tasks distributed on a cluster-wide level rather than locally between attached disks. After losing a single disk, one can now re-create missing file or block replicas in parallel, involving many more target disks at the same time, which dramatically reduces the time until full redundancy has been reestablished.

Example for this approach are the recent cloud-storage systems: the Hadoop file system (HDFS), OpenStack/SWIFT, AMAZON/S3 all achieve scalable redundancy in

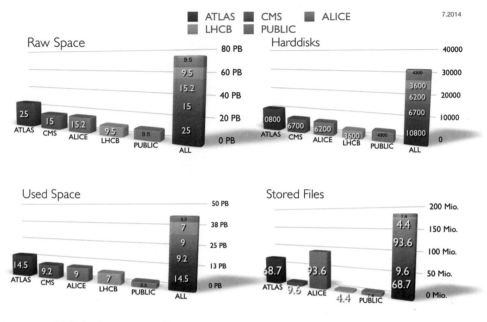

Fig. 7. – EOS deployment at CERN.

software with either simple replication or erasure encoding on subfile level. Also the EOS storage system, developed from 2010 at CERN, follows a similar approach and uses file replicas or block erasure encoding to aggregate disk drives from a large storage cluster which can spread even different geographical sites [7].

2˙2.4. The EOS storage system at CERN. The EOS development has been initially targeted on the specific use case of large scale physics data analysis. Figure 7 describes the size of the current EOS deployment at CERN In this environment several design and implementation choices have been made:

– re-use of the XROOTD framework

The XROOTD project, initiated at SLAC, had been developing a mature software framework for building distributed I/O servers. The flexible XROOTD software design allowed to introduce even major extensions as software plugins. This made XROOT an excellent starting point for the EOS development.

– in-memory namespace

With an expected scale of hundreds of petabytes, the EOS deployment extended the typical scale of XROOT deployments in 2010. Hence several key components of XROOT have been replaced in the EOS system: For example, XROOTD performs file lookup operations by issuing a broadcast query to all participating storage servers, which may respond with a file location respond within a timeout period.

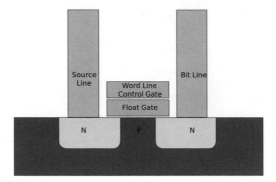

Fig. 8. – Basic flash memory cell (source: wikipedia).

To achieve a fast and reliable file lookup in a large EOS setup, this approach has been replaced by constructing an in-memory namespace. This new component gives excellent lookup performance, since the complete namespace of LHC experiments (several hundred million files) can be accessed from RAM (typical 256 GB) via fast hash operations.

– file level data redundancy

Similar to HDFS and other recent systems, EOS does not delegate the responsibility for data redundancy to a lower-level RAID setup, but implements replication and erasure encoding on file level on the basis of cost effective JBOD storage.

2˙3. *Flash memory.* – Already three decades ago Toshiba introduced the so-called *Flash Memory* —a new type of non-volatile memory to the storage media hierarchy, which has very interesting performance and power consumption characteristics. A basic flash storage cell is shown in fig. 8.

A MOSFET transistor with a floating (isolated) gate is used to store either a single or multiple charge levels per memory cell (SLC/MLC). The stored charge can then be "sensed" (read-out) via the transistor and remains stable without requiring external energy. Practical setups usually use bit lines organised as NAND gates (see fig. 9) to maximise the structural density and can be addressed *e.g.* by page, word and cell. The process of writing and erasing flash cells is based on tunnel injection or release on page level.

The flash storage density follows the transistor density (*e.g.* Moore's law). In comparison to magnetic disks, flash has many advantages, such as the absence of moving parts, a smaller form factor and a higher power efficiency. Figure 10 shows the estimated evolution of current (2D) NAND flash in comparison to normal DRAM and to 3D geometries, which are under development.

On the other hand, flash devices have depending on their design a more limited endurance: typical flash devices are limited to 5–100 k erase/write cycles and require a quite complex flash controller, which actively manages data placement and internal transfers to limit the impact of endurance constraints.

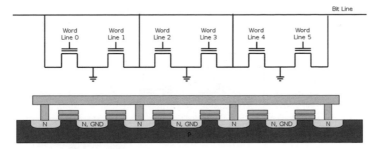

Fig. 9. – Flash memory: NAND Flash Bit Line (source: wikipedia).

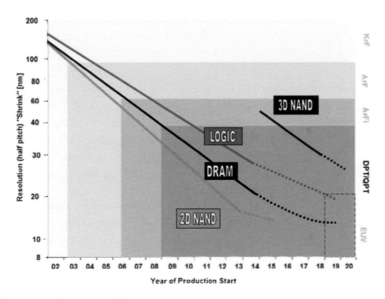

Fig. 10. – Flash areal density evolution.

The page based writing and active wear leveling imply several, sometimes unexpected and undesired, side effects. Since erase operations are page based, the ratio between read and write rates is quite asymmetric. The internal reorganisation after an user update is shown in fig. 11. One needs to take into account the so-called *write amplification* —the factor between user changes and resulting flash memory changes. During benchmarking operations, one needs to be aware that block recycling operations can cause large internal data transfers, which impact user I/O operations. In general, reproducible and relevant performance studies are made more difficult by the fact that past I/O operations and used volume all influence flash access performance.

Flash memory enters the HEP storage hierarchy in a number of different packaging options. Mobile devices such as user laptops and tablets come with integrated flash storage. On the desktop and server side, flash memory is usually integrated via solid state disks

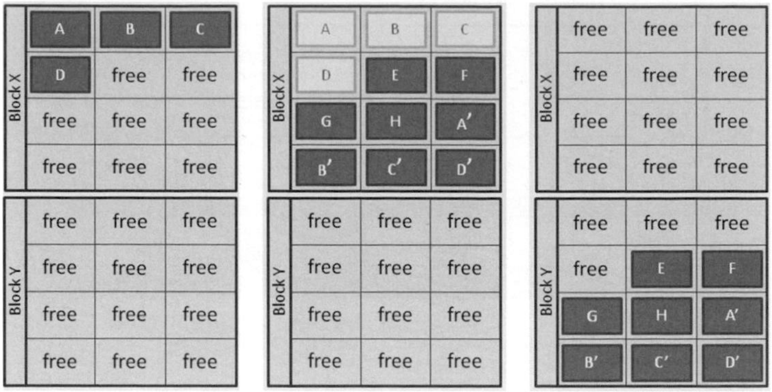

Fig. 11. – Write amplification. Internal data updates as consequence of a user update (source: wikipedia).

(SSD), which embed flash modules in the mechanical form factor of a magnetic disk drive and also utilize the traditional interface and protocols (*e.g.* SATA or SAS). This drive level integration provides convenient compatibility with (pre-)existing computer systems, but the limitations of the disk access protocol can also significantly constrain the achievable performance (throughput or I/O operation). High-performance flash applications therefore usually use a more direct integration approach via bus extension cards.

2˙3.1. Hybrid disks. A further packaging option is to integrate flash memory inside a magnetic disk device to create a so-called hybrid disk. These devices internally manage the transfer between the flash and magnetic media based on the observed data access patterns. This packaging option has some advantages for systems with *e.g.* limited mechanical space or drive connectivity, but implies a fixed ratio between magnetic and flash volume, which can be constraining. Figure 12 shows a recent overview on magnetic and hybrid disk perfromance and prices, which demonstrates the spread between volume oriented archive drives and performance oriented hybrid drives.

A further and more flexible approach for the integration of flash memory with traditional magnetic disk are multi-tier file systems (*e.g.* ZFS, Apple Fusion Drive, MyLinear/GreenDM) which integrate magnetic and flash storage devices to form a single file system that transparently moves data between the two storage tiers based on recent use and available free capacity on each tier. In this software based solution, the ratio between both storage types and the management policies can be adapted in a more flexible way to the application specifics.

2˙4. *Magnetic tape*. – Magnetic tape is positioned on the other side of the performance and cost spectrum. Tape media has been deployed since the very beginning of scientific computing. Due to its linear media organisation and the mechanical separation between media and access electronic also here several important advantages exist. Today's tape cartridges easily reach capacities of several TB per unit and still operate at many orders

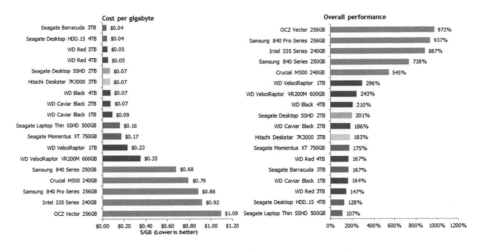

Fig. 12. – Disk performance and price spectrum (including hybrid devices).

lower areal densities than magnetic disk media (see fig. 13) and also at much lower price per storage capacity. Tape media is physically disconnected from its data access drives. This allows (in contrast to disk systems) to increase the available storage volume (by adding media cartridges) without affecting the archive power consumption. The separation between media and drives further allows to increase the storage density via

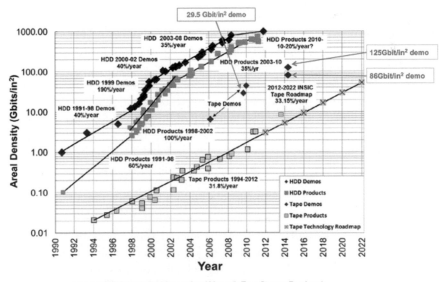

(Source: INSIC 2012-2022 International Magnetic Tape Storage Roadmap)

Fig. 13. – Evolution of disk and tape areal density.

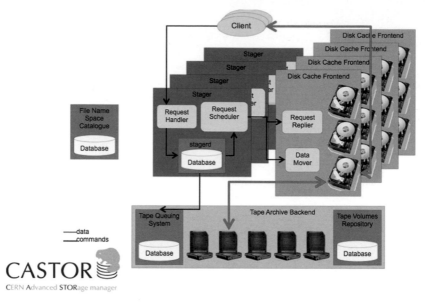

Fig. 14. – CASTOR architecture.

drive upgrades without replacing already acquired media. Modern tape drives access data on many tape tracks in parallel and hence access speeds can easily reach $250\,\mathrm{MB/s}$. Already today this rate exceeds the transfer capabilities of a single magnetic disk and current predictions expect this gap to increase. In contrast to high sequential access rates, the latencies for direct (random) access to data on tape is very significant ($O(10\text{--}100)\,\mathrm{s}$) and vary only slightly with tape drive and library technology. This latency is result simply from the fact that a tape cartridge has to be retrieved within a robotic tape library and a free tape drive has to be found and further the linear media has to be positioned before finally starting any user I/O. For many applications, apart from data archives, these latencies are prohibitive, but tape systems enjoy a continued interest as backup and archive tier due to their continued price advantage (see fig. 15).

2'4.1. An example archive: the CASTOR system. At CERN the archival tape function is provided by the CASTOR system [5], which has originally been designed as Hierarchical Storage System (HSM). A schematic view of the system is shown in fig. 14. Client data access is provided via a disk cache which is managed using a global file catalogue and a complex scheduling component which aims to collect sufficient user requests for tape based data to insure efficient utilisation of the shared tape nback-end. Newly created data is automatically transfered from disk to tape. Data which is not available on disk is scheduled for retrieval. The disk cache which mediates user access is managed automatically, based on usage pattern and available capacity. In order to implement the strict archive reliability requirements and to maintain consistency for the potentially long transfer and scheduling latencies a relational database is used.

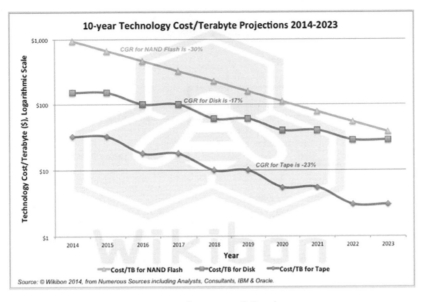

Fig. 15. – Tape and disk price predictions (source: wikibon).

3. – Data organisation

Hand in hand with the organisation of storage discussed above, there have been significant advances also in structuring and organising data. In contrast to the discussion above which mostly treats data as opaque byte stream with a named "file" being the main (only?) higher level concept, we consider here the logical relationship between different data elements and the application specific management of data movements between permanent storage and memory and on a larger scale the data movements among different computing sites. Both of these data management activities make higher use of the storage infrastructure to implement the real science workflow.

3'1. *Databases*. – Databases and relational databases in particular have been used in the HEP computing since several decades, but due to their complexity and/or associated costs only in well encapsulated problem domains such as meta-data catalogues and calibration databases.

Relational databases provide an attractive set of high level functions to the application developer, including:

- Consistent data changes in an environment with concurrent modifications through ACID transactions

- A simplified model with relational tables (see fig. 16) for describing data relationships, which has enabled automated planning and optimisation of data acces described in a structured query langue (SQL)

- Fast access to disk resident data with volumes larger than real memory using *e.g.* Bayer trees (see fig. 17).

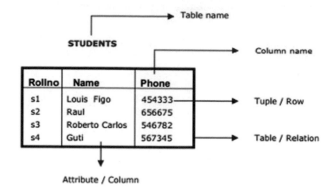

Fig. 16. – Relational tables.

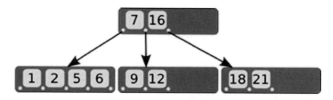

Fig. 17. – Disk access using a Bayer tree.

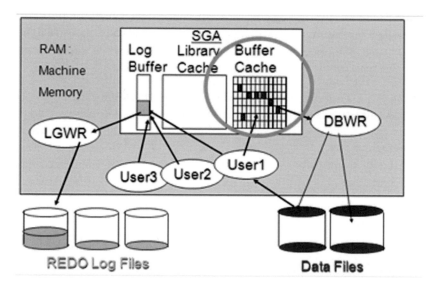

Fig. 18. – Oracle server architecture (source: wikipedia).

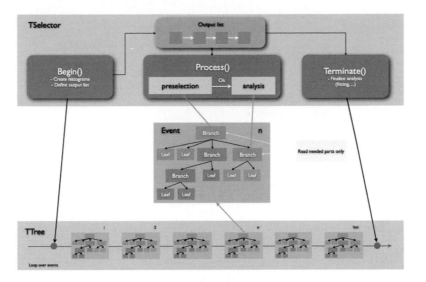

Fig. 19. – Processing event object trees with ROOT.

In particular the implementation of the first two functions requires a very significant development effort (see fig. 18 for a schematic view of consistency management via redo logging in Oracle). Still, the use of relational systems for HEP applications is limited to the area of meta-data handling for several reasons:

– Most HEP experiments follow a strict data management policy that forbids to modify measurement data, but mandates instead to create additional data versions. This approach greatly simplifies data management as data becomes essentially read-only soon after it has been collected or produced.

– The efficient design and use of transactional systems requires specific training and experience. These specific skills can only be assumed for a fraction of the scientific developer community.

– SQL as implementation language of the relational model shows limitations in describing the complex hierarchical data models of LHC experiments. SQL is also not widely used by the science community and would constrain their active contribution to the experiment software base.

– Given the fast growing volume of available RAM in modern computers, many problems have evolved from disk access problems into simpler memory lookup problems, which can now be solved more effectively with other access methods (*e.g.* hashing, in-memory search algorithms).

3˙2. *C++ persistency with ROOT.* – The system which is used to manage the bulk of LHC experiment data is the ROOT framework [4]. ROOT uses C++ introspection to

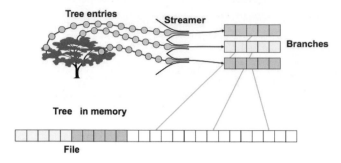

Fig. 20. – Physical data clustering by object type.

automatically derive the data description and internal relationships from the corresponding C++ implementation files. This process is well adapted to the skill-set and workflow of the large software developer community in today's HEP experiment Collaborations. ROOT organises the the many data objects which form a single particle collision event in memory as tree of C++ objects (see fig. 19). Inside the stored file data is layed-out in physically contiguous areas (branches —see fig. 20 and 21) either by object type or by single attribute. This column-store approach has been proven to facilitate the often very selective reading during the physics analysis phase.

One potentially limiting side effect of the rich internal structure of ROOT data files is the non-sequential I/O position change, as data is read from a file with several branches. In a naive implementation, the client application would retrieve data from multiple (branch) locations in the file and hence execute many small reads interleaved with seek operations.

This would has several negative side effects:

– The frequently changing read position would affect the efficiency of I/O caching and read-ahead algorithms present in most operating and storage systems and in fact also in some remote I/O protocol implementations.

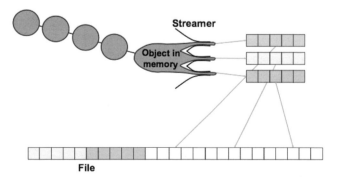

Fig. 21. – Data clustering by attribute.

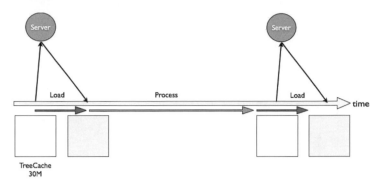

Fig. 22. – Alternating data loading and processing steps of a remote client.

– A large number of small I/O requests would in a wide-area-network (WAN) environment with larger round trip times (RTT $\sim$ 10–100 ms) accumulate significant network latency. In a naive single-threaded implementation, the wait time would alternate with other processing and hence delay total program execution (see fig. 22).

To reduce the number of network round-trips and the effect of accumulated network latency the ROOT system uses the following optimisations:

– The ROOT framework implements a predictive read-ahead cache as part of the client process. This component pre-calculates the file locations of future request in used branches, which are determined in a short training phase at the start of each job. This information is then used to submit large requests for groups of offset, length pairs in one network round trip (vector-read).

– The handling of the above vector-read request takes place asynchronously in a separate read-ahead thread. This allows to overlay the network latency with other

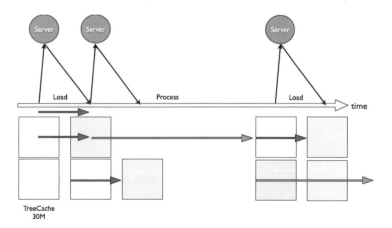

Fig. 23. – Overlapping data access and processing by using a read-ahead thread.

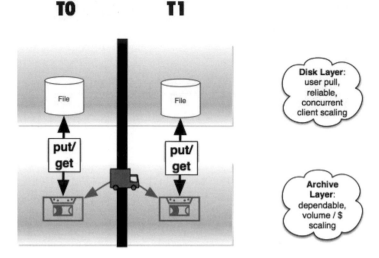

Fig. 24. – Disk and archive layers at two disconnected sites.

CPU intensive tasks such as data decompression or analysis calculations (see fig. 23) in the same process.

4. – Data management in grids and clouds

Data management in high energy physics has a long tradition, going back to the first electronic detectors and —at the time— small collaborations of physicists involved in both construction and analysis. From the start, most computing workflows used magnetic tape to implement a dependable archive at low volume price. This archive needed to be complemented by a disk layer that can support random data access patterns generated by larger groups of concurrent production and analysis processes. Initially, user operations were relatively simple and often limited to put and get operations moving files between disk and tape. In the few cases that required multi-site collaborative work data was distributed via the physical shipment of export tape media from source to destination site (see fig. 24).

Since then the infrastructure has been improved in terms of usability and scalability: Todays distributed setups are used by millions of jobs per day from thousands of physicists located at hundreds of institutes world-wide. On the macroscopic scale this required that data transfers between the sites had to be completely automated using a distributed File Transfer Service (FTS), which has replaced physical media exchange.

The MONARC project first proposed and modelled this multi-tier site grid for global data exchange [3], which is today realised in the World-Wide LHC Computing Grid. In this model, CERN fulfils the role of Tier 0 and archives all detector raw data and distributes a further complete copy across some 12 Tier 1 sites. The Tier 1 centers currently maintain a secondary archive copy of their data fraction on tape and serve

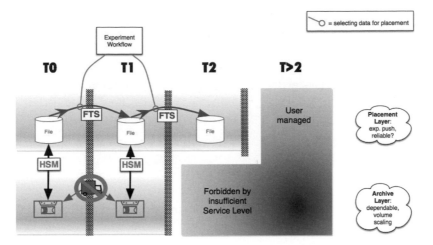

Fig. 25. – Initial roles of grid sites.

higher Tier sites in their region. A schematic overview of the different storage services at the different tiers is shown in fig. 25.

On the scale of user interaction with the storage system, the explicit user driven put/get operations to exchange data between disk layer and archive layer were replaced initially with a so-called Hierarchical Storage Management (HSM) system.

The experiment specific data management strategy —*e.g.* which datasets should move to which sites/user communities— is implemented via instructing FTS according to current experiment workflow goals. The schema also shows that Tier 2 are currently not implementing a reliable archive layer (due to the significant investment for a reliable tape infrastructure), but only managed disk space. On Tier 3 and above, no centrally organised disk storage is expected since the available personell resources (and hence the available service level) are too low. Data copies on the tier are hence managed directly by their end-users.

4˙1. *The CAP theorem*. – One of the important changes in the distributed computing area during the last decades was the realisation that continued scaling of distributed computing services can only be maintained by reducing either:

– the consistency level provided

– the availability of the system

– the tolerance against network partitioning

This observation has been formulated in a concise way in the so-called CAP conjecture/theorem by Eric Brewer. The theorem states that out of *consistency, availability* and *partition tolerance* not all three can be achieved in a single system (show in a schematic way in fig. 26). This implies for example that distributed ACID transactions at scale are

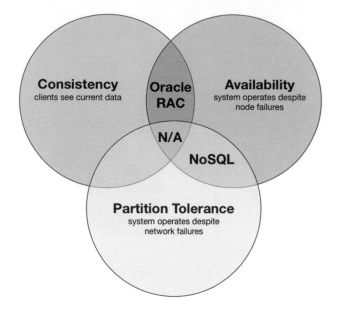

Fig. 26. – Brewer's CAP theorem.

not just difficult, but they rather can not exist. The realisation of this computer science "exclusion principle" has lead to a significant differentiation of computing systems, since depending on the main focus (consistency, tolerance to partitioning) different systems need to be constructed at larger scale. From this perspective, the CAP theorem can be seen as the defining principle for the large spectrum of today's cloud computing services.

4˙2. *Cloud storage*. – The large scale storage area has been affected by the CAP theorem in several ways. One example is the area are the different attempts to simplify the semantics of POSIX file systems, which are increasingly difficult to scale. In particular their meta-data components and hierarchical namespace show performance issues at larger scale. POSIX functions such as keeping a consistent last-modification-time, hierarchical access control lists and distributed lock support are therfore often omitted to achieve scalability. Several different cloud storage systems have been proposed, which outperform traditional POSIX systems at scale, but at the price of strategically avoiding some "CAP"-violating functionality combinations (see fig. 27).

Simple Storage Service: Amazon S3

S3 [10] simplifies the POSIX file name semantics drastically by reducing the file (and hence namespace) operations to only *put*, *get* and *delete*, which are in fact sufficient to implement a large fraction of HEP use-cases. S3 does not provide consistent iteration over "directories" or a directory rename operation, nor does S3 provide atomic operation across S3 container boundaries.

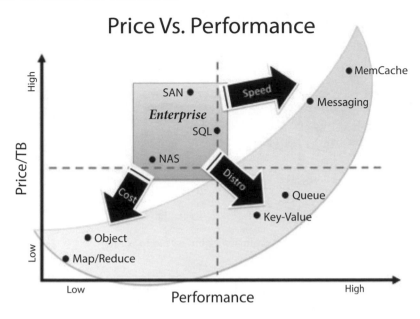

Fig. 27. – Focus specialisation in large systems (source: blog R. Hirschfeld).

HDFS and map-reduce: Apache Hadoop

With similar semantic simplifications (no update) and limited meta-data consistency, the Hadoop [12] File System (HDFS) acts as basis for a suite of higher level Hadoop components. File redundancy is achieved via file replicas, which are spread over cluster nodes to increase the data availability in case of disk or host failures. Data locality is exploited when scheduling larger tasks, which are split into units which execute, if possible, close to a disk containing a replica of their input data. From this perspective, Hadoop breaks with the traditional organisation of separate storage and processing services. Hadoop instead provides a integrated computing fabric that supports the execution of large data intensive workloads in a highly parallel way using *map-reduce* as directly supported workflow primitive.

Distributed key-value systems

On the other side of the complexity axis also dedicated "small"-object storage services emerged, which drop the concept data update and of hierarchical filenames completely and implement highly scalable key-value stores (or object stores) [11]. These systems scale horizontally by distributing the key space onto many nodes using the concept of a distributed hash-table (DHT). Redundancy can be achieved on the key-value pair level by coupling a small number of storage nodes in redundancy groups, which autonomously organise re-replicating, if one of their members nodes should fail.

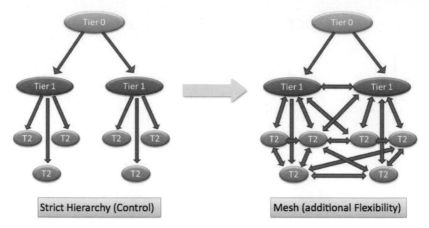

Fig. 28. – Data management strategy evolution: from a tree to a mesh.

It should be noted that the above implementation techniques are not mutually exclusive and many systems use several of the above approaches. The Huawei UDS storage system for example uses a distributed key-value store on the system level to implement a scalable S3 service on the user level.

A similar evolution to cloud-like approaches also took place in the *data management* area. After an initial LHC deployment phase with strictly hierarchical data transfers (from Tier 0 to Tier 1 to Tier 2, etc.) based on the assumption of data availability at all sites, both concepts turned out to lead to suboptimal system scaling and efficiency:

– By 2010 it became increasingly clear that the evolution of network availability and price was actually more positive than assumed in multi-tire simulations by the MONARC project around 2000. Relaxing the application access to also non-local data was tried and shown to increase the efficient use of the available storage volume.

– Strict availability of all placed data in a world-wide grid was difficult to fulfil. The autonomous storage systems at the participating sites regularly exposed temporary unavailabilities due to unavoidable service interventions or localised hardware/software failures. The storage interface to the application programs was hence adapted in order to react more flexible to a small fraction of locally unavailable data.

As a consequence, the data management strategy evolved to allow

a) Also non-local file access (via the wide-area network) in case some input data was temporarily not available at a grid side (see also fig. 28).

b) Federated access to non-local data. In case a running job discovered some of its input data to be locally unavailable, data access protocols such as XROOT [6] allowed to find alternative replicas within the local region, continent or even world-wide (see fig. 29). In the meantime, this approach has been shown to allow the

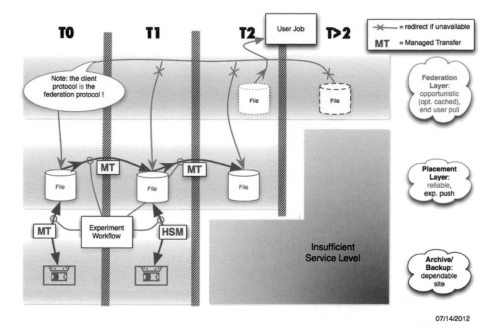

Fig. 29. – Federated grid tiers.

operation of pure CPU sites (without any reliable local storage resources) and also the independent use of all CPU resources at a grid site, while the local storage system was temporarily unavailable due to a maintenance intervention.

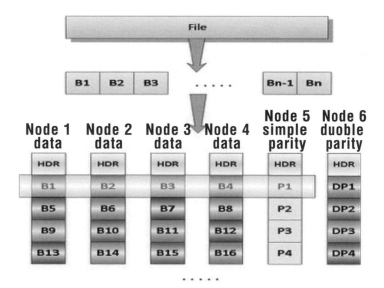

Fig. 30. – RAIN storage layout in EOS.

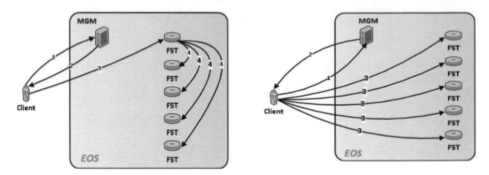

Fig. 31. – RAIN reading modes in EOS.

4˙2.1. RAIN storage. The redundancy concepts of traditional RAID systems have been extended already in 2004 by NASA/JPL to form Redundant Arrays of Independent Nodes (RAIN) [8]. As shown in fig. 30, these networked storage clusters split stored files into chunks $(B_1 \ldots B_n)$, which are distributed to storage nodes on a local area network. Similar to RAID systems, one can adjust the balance between storage overhead, performance and redundancy using erasure encoding techniques.

Also different data access modes can be implemented, which affect the achievable scalability in number of concurrent clients and the throughput per client.

Figure 31 shows on the left a mode in which one of the storage nodes acts as a proxy on behalf of the client. This node collects all required data chunks, can perform decoding repair calculations and returns the data back to the client. On the right side an alternative approach is shown. Here the client process connects in parallel to all involved storage nodes and assembles the file data from individual chunks and parity blocks.

4˙2.2. Multi-site clustering and geo-localisation. A further important area of recent work has been the support for clustered storage which can span several geographically disjoint sites. The EOS system at CERN is using today disk server nodes, which are partially located in Meyrin, Switzerland and partially in Budapest, Hungary. The two sites are connected via two dedicated $100 \, \mathrm{Gbit \, s^{-1}}$ network lines, which expose a significantly larger round trip time (some 25 ms) than local area clusters.

Designing and operating a storage system in this environment requires additional attention in several different areas:

– Bandwidth constraints: due to the lower connectivity limits on WAN connections some additional planning between large scale storage users and storage operation teams is required to avoid saturating the connecting links.

– Redundancy and availability: the geographical separation between the disk servers may allow to provide additional availability since the disjoint sites share fewer common failure modes than a single larger site. To exploit this advantage, the storage system needs to systematically distribute the redundant mirror or erasure chunks between the envolved storage sites. This policy based placement requires a detailed description of the location of all storage components. The effective use of the geographically distributed data parts requires additional care when selecting alternative data replica locations with respect to a given client location. Moreover, the resource planning for CPU and storage needs to take into account the additional efficiency impact of separating larger fractions of computing and storage resources.

– Latency sensitivity: distributed systems, which are geographically split via a significant round-trip-time (RTT) are generally exposed to significant efficiency impact from accumulated network latencies. While larger sequential data transfers can typically use the available bandwidth efficiently, this is not the case for shorter connections (due to the impact of TCP window size) and for high-frequency protocol exchanges (due to the accumulated round trip time).

While already today larger systems like EOS at CERN are operated successfully in multi-site mode and provide a set of geo-localisation policies to their user communities, this area is still under active development. It is for example not clear yet, whether erasure encoding techniques can be provided in an effective and operationally stable way when data chunks need to be spread over site boundaries. For this reason, CERN currently deploys in EOS the erasure encoding and multi-site functions only as alternative options.

5. – Storage market evolution and technology trends

Looking at the medium term future of distributed storage systems, several factors need to be taken into account to evolve the scale and efficiency of the current systems. Today, the relevance of CERN (and scientific computing in general) in terms of market share is low compared to many larger commercial computing deployments. This means that scientific computing systems need to be constructed in an opportunistic way from components and technologies that are supported by large external markets. At the same time, the number of different technology providers has been continuously consolidating. For an established market, such as magnetic disks, the evolution is show in fig. 32. Only very few companies can economically sustain the high research and development costs to participate in a market which expects continued exponential volume growth. For the science community, this means that careful continous evaluation of upcoming technologies is a requirement in order to profit from upcoming technology changes and to avoid the risk of surprises.

On the disk technology side, as an example, the evolution to increased areal density is driven by improvements in the recording technology. Figure 33 shows the exponential growth and the main technology changes during the last 25 years.

The predicted density improvement in this figure is connected on the introduction of *heat assisted magnetic recording* (HAMR), a technique that uses a laser to heat-up the recording area to temporarily change its coercivity. Figure 34 shows a schematic

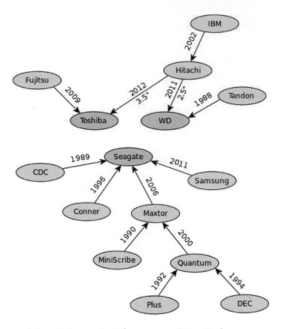

Fig. 32. – Consolidation of the disk market (source: wikipedia).

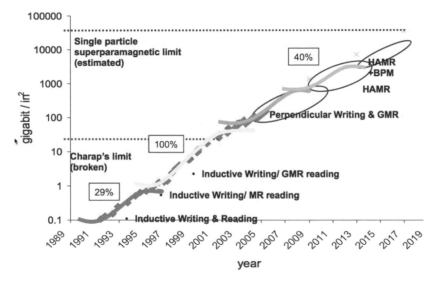

Fig. 33. – Magnetic density evolution.

view of the recording head and media in comparison to the currently used perpendicular recording technique.

A further relevant technique to achieve the continued density growths is the so-called shingled magnetic recording (SMR). This approach exploits the fact that magnetic read-

Heat Assisted Magnetic Recording (HAMR)

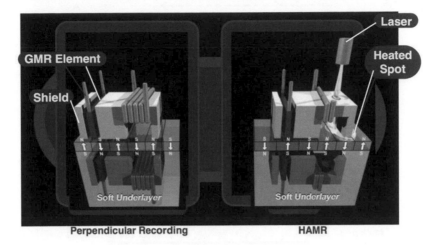

Fig. 34. – Evolution in magnetic recording techniques.

ing heads can be constructed at smaller width than required for recording heads. As a result, one can increase the track density on the media by writing consecutive tracks in an overlapping fashion, similar to roof shingles (see fig. 35). The narrow reading head will still be able to retrieve information from each individual track.

In case of a later data update though, a complete group of overlapping tracks (a band) needs to be relocated in a process similar to *e.g.* the page based data relocation in flash memory. The volume gain with the shingled approach is significant ($\sim 25\%$) and can be fully available to applications with limited or no update semantics (*e.g.* video recording, the collection of sensor data or archive use cases). For use cases requiring the update semantics of traditional disk drives, a shingled disk manages the internal data relocation, but this process will increase I/O latency and decrease the usable volume.

A interesting approach for integrating shingled drives is their direct use to form distributed key-value storage. Also key-value systems, for scalability reasons, share the preference of shingled disks to avoid any update semantics. A concrete system of this kind has been proposed first by Seagate with their Kinetic disk. This device offers ethernet connectors instead of the traditional local disk attachment (SATA or SAS). This allows to cluster a large number of disks without the intermediate POSIX file system layer and without individual storage servers (see fig. 36). Instead, each kinetic disk provides an open key-value API, which is being standardised under the auspices of the Linux Foundation with multiple disk and storage system vendors [13].

Also in the area of shingled media and object drives, additional work will be required to confirm the possible advantage of this approach for science workloads and equally important, to confirm that the commercial interest outside of science will be sufficient to sustain these new storage products.

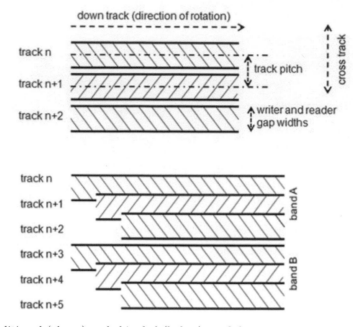

Fig. 35. – Traditional (above) and shingled (below) track layout.

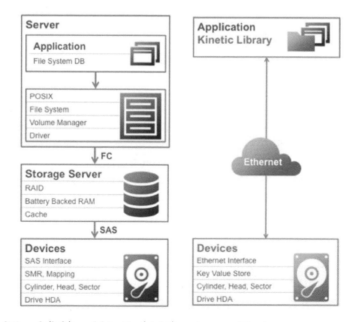

Fig. 36. – Traditional (left) and kinetic (right) system architecture.

REFERENCES

[1] MOORE G., *Electronics*, **38** (1965) 4.
[2] HENNESY J. and PATTERSON D. (Editors), *Computer Architecture - A Quantitative Approach*, fifth edition (Elsevier) 2012.
[3] *Models of Networked Analysis at Regional Centres for LHC Experiments*, in MONARC Phase2 Report, CERN/LCB 2000-001, 2000.
[4] BRUN R. and RADEMAKERS A., *Nucl. Instrum. Methods Phys. Res. A*, **389** (12) 1997.
[5] LO G. PRESTI *et al.*, *CASTOR: A Distributed Storage Resource Facility for High Performance Data Processing at CERN* in *Proceedings of the 24th IEEE Conference on Mass Storage Systems and Technologies* (2007).
[6] HANUSHEVSKY A. *et al.*, *WSEAS Trans. Comput.*, **4** (2005) 348.
[7] PETERS A. and JANYST L., *J. Phys.: Conf. Ser.*, **331** (2011) 052015.
[8] BOHOSSIAN V. *et al.*, *Computing in the RAIN: A Reliable Array of Independent Nodes*, Caltech technical report No. 26045 (1999).
[9] BREWER E. A., *Towards Robust Distributed Systems*, in *Proceedings of the Nineteenth Annual ACM Symposium on Principles of Distributed Computing*, Vol. **7** (ACM, New York) (2000).
[10] AMAZON S3 at http://aws.amazon.com/s3.
[11] DECANDIA G. *et al.*, *ACM SIGOPS Oper. Syst. Rev.*, **41** (2007) 205.
[12] Apache Hadoop at http://hadoop.apache.org.
[13] Kinetic Open Storage Project at http://www.openkinetic.org.

Proceedings of the International School of Physics "Enrico Fermi"
Course 192 "Grid and Cloud Computing: Concepts and Practical Applications",
edited by F. Carminati, L. Betev and A. Grigoras
(IOS, Amsterdam; SIF, Bologna) 2016
DOI 10.3254/978-1-61499-643-9-185

Advanced networking for scientific applications

A. BARCZYK(*)

California Institute of Technology - Pasadena, CA, USA

Summary. — This paper provides an overview of recent ideas and novel paradigms in data networking, with some discussion on how they can be leveraged in modern scientific applications. In it, we discuss the dynamic circuit services providing bandwidth guarantees to the application, the Software Defined Networking principle and the OpenFlow protocol, showing a number of possible application scenarios. We conclude with a glimpse of the Information Centric Networking paradigm, one of the Future Internet Architecture directions being researched today.

1. – Introduction

Distributed computing systems are today the work horse of many scientific projects. Distributed codes are used in simulation studies, design of complex instruments, and the analysis of collected data. Networked connectivity forms the basis of any such decentralized processing system. While the first networks were focused on providing connectivity between a pair of en-hosts by "putting bits on the wire", network functions have evolved very rapidly by adding complex higher level services, ranging from dynamic address allocation, name and address lookup, and up to allocation of bandwidth based on application demand.

In general, we distinguish two basic switching techniques —circuit or packet switched. In circuit switched networks, end-to-end communication channel is created before data

---

(*) E-mail. Artur.Barczyk@cern.ch. Now at Cisco Systems, Inc.; e-mail: artbarcz@cisco.com

is sent from source to destination. The prominent example of this technique is the classic telephone network. It was the first technique developed, fitting the requirements of analog signal transmission of that time. Circuit switching is also used in modern digital networks forming the so-called transport technology underlying the Internet today —SONET/SDH and OTN are examples of circuit-based technologies.

Packet switched networks on the other hand transport data in chunks called frames or packets. Each frame or packet starts with a header containing the destination (as well as source) address, together with possibly additional information intended for the switching elements, followed by the user payload. A data path does not need to be established before packets are sent —each network device forwards the incoming packets towards the destination based on information in its forwarding database.

The OSI reference model includes 7 layers: physical (1), data link (2), network (3), transport (4), session (5), presentation (6) and application (7). In this model, communication happens between partner entities within the same layer, while information within a network node is passed up and down the layers. Not all network devices need to implement all layers. An Ethernet switch operates at layers 1-2, while a router only needs to implement layer 1, 2 and 3 functionality. The OSI model was not implemented in network devices in the strict sense, but proved very powerful as a reference scheme in engineering and design, hence engineers often refer to routing as Layer 3, switching as Layer 2, applications are Layer 7, etc. Excellent explanation of the OSI model as well the simpler, and widely adopted TCP/IP architecture layers can be found in *e.g.* [1], while a good introductory textbook on the basics of networking in general is *e.g.* [2].

An important concept in packet networks is the locality of action —each switch or router in the path of a packet examines the header, and takes a decision what to do with it. Wile this approach is one hand very flexible and provides a rather robust fabric, it brings also the challenge of having a consistent treatment of packets along the path, and is possibly hard to analyse (and fix) in case of performance problems. Techniques developed such as in Multi-Protocol Label Switching (MPLS) help here. In MPLS, a "label switched path" is set up before the first data packet is transmitted, and the setup can include configuration requests such as bandwidth specification. As such, MPLS is an example of circuit emulation —once the path is set up, each router on the way forwards the incoming traffic along it. Generalized MPLS (GMPLS) extends the MPLS concept beyond packet switching networks. For more details on (G)MPLS see, *e.g.*, [3] and/or [4].

2. – Application-network interactions

In IP networks, routers have access to only a limited amount of information regarding the intent or requirements of an application running on the end-system. At Layer 2, The Class of Service (CoS) field in the frame header, as defined by IEEE 802.1p standard can be used to differentiate traffic using 8 priority levels. At Layer 3, the Differentiated Services (DiffServ) technique was developed in order to provide a mechanism for traffic classification and management. The Differentiated Services field in the IP header is used for this purpose, with a Differentiated Services Code Point (DSCP) offering up to 6 bits for the definition of traffic classes. Both of these mechanisms provide means for the end-system or application to provide some degree of information on the data being sent. Network nodes can be configured to react to the classification in pre-defined ways.

In practice, the means for congestion avoidance inside the network are rather limited, and in fact, congestion control in the now ubiquitous TCP/IP protocol suite is done in the end-systems at Layer 4. Most common algorithms are based on detection of packet loss and re-transmission of the not acknowledged packets. More advanced ones such as FAST TCP [6] use time stamp information and react to variations in packet arrival times, thus potentially avoiding packet loss. However a fundamental issue with TCP/IP, in the context of high-rate data movement, is its great strength in the general case — the underlying fairness, treating all packets in the same way. This implies that under appearance of congestion condition, small and large flows within the same QoS category will experience the same packet loss leading to performance degradation. The impact on the application is of course different —a high throughput ftp session will see major degradation as a result of packet loss, while a web session will just appear a bit slower.

While TCP was designed with wide area connectivity in mind, the progress in network technology and channel bandwidth since its conception has been enormous. Even the most sophisticated congestion control algorithms available inside TCP show their limitations at very long distances (1000s of kilometers) and/or when using fat pipes (10+ Gbps). The large round trip time (RTT) in the tens to hundreds milliseconds range dictates the reaction time of the algorithm. To illustrate, a 40Gb connection between two servers with an RTT of 100 ms (*e.g.* between Europe and U.S.), transports 500 MB of data during a single round trip time.

Worth mentioning at this point is the approach of breaking up very long distance TCP connections into buffered multi-hop transfers. Routers equipped with enough storage capacity for temporarily storing the data packets act as relays The advantage is the lower latency in ACK reception, and thus faster re-transmission in the case of packet loss. Obviously this requires the infrastructure to be deployed in the network, either through new router hardware equipped with sufficiently large amounts of storage for buffering each TCP flow as well as operating at layer 4, or dedicated high-performance storage nodes distributed within the network. One such application is Phoebus [5] developed at the University of Delaware, and trialled out in the Internet2 R&E network in the USA.

2‘1. *Dynamic Circuit Networks.* – In addition to classifying and managing traffic based on fields in the frame of packet header, the NREN community has been investigating the potential for even more powerful means of providing quality of service to their user community. This is done through providing bandwidth guarantees to the client systems and applications using circuit emulation. This approach is known as Dynamic Circuit Networks([1]) —an emulation of circuit networking using packet switched technology. The use case for circuit emulation with bandwidth allocation comes from several observations: To start with, scientific instruments generate increasingly large amounts of data, hence, sci-

---

([1]) Also known as Lightpaths and Bandwidth on Demand (BoD) networks.

ence data movement often involves large data volumes, in the multi-gigabyte to terabyte range per data transfer operation. The LHC experiments, for example, are distributing 100 PB of data over the network each year, expected to increase by 1-2 orders of magnitude with the advent of the High-Luminosity LHC around 2020. This data is then processed at the destination sites, steered by powerful but complex workload management systems such as, *e.g.*, PanDA [23]. For efficient workload management, efficient transfers with deterministic execution times are important. To achieve high rates, dedicated transfer nodes are deployed at computing sites. These nodes are tuned to send data at 10 or nowadays even 40 Gbps. 100 Gbps and more, streamed from a single server equipped with SSD storage has been demonstrated.

Hence we see the capability to send data efficiently at high rates between research computing sites. On the other hand, IP's Quality of Service features can provide different classes of traffic, differentiating, and possibly treating flows differently based on bits in the IP header set by the user application. However, the network does not distinguish between "small" and "large" flows, and in congestion conditions, packets are dropped randomly (within a class of service). On the end-hosts, TCP congestion control applies the same mechanisms to any data stream. The resulting effect is that small flows can disrupt large flows, and the effect on large flows can be significant.

Second observation is that bandwidth reservation creates a virtual private resource for a single user or use case. Traffic separation allows the user (or application) to ignore the requirement of fairness and send data as fast as he can. Or, to put it differently, 90% utilization on a shared link results in very bad user experience, while 90% utilization of a dedicated point-to-point channel constitutes a well used resource. At the transport layer, the application can use either aggressive flavours of TCP such as *e.g.* FAST TCP [6], or use UDP-based transfer tools altogether, where congestion control can be neglected and only lost data re-transmitted as quickly as possible.

In order to support high data transfer performance, networks for research applications have to distinguish themselves by providing very low loss rate links, line-rate equipment and design the network such as to minimise probability of congestion. In addition, Dynamic Circuit Network services give them the possibility to separate the traffic and partition their network in a way that negative impact of one user on another is avoided.

3. – Inter-domain aspects

Network connections between end-hosts in different physical location are crossing in most cases multiple domains. For example a connection between a host in the CERN data center and a workstation at Caltech involves the local data center network at CERN, several R&E network domains such as SWITCH, GEANT, Internet2 and CENIC, and the campus network at Caltech. Each of these domains is administered independently, and each operating organization has its own policies and service definitions. Peering agreements between the connecting organizations defines the connectivity, use policies, and service characteristics between the domains. Based on the commercial world's example of service provider networks, these agreements are typically bilateral.

For an application such as *e.g.* gridtfp or FDT, what matters is however the service provided over the entire path between the server and client host. In standard IP routed networks, the quality of the end-to-end service depends on the configuration of each of the domains and the agreements between them —something typically the end user has no control over. The data transfers over the general-purpose internet are usually short lived and/or of low throughput compared to data movement created by, *e.g.*, the LHC experiments. Research and Education Networks (NRENs) therefore are much more sensitive to the end-to-end performance requirements of their users, and collaborations between them have to focus on performance in addition to pure connectivity. The physical locations (facilities, network elements) where networks "peer" are thus of high importance, and since often operated by independent entities from the network operators, have to be included in the end-to-end view.

3`1. *Networks and exchange points*. – Facilitating the connectivity, Internet Exchange Points provide "meeting points" for service provider networks, where a domain can interconnect through a switch with one or more peering partners at the same location. In addition to commercial exchanges, such as AMS-IX, etc., the research network community has put in place several exchanges dedicated to serving research and education traffic. The facilities providing Layer 1 and Layer 2 services are known as Open Lambda Exchanges.

The Global Lambda Integrated Facility (GLIF) [7] is a collaboration of organizations supporting networking for research applications. GLIF's declared vision is to promote the paradigm of lambda networking, also known as dynamic circuit networking, in support of data-intensive science, and it does so through fostering collaboration on development, testing as well as operational best practices. Many of the GLIF participants operate so-called GLIF Open Lightpath Exchanges known as GOLEs. The GOLEs implementing automated dynamic provisioning through the NSI protocol described below, are known as AutoGOLEs. Figure 1 shows a map of the AutoGOLEs and their interconnecting network links(²).

3`2. *OGF network services interface*. – Many R&E network operators have been developing dedicated services to satisfy the special needs of the researchers and scientists at the institutes and laboratories connected to their networks. To mention are certainly OSCARS, DRAC, DRAGON, AutoBAHN, Phosphorus. As mentioned above, today's large scientific collaborations do not stop at country or even regional scope, and often require good network services between domains. Several organizations and working groups have thus been engaged in the development of common protocols and services. DICE in the transatlantic area was an attempt at defining and delivering uniform inter-domain services, and defined the Inter-Domain Control Protocol (IDCP), but was constrained to only the handful of participating network organizations.

In order to address the above issues, a working group within the Open Grid Forum has been created, tasked with defining a standard set of protocols for inter-domain network

---

(²) The number of "standard" GOLEs and the network infrastructure provided by GLIF participants is however much larger, see, *e.g.*, http://www.glif.is/publications/maps/.

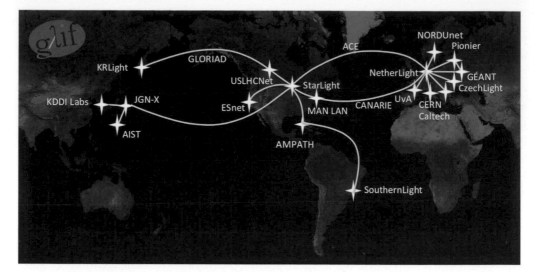

Fig. 1. – The global topology of Automated GLIF Open Lightpath Exchanges (AutoGOLEs) as of 2014, interconnecting many major R&E networks.

services. Circuit setup and management is only one of the possible and necessary services, hence the group was named "Network Service Interface" group, to reflect its broader role.

The published Network Services Framework [8] defines the Network Services Agent (NSA), the Network Services Interface (NSI), the NSI protocol as well as the very notion of Network Services and the Inter-Network Topology. Communication between NSAs crosses the Network Service Interface by means of NSI Message exchanges, as visualized in fig. 2.

As shown in fig. 3, NSAs can be interconnected to form a hierarchical structure. Depending on the position of an NSA in the hierarchy, it can carry out one or more of the basic functions: the *Requester Agent* requests service from a *Provider Agent* which services the requests, while the *Aggregator Agent* has more than one child NSA, and aggregates the responses from each of them. This happens when a larger domain is divided into sub-domains for management reasons, or when regional networks provide aggregation service for their clients or local partner networks.

The first NSI service to be standardized is the Connection Service (NSI-CS) [9]. As the name indicates, this is the service providing a connection between end-points called Service Termination Points (STPs). Other services in preparation are the Topology Service (NSI-TS), or the Discovery Service (NSI-DS), and later extensions to monitoring, verification and other services needed to operate inter-domain connections.

The NSI-CS is built upon an advance-reservation protocol. The connection request, issued by the Requester NSA (which could be part of middleware or a user application), has to contain only the two end-points of the connection. Additional parameters can be provided specifying the start time and end time of the reservation period, the requested bandwidth, and if needed for the end-point connectivity, VLAN IDs for each termination point.

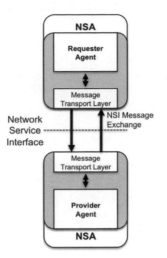

Fig. 2. – Network Service Agents (NSA) interact through the Network Service Interface (NSI).

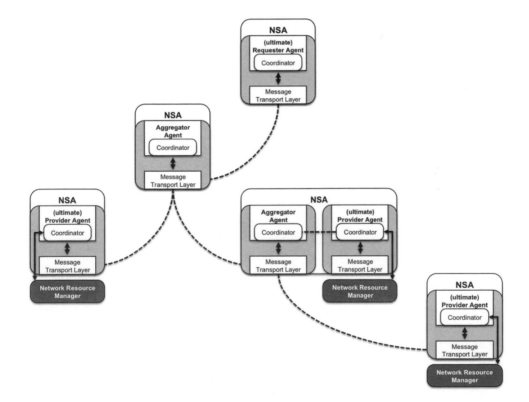

Fig. 3. – Example of a hierarchy of NSAs.

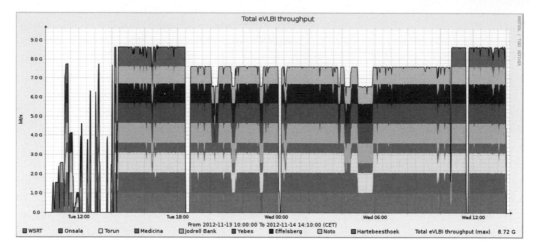

Fig. 4. – Example of data streaming from multiple radio telescopes towards the correlator site.

3˙3. *Use cases*. – This section presents two use cases for dynamic circuit networks, one showing the advantages of bandwidth provisioning for fast data transfers between data centers, and one addressing the needs of jitter sensitive applications.

3˙3.1. eVLBI. One particularly successful application of dynamic circuit network has been developed in order to facilitate Very Large Baseline Interferometry, VLBI [10], observations. In this important technique in astrophysics research, signals from multiple radio telescopes are combined, forming a single large observation facility. The resolution of the resulting image depends on the distance between the telescopes —in general, the larger the distance, the higher the resolution. The sensitivity increases with the number of telescopes.

Custom-build supercomputers are used for correlating the received data. One such facility is operated by the Joint Institute for VLBI in Europe (JIVE) in The Netherlands. The European VLBI Network uses telescopes in several countries around the globe, such as UK, The Netherlands, Germany, Poland, Sweden, Finland, Italy, South Africa, China and others.

Traditionally, VLBI data has been recorded on tapes or disk drives, and sent to the correlator site for processing. In a new scheme, called e-VLBI, data from the telescopes participating in the observation is delivered to the correlator in real-time using the network. The advantage is the faster evaluation time, short reaction time to instrument issues as well as the possibility to define new observation parameters based on current measurement.

The data rates from today's radio telescopes are around or below 1 Gbps, which can be well handled within today's R&E networks [11]. The data flows are very regular over time, as shown in the example measurement in fig. 4. The application, correlating multiple streams of data however is sensitive to jitter, as delay in packet delivery on one particular stream causes backlog of the entire data input. On the other hand, similar to audio and video streaming, the application is less sensitive to low rate of packet loss. Dedicating capacity within the network through the use of dynamic circuits is therefore a good match of technology and requirements.

3˙3.2. ANSE. The ANSE project [12] has been focusing on interfacing advanced network services, like bandwidth provisioning, with scientific data and workflow management applications such as those being used in the LHC experiments. These services allow the applications to observe and to react to the status of the network, *e.g.* through interfaces to the MonALISA [20] and/or PerfSONAR [21] monitoring systems, or to execute some level of control, *e.g.* as provided by capacity allocation systems such as OSCARS [22] or NSI-based systems such as OpenNSA.

As part of the ANSE project, the CMS experiment at CERN has extended the data placement management toolkit PhEDEx [19], which manages the scheduling of all wide-area network transfers, by an interface to dynamic circuit provisioning. The integration of dynamic circuit provisioning with PhEDEx primarily serves two purposes: to provide determinism in data transfers and a possibility of strict prioritisation of transfers are the transport level. Determinism is achieved through the creation of dedicated channels for a particular transfer of a dataset, thus avoiding resource contention and congestion effects. On the other hand, circuits can be set up for high priority transfer requests, bypassing a possibly busy default routed path. Fine tuning can be achieved by requesting higher-bandwidth channels for higher-priority transfers.

PhEDEx itself consists of an Oracle databse, a website-based data service, a set of central agents running at CERN, and a set of site agents for each PhEDEx site. Circuit requests can be either issued by the FileDownload agents running at the sites, or by the central FileRouter agent. In the first case, since the local agents have no global system view, the circuit is requested when the transfer is starting. This "Bandwidth on Demand" mode has the advantage of ease of implementation, but as the circuit is provisioned only in case resources are available at the instant the request was issued, no advance planning is possible. The integration of circuit provisioning with the central agents, having a global view of the transfer requests being executed as well as pending, allows to schedule the resources in advance, and in this way optimize the global data movement and subsequently the entire workflow.

The local reservation at FileDownload agent level was implemented in the initial phase of the project. Figure 5 shows the throughput plots during a test transfer between two sites equipped with dynamic bandwidth provisioning capability and the extended version of PhEDEx. The blue plot shows the throughput of the transfer using the default, routed path, on which 5 Gbps background traffic has been added, resulting in 5 Gbps remaining capacity for the transfer. The red plot results when a dedicated path of 10 Gbps is requested: the transfer is smoothly directed onto the new path, and proceeds at the requested rate.

Details of the setup and the results have been published in [12].

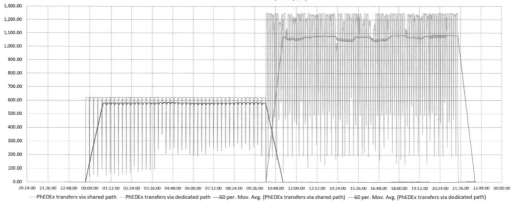

Fig. 5. – Data throughput during PhEDEx data transfers between two prototype sites. Use of default path in blue, dedicated circuit in red.

4. – Software defined networking

Traditional networks are built from elements —switches, routers— typically running proprietary implementations of protocols and algorithms. Even if the protocols themselves are open and available to the public, the implementation is not. This gives the hardware vendor the advantage of control and differentiation of products, but new developments, improvements and bug fixes are delivered at the pace of the providing company. Innovation is slow, and possibilities to trial or experiment in real user environment are hard to find. A new approach to networking, Software Defined Networking (SDN), aims at facilitating innovation through decoupling of control and forwarding functionality. With centralized control and programmatic interface using standard based protocols, SDN opens up the network to innovation in a way not seen before. Some draw parallels with the computing industry's transition from mainframes towards workstation and personal computers.

4‘1. *Separation of control and data plane*. – Each network device operates several processes, the forwarding of packets being only one of them. In general, we distinguish between data plane processes which perform inspection, forwarding or dropping of incoming frames or packets, and control plane processes which are responsible for building the topology and forwarding tables in the device. Figure 6 outlines the interactions between network elements in the control and data planes.

While in traditional networks operating today, the control functionality is integrated in the same device([3]) as forwarding functions, the underlying principle in SDN is the

---

([3]) Internally, however, the control functions are executed on dedicated control elements or modules.

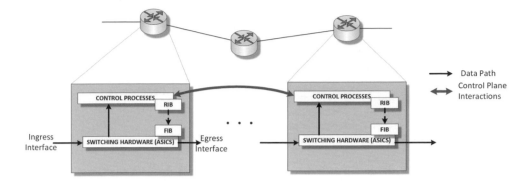

Fig. 6. – Distributed control plane interactions between network devices with integrated control plane.

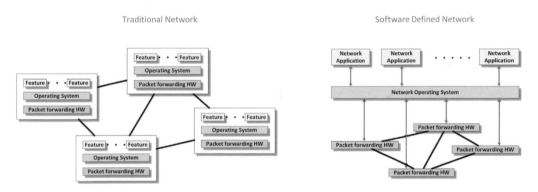

Fig. 7. – On the left, a traditional network with devices performing both forwarding and control functions. Software Defined Networks, on the right, decouple control from forwarding functionality, with applications running on top of a network OS, on control servers external to the network devices.

decoupling of control and data plane functionality. The difference in approach is shown in fig. 7. In an SDN network, the hardware in the data plane (blue boxes) is dedicated to classification and forwarding of incoming packets, while all the algorithmic intelligence is located in servers executing the controller code external to the switching device.

Decoupling the control functions from the forwarding hardware offers several advantages:

– Possible centralization of control functionality: In the basic model of SDN, a single controller entity has the complete overview over and access to all devices in the network. Operationally this results in less interventions —only one device (the controller) needs to be reprogrammed, while traditional switched and routed networks require configuration changes in each and single device

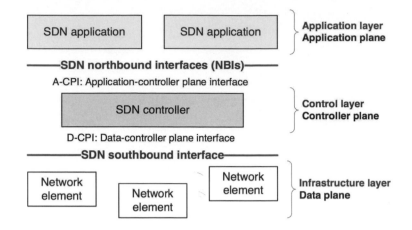

Fig. 8. – Basic SDN components as defined in the ONF SDN architecture specification [15].

– Reduction in operational complexity: In traditional networks, routing processes on each node synchronize their state through message exchange between them. This makes large networks complex to manage, while a single controller having the complete overview over the entire network can avoid much of this complexity.

– Diversity in control function provider space: especially if the communication protocol used between the network element and the controller is open and standardized, the controller can execute third-party code, independent of the hardware vendor(s). A new business and service model can evolve, fostering diversity. Data centers can deploy hardware from different vendors, based on the particular requirements, but managed by the same controller. They can freely choose the hardware based on hardware specification (forwarding rate, buffer space, cost, etc.), and the controller software provider based on different criteria such as functions, reliability, cost, etc.

The SDN architecture, as described by the ONF in the SDN Architecture specification [15], defines 3 layers: an *application layer (plane)*, a *control layer (plane)* and *infrastructure layer (data plane)*. The interfaces between them are defined as *South-bound* and *Noth-bound* interfaces, for the data-control plane and application-control plane interfaces, respectively. Figure 8 shows the relations in a pictorial way.

As mentioned above, decoupling the control functions allows to centralize the intelligence of the network in a single controller entity. In order to avoid introducing a single point of failure in the network, the central controller is a logical unit, while High-Availability techniques are used across a physical cluster of nodes. One example of this approach is the implementation of the OpenDaylight controller.

The application of SDN principles to the Wide Area Networking has additional challenges in the form of dealing possibly large latency in communication between the network nodes and the controller, as well as the need to address administrative diversity —while

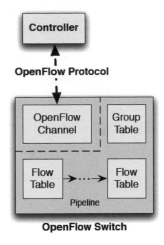

Fig. 9. – The logical components of an OpenFlow switch [16].

it is natural to assume that inside the data center there is a single authority administering a single domain, this is mostly not true in the case of interconnecting data centers, or connecting remote user equipment. The most notable exception here is Google's B4 network [18], which interconnects Google's data centers on multiple continents though an SDN network under a single administrative domain. In general, however, inter-domain SDN is an active topic of research and development today.

4′2. *OpenFlow*. – OpenFlow [13] is the open standard for SDN, defining a framework that includes the protocol for communication between the controller and network devices, and definition of the packet processing within the switch based on flow tables. It currently is the most widely used protocol in SDN implementations. The standardization body for OpenFlow is the Open Networking Foundation [14].

Figure 9 shows the components as defined in OpenFlow v1.3. Flow tables and group tables are used for packet look-up and to store forwarding decisions. In order to support complex patterns and operations, processing of multiple tables can be pipelined.

A control channel is defined for the purpose of adding, updating and removing flow table entries, based on the communication with the OpenFlow controller, though the OpenFlow protocol.

The flow table structure is shown in fig. 10. A packet received by an OpenFlow switch will be matched against the entries in the first table (flow tables are numbered starting from 0). If a match is found, the action set is updated with the instructions in the corresponding field in the table. If the instructions contain a "goto-table" instruction, processing of the frame continues with that table. If not, the entire action set is executed. If no match is found in a table, the packet is matched against a "miss-flow" entry. This miss-flow entry could *e.g.* instruct the switch to forward the packet to the controller, a default action mimicking the behaviour of a learning switch.

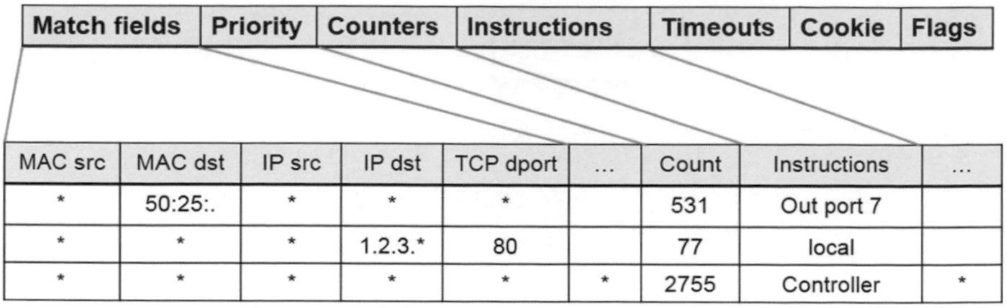

Match fields						Priority	Counters	Instructions		Timeouts	Cookie	Flags
MAC src	MAC dst	IP src	IP dst	TCP dport	...		Count	Instructions	...			
*	50:25:.	*	*	*			531	Out port 7				
*	*	*	1.2.3.*	80			77	local				
*	*	*	*	*	*		2755	Controller	*			

Fig. 10. – The structure of the OpenFlow tables with example entries.

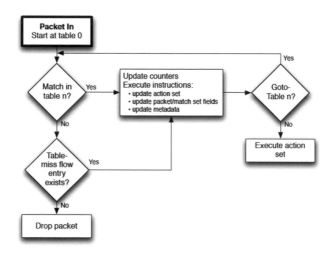

Fig. 11. – Packet processing flowchart as defined in the OpenFlow specification v1.3 [16].

If on the other hand no miss-flow entry is defined, the switch's default action is to drop the packet. This feature is important in systems where only predefined flows are to be processed, and unknown traffic should be rejected.

The packet flow chart through an OpenFlow switch is shown in fig. 11.

The instruction set defined in the OpenFlow specifications v1.3 contains the following instructions: APPLY actions, CLEAR actions, WRITE actions, METER actions, GOTO table. Some of the actions defined are: OUTPUT on port, DROP, PUSH tag, POP tag —with tags referring to VLAN, MPLS or PBB tags.

4˙3. Programmable networks. – The powerful new concept in SDN is that the network devices expose a, preferably standard, interface to third-party applications. The switching behavior of a device from a particular equipment vendor is determined by algorithms and applications executed on the controller device, and possibly developed by a different entity than the hardware manufacturer. It is the key enabler for accelerated innovation in development of network functionality and services.

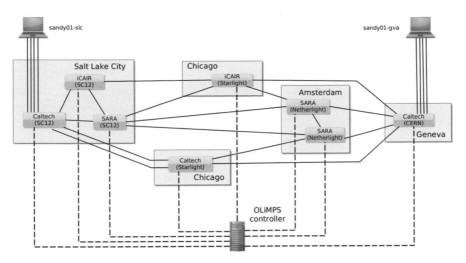

Fig. 12. – The OLiMPS demonstration topology during SC'12 conference.

4˙4. *Use case example: multipath.* – The Openflow Link-layer Multipath Switching (OLiMPS) project has been investigating the use of multipath connectivity with a focus on the Wide Area Networks. The application space ranges from data-center bridging at Layer 2 to the support of robust inter-domain connectivity over multiple physical links. The intended benefits are either increased end-to-end bandwidth, or increased reliability through multiple path diverse connections, or both.

OpenFlow out-of-band control allowed to construct a robust multipath system without modifications to the layer-2 frame structure, and resulted in flexible operation as compared to traditional multipath techniques, which require significant control overhead and/or are constrained to paths with equal characteristics. The centralized view available in OpenFlow also simplifies the control of all flows and a network-wide traffic optimization.

An implementation based on the Floodlight controller has been trialled in the WAN during the SuperComputing 2012 conference, on a topology shown in fig. 12, resulting in efficient load balancing over all available paths between Geneva, Switzerland and Salt Lake City, USA.

The project has subsequently evaluated several load balancing algorithms, including round-robin, hash-based, equalizing flow numbers, and in particular an application-aware path selection algorithm. The latter took into account the information provided by the application, indicating the size of the data set to be transferred between the end-points. The algorithm optimized the distribution of flows over the possible paths, using the total time to completion of all transfers as the metric. While the results [17] show improvement over standard multipath techniques, the approach taken in this study would not have been possible using standard network equipment. It thus highlights the power of SDN and OpenFlow in particular in network-related research.

5. – Information centric networking

Information Centric Networking (ICN) is a new, green-field approach to the internet architecture. Sometimes used synonymously, Content-Centric Networking (CCN) and Named Data Networking (NDN) [25] are currently the two flagship projects in this space. In this paper, we shall use ICN as an umbrella term to mean the concepts common to all of the projects and initiatives. In this, we shall follow the terminology used by the ICNRG [26], a working group within the IRTF, dedicated to the development of concepts related to ICN.

Today's Internet is based on protocols which evolved from concepts modelled on the telephony network. As the underlying principle, a network connection connects two end-points of the communication channel. For example, a web browser running on a client PC, receives its data from a web server identified through the address field, while the URL used to identify the website contains the domain name of the server, which is translated into an IP address belonging to the server.

For most of today's applications however, the physical or location of the desired data is irrelevant. For a video streaming application for example, running on a tablet computer, the location of the source of the date does not matter. In fact, this was recognized long time ago, and has been developed and commercialized widely as Content Distribution Networks (CDN). Companies providing CDN services, such as, *e.g.*, Akamai, are operating many servers on all continents and many countries and regions. CDNs replicate the content from a provider node to as many cache nodes as deemed necessary for good performance. A user request is redirected to the nearest cache, and the requested data is provided from this server, completely transparent to the user, but with a potentially much lower latency. Effectively, what really matters to the application is the content (and its authenticy), not where it comes from.

5`1. *Named data networking*. – Named Data Networking, or NDN, is a project funded since 2010 by the U.S. National Science Foundation, as one of four projects in NSF's Future Internet Architecture program. NDN makes use of the CCN architecture, where CCN stands for Content-Centric Networking. The initial methods were investigated at the Palo Alto Research Center (PARC) in the CCN project, based on ideas expressed by Van Jacobson [24].

In NDN, the underlying principle is the naming of the data rather than end-host in the communication —the NDN network delivers data identified by its name to the requesting client. To do so, NDN defines two basic types of packets: Interest Packets (IP) used by a client to express interest in a named data object, and Data Packets (DP) carrying the requested content towards the client.

Within the NDN network, the routers operate three data structures: the Forwarding Information Base (FIB) holding information on where to forward particular requests, the Pending Interest Table (PIT) which stores the received but not yet satisfied requests, and the Content Store (CS) where through-going content is cached. The tables are shown in fig. 13.

FIB	
Prefix	**Face(s)**
/data/higgsgg/aod	0,3,7
/mc/higgsgg/aod	0,2

PIT	
Name	**Face(s)**
/data/higgsgg/aod/2012/run17068/4	5

Content Store	
Name	**Data**
/data/higgsgg/aod/2012/run17068/1	...
/data/higgsgg/aod/2012/run17068/2	...

Fig. 13. – Data structures used in an NDN router, with some (fictional) example entries.

The FIB is populated based on information obtained from data publishers, and distributed by means of, *e.g.*, routing protocols. It contains the prefix for the data, and the Faces([4]) through which the next hop towards the published content can be reached.

An incoming interest packet received on a Face is first compared with the content of the Content Store. If the requested data is present locally, a Data Packet is created as a response, and sent out on the Face on which the interest was received. If not, the PIT is checked for presence of previous, not yet satisfied requests for the same object. If no previous request is registered in the PIT, a new entry is created, listing the data name and the face on which the request was received. The interest frame is then forwarded towards the publisher. If on the other hand an interest is already pending for the same data, the incoming Face is added to the corresponding entry in the PIT, and the interest packet is discarded.

Once the interest packet reaches a node which has the content, whether it is the original publisher, or an NDN router caching the data, this node sends back a Data Packet on the Face it received the interest on. A router receiving the DP, performs a lookup in the PIT, and forwards the DP on all the faces listed in the corresponding PIT entry. This mechanism guarantees symmetric forwarding (data packets always follow the path the interest packets created), as well as implements a multicast like named data distribution for content which is requested by multiple clients over a short period of time.

The process of Interest and Data packet forwarding is shown in fig. 14. On the left, the original Interest packet is forwarded all the way to the data provider, because the requested data is not cached in the network. Data packets travelling back from the provider to the client are cached in the network nodes along the path. On the right side, a subsequent Interest is satisfied from the cache of the first NDN node, thus reducing the network utilisation over all, as well as the load on the data provider node.

For more detailed information also regarding issues such as authentication, data and request privacy, use cases and other related topics, the NDN web site [27] contains list

---

([4]) NDN terminology uses "Face" as a generalization of Interface. A Face can be a physical port, a logical port, or an application interface.

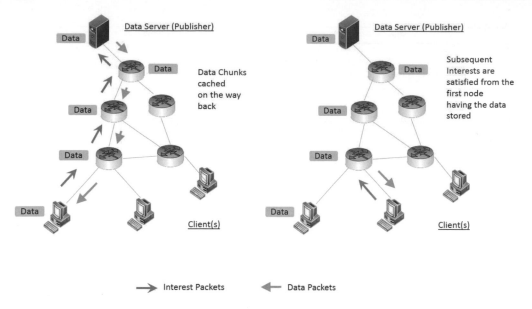

Fig. 14. – Interest and Data packet forwarding in the NDN network.

of in-depth publications, as well as link to the global NDN testbed, where interested researchers can participate.

6. – Summary

Modern data-intensive science applications are generating and processing Petabytes of data on daily basis, and the data volumes are bound to grow even further with the appearance of more sophisticated and more precise instruments. In order to support these applications, network operators need to stay at the forefront of technology development, sometimes by constructing novel services, sometimes by carrying out and supporting research and development activities. Much can be gained by the development and use of new interfaces, through which the applications can interact with the network elements, forming one optimized system for data-intensive research. This paper presented also some of the standard protocols which have recently caught attention, such as the OGF Network Services Interface, or the OpenFlow protocol. The latter framework is an important driver of the Software Defined Networking paradigm, which has brought recently many changes to the way networks are built and operated. In addition, going beyond the internet as we know it today, several initiatives have formed to investigate the possible "Future Internet Architecture". Some of them, like the Information-Centric Networking paradigm presented in this paper, are drawing on the experience from today's internet, but redesign it at a fundamental level. It is the activities like these which set the Research and Education Network operators apart from the commercial service providers, and open up the possibility for the researcher to include the network as an active element in the instrument design.

REFERENCES

[1] STALLINGS W. S., *Data and Computer Communications*, 10th edition (Prentice Hall) 2013.
[2] TANNENBAUM, *Computer Networks*, 5th edition (Prentice Hall) 2010.
[3] MINEI I. and LUCEK J., *MPLS-Enabled Applications: Emerging Developments and New Technologies* (Wiley, 2010).
[4] FARREL A. and BRYSKIN I., *GMPLS: Architecture and Applications* (Morgan Kaufmann, 2005).
[5] KISSELM. SWANY E. and BROWN A., *J. Parallel Distrib. Comput.*, **71** (2011) 266.
[6] WEI D. X., JIN CH., LOW S. H. and HEGDE S., *IEEE/ACM Trans. Netw.*, **14** (2006) 1246.
[7] THE GLOBAL LAMBDA INTEGRATED FACILITY, `http://glif.is`.
[8] OPEN GRID FORUM, NETWORK SERVICES INTERFACE WORKING GROUP (NSI-WG), *GFD-I-213: Network Services Framework v2.0*, available online at `http://www.ogf.org/documents/GFD.213.pdf`.
[9] OPEN GRID FORUM, NETWORK SERVICES INTERFACE WORKING GROUP (NSI-WG), *GFD-R-P212: NSI Connection Service v2.0*, available online at `http://www.ogf.org/documents/GFD.212.pdf`.
[10] CAMPBELL R. M., *So You Want to Do VLBI*, in *4th EVN VLBI School, 1999*.
[11] BOVEN P., *Full steam ahead - 1024Mb/s data rate for the e-EVN*, 2008.
[12] LAPADATESCU V., WILDISH T. *et al.*, *Integrating Network Awareness and Network Management into PhEDEx*, in *Proceedings of ISGC 2014, Taipei, Taiwan, 2014*, PoS (ISGC 2014) 021.
[13] MCKEOWN N., ANDERSON T. *et al.*, *SIGCOMM Comput. Commun. Rev.*, **38** (2008) 69.
[14] OPEN NETWORKING FOUNDATION, `https://www.opennetworking.org`.
[15] OPEN NETWORKING FOUNDATION, *SDN Architecture*, Issue 1, June 2014.
[16] OPEN NETWORKING FOUNDATION, *OpenFlow Switch Specification*, available online at `https://www.opennetworking.org`.
[17] BREDEL, BOZAKOV Z., BARCZYK A. and NEWMAN H., *Flow-Based Load Balancing in Multipathed Layer-2 Networks using OpenFlow and Multipath-TCP*, in *Proceedings of the ACM HotSDN, 2014, Chicago, USA*.
[18] JAIN S., KUMAR A., MANDAL S., ONG J., POUTIEVSKI L., SINGH A., VENKATA S., WANDERER J., ZHOU J., ZHU M., ZOLLA J., HLZLE U., STUART S. and VAHDA A., *B4: experience with a globally-deployed software defined WAN*, in *Proceedings of the ACM SIGCOMM 2013 Conference*.
[19] REHN J., BARRASS T. *et al.*, *PhEDEx High-Throughput Data Transfer Management System*, in *Proceedings of the CHEP 2006 Conference*.
[20] LEGRAND I. *et al.*, *Comput. Phys. Commun.*, **180** (2009) 2472.
[21] TIERNEY B., METZGER J., BOOTE J., BOYD E., BROWN A., CARLSON R., ZEKAUSKAS M., ZURAWSKI J., SWANY M. and GRIGORIEV M., *perfSONAR: Instantiating a Global Network Measurement Framework*, in *4th Workshop on Real Overlays and Distributed Systems (ROADS'09) co-located with the 22nd ACM Symposium on Operating Systems Principles (SOSP), January 1, 2009*, LBL-1452E.
[22] GUOK C., ROBERTSON D., THOMPSON M., LEE J., TIERNEY B. and JOHNSTON W., *Intra and Interdomain Circuit Provisioning Using the OSCARS Reservation System*, in *Proceedings of the 3rd International Conference on Broadband Communications, Networks and Systems, 2006, BROADNETS 2006* (IEEE) 2006.
[23] MAENO T., DE K., WENAUS T., NILSSON P., STEWART G. A., WALKER R., STRADLING A., CABALLERO J., POTEKHIN M. and SMITH D., *J. Phys.: Conf. Ser.*, **331** (2011) 072024.

[24] Jacobson V., Smetters D., Thornton J., Plass M., Briggs N. and Braynard
      R., *Networking named content*, in *Proceedings of the 5th ACM International Conference
      on Emerging Networking Experiments and Technologies (CoNEXT 2009) Rome, Italy,
      December 2009* (ACM) 2009.
[25] Zhang L., Afanasyev A., Burke J., Jacobson V., claffy kc, Crowley P.,
      Papadopoulos Ch., Wang L. and Zhang B., *Comput. Commun. Rev.*, **44** (2014) 66.
[26] Internet Research Task Force, Information-Centric Networking Researh
      Group (ICNRG), https://irtf.org/icnrg.
[27] Named Data Networking, project web site: http://www.named-data.net.

Proceedings of the International School of Physics "Enrico Fermi"
Course 192 "Grid and Cloud Computing: Concepts and Practical Applications",
edited by F. Carminati, L. Betev and A. Grigoras
(IOS, Amsterdam; SIF, Bologna) 2016
DOI 10.3254/978-1-61499-643-9-205

Networking for high energy physics

H. B. Newman(*), A. Mughal, I. Kassymkhanova, J. Bunn, R. Voicu,
V. Lapadatescu and D. Kcira

California Institute of Technology - Pasadena, CA, USA

Summary. — This report, and the accompanying reports of the Standing Committee on Inter-regional Connectivity (SCIC), a technical panel of the International Committee on Future Accelerators (ICFA), serve as comprehensive lecture notes, updated to February 2015, for the lectures on Global Networking delivered at the Varenna Summer School in July 2014. The full set of reports including the accompanying Annexes, Monitoring Working Group report and presentation slide deck may be found at `http://cern.ch.icfa-scic`.

1. – Introduction: Networks for HEP and the LHC program

A major milestone in the history of physics was passed in July 2012, with the discovery of a new boson at a mass of 125 GeV, which was confirmed as the Higgs Boson of the Standard Model (SM) in March 2013. This contributed to the 2013 Nobel Prize being awarded to Englert and Higgs that year. Following the discovery, along with intensive preparations for LHC Run2 at higher energy and luminosity, the LHC experiments have continued their searches for the first signs of new physics beyond the Standard Model in the Run1 data, and ATLAS and CMS have made increasingly precise and sensitive measurements of the boson's properties.

(*) E-mail: `newman@hep.caltech.edu` (lecturer)

In addition to the outstanding performance of the LHC accelerator and the experiments, the outstanding physics results would not have been possible without the excellent performance of the worldwide grid and network infrastructures, that coped well with the massive data flows generated as physicists throughout the world worked to distribute, process, and collaboratively analyze the data both during LHC Run1 (2009–2012) and Long Shutdown 1 (2013–2015) which is now drawing to a close.

The data volumes generated, stored and transported over continental and transoceanic networks among the Tier0 at CERN, the 11 Tier1 national centers, 160 Tier2 centers and 300 clusters serving individual physics groups, continued to grow exponentially throughout the LHC run, and reached several hundred petabytes in 2012–2014. During the long shutdown LS1 now underway, network usage continued at an impressive pace, with little or no recession in the data flows supporting physics analysis.

This Executive Summary and the major themes covered in sect. **1** of this report serve as an introduction to the extensive set of reports of the ICFA Standing Committee on Inter-regional Connectivity (SCIC) for 2015. This report is accompanied by 1) a separate report of the SCIC Monitoring Working Group led by Les Cottrell (SLAC) that summarizes the work of that group and provides in-depth coverage of the state and evolution of connectivity to sites in all world regions, 2) a set of 31 Annexes presenting the status and plans of the major continental, regional, and intercontinental Research and Education Networks, all of which are new or updated to the beginning of 2015, and 3) a complete 240 slide presentation.

The presentation, in addition to covering highlights from the full set of reports, provides additional important information on the main developments and ongoing changes in the vision of networking and distributed computing for our field, and associated rapid developments in the scale and character of networking in the world at large that affect both our field and our daily lives. These are introduced in sect. **1** of this report.

Section **2** of this report presents SCIC's Conclusions, Recommendations and Requests to ICFA for 2015. Sections **3** to **4** of the report contain highlights extracted from the Annexes, and the Monitoring Working Group.

While the SCIC annual reports have tended to focus on the LHC program, which dominates the picture of global networking and worldwide-distributed computing for HEP for the next several years, it is important to realize the important needs of other major programs, including Belle II and the Fermilab neutrino program now, and the ILC in the future.

Beyond our own field, astrophysics projects such as LSST([1]) and SKA([2]), and other data intensive fields of science (probing the genomes of humans and other species, the

---

([1]) The Large Synoptic Space Telescope. See http://www.lsst.org/lsst/science/ development and http://www.lsst.org/lsst/science/petascale.
([2]) The Square Kilometer Array (SKA). See https://www.skatelescope.org/system-engineering and W. Johnston, "The Square Kilometer Array —A next generation scientific instrument and its implications for networks", available at https://tnc2012.terena.org/core/ presentation/44. Also see slides 209–214 in the accompanying deck.

nature and evolution of our earth, its atmosphere and climate, and grand challenge advanced scientific computing with distributed exascale systems), are projected to have networking needs as large as those of our field by approximately 2020, and they may eclipse our field's needs by the time the High Luminosity LHC program starts in 2025. Overall, the historical exponential growth trend of network usage by our field and others is projected to continue, and perhaps accelerate in some disciplines and in some of the more advanced world regions.

This raises the prospect that the needs may outstrip the affordable network capacity in spite of the rapid advances of networks and data servers across multiple technology generations. Other studies have shown that the computing and storage requirements of the LHC program also will create similar budget pressures. If these projections are realized, then two foreseeable consequences are

- HEP and other fields which are the major users of R&E networks will need to make the best use of their network, computing and storage resources. A corollary is that the use of all three classes of resources will need to be well-coordinated in order for their use to be optimized. As a consequence a new class of globally distributed integrated system would need to emerge before the HL LHC starts, and perhaps within the next five years.

- HEP will increasingly need to compete with other fields for the use of R&E network resources.

A number of efforts moving towards the development of the new class of worldwide systems, or its precursors, are evident in this year's SCIC reports. A major theme in the networking field both in academia and industry, that is helping to enable the trend towards such systems, is Software Defined Networking (SDN)(^{3}) SDN (discussed further in sect. 1'10, below) replaces rigid, proprietary, hardware based network architectures and services by deeply programmable, software-driven, virtualized and integrated systems based on open, vendor-neutral standards.

One of the main focal points of the SCIC since 2002 is the Digital Divide in our community and the world at large, as it affects our field as well as other fields of science, which is discussed further in the following section and in sect. 1'12. High energy physics is global, and thus limitations such as limited network connectivity and capability that impede one region from collaborating effectively, or developing effective HEP groups at all, are of great concern to us all.

1'1. *The SCIC and Digital Divide issues.* – A major part of the SCIC's work on Digital Divide issues continues to be carried out by the SCIC Monitoring Working Group, led by

---

(^{3}) There is a large well-developed literature on SDN and an associated set of developments known as Network Function virtualization (NFV). For an introduction, see for example: https://www.opennetworking.org/sdn-resources/sdn-definition, and https://www.opennetworking.org/images/stories/downloads/sdn-resources/solution-briefs/sb-sdn-nvf-solution.pdf.

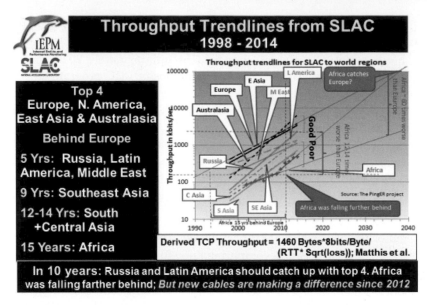

Fig. 1. – SCIC Monitoring WG data 1998–2014, and forward projections from the PINGER project of Les Cottrell *et al.* PingER, the Ping End-to-end Reporting Project, http://www-iepm. slac.stanford.edu/pinger/.

Les Cottrell of SLAC. The remarkable, wide ranging work of this group in quantifying the Digital Divide, tracking its evolution throughout the world with a system of beacons and monitors, with data going back to 1995, has allowed us to identify and focus on rising problems affecting certain world regions or countries, most notably Africa, as well as sudden problems provoked by major world events, such as cable cuts caused by undersea earthquakes in the Mediterranean, the Fukushima-Daiichi nuclear disaster in Japan following the 2011 Tohoku earthquake and tidal wave, and the temporary loss of Internet connectivity following political upheavals in Syria and Libya, and other countries in the Middle East.

The work of the Monitoring WG, discussed further in sect. 1˙12 below and in depth in the dedicated report of this working group, also has provided us with the crucial ability to track whether developments in a given region are allowing that region to catch up to the more advanced regions of the world in terms of network capability, or are falling farther behind. In addition to the SCIC's own efforts with its partners to spread the knowledge of advanced network technologies, network monitoring and distributed system software development methods, and high throughput methods to handle large datasets, it is hoped that this data will further motivate inter-regional as well as regional efforts to bring the disadvantaged regions to a state of greater equality, where scientists in those regions can collaborate effectively, take part in the process of exploration and discovery, and grow and mature their scientific communities as a result.

As foreseen over the last decade, and as illustrated in figs. 1 and 2, as the research and education network infrastructures have progressed in the more economically and

RedCLARA: Extra-regional Connectivity to Participating Latin American Networks		Marco Teixeira (RNP)
Latin American Country	**NREN Organization**	**RedCLARA Connectivity (Gbps)**
Argentina	INOVARED www.innova-red.net	*0.500*
Bolivia	ADSIB www.adsib.gob.bo	*Off*
Brazil	RNP www.rnp.br	6.0
Chile	REUNA www.reuna.cl	*1.350*
Colombia	RENATA www.renata.edu.co	*0.500*
Costa Rica	CR2Net www.conare.ac.cr	*0.400*
Ecuador	CEDIA www.cedia.org.ec	*0.223*
El Salvador	RAICES www.raices.org.sv	*0.125*
Guatemala	RAGIE www.ragie.org.gt	*0.125*
México	CUDI www.cudi.edu.mx	*0.200*
Panama	PANNET/SENACYT www.redcyt.org.pa	*Off*
Paraguay	ARANDU - www.arandu.net.py	*Off*
Peru	CONCYTEC www.raap.org.pe	*Off*
Uruguay	RAU www.rau.edu.uy/redavanzada	*0.155*
Venezuela	REACCIUN www.cenit.gob.ve	*0.300*
Inter-regional Connectivity to Latin American NRENs via RedCLARA is hardly increasing or getting worse. *A pricing/policy issue*		

Fig. 2. – Extra-regional connectivity of Latin American NRENs in RedCLARA. RedCLARA Cooperación Latino Americana de Redes Avanzadas (Latin American Cooperation of Advanced Networks), http://www.redclara.net/index.php/en/we-are/about-redclara.

technologically advanced world regions, other regions including much of Southeast Asia, South Asia, Latin America and especially Africa have lagged behind. This is in spite of the fact that important progress on an absolute scale has been made in the less advantaged regions, through inter-regional outreach efforts such as those of GÉANT([4]) and Internet2([5]), regional consortia such as APAN([6]) and the TEIN3([7]) network in the Asia Pacific Region, key projects such as the GLORIAD([8]) optical ring around the earth, AmLight (Americas Lightpaths([9])) between the U.S. and Latin America, within Europe through the use cross-border optical fibers, and within Latin America through

---

([4]) GÉANT is the pan-European research and education network that interconnects Europe's National Research and Education Networks (NRENs), www.geant.net.

([5]) Internet2 is a member-owned advanced network and technology community founded by the leading higher education institutions of the U.S. In addition to over 440 member universities, corporations, government research agencies and not-for-profit networking organizations —the broader Internet2 community includes over 93000 institutions across the U.S. and international networking partners representing more than 100 countries; www.internet2.edu.

([6]) The Asia Pacific Advanced Network, http://www.apan.net.

([7]) TEIN3, the Tran-Eurasi Information Network, http://www.tein3.net.

([8]) The "GLORIAD" advanced science internet network, conceived as an optical ring encircling the northern hemisphere, was launched in 2004 by the U.S., China and Russia, and expanded its reach in 2005 —to Korea, Canada and the Netherlands— and in 2006 to the five Nordic countries of Denmark, Finland, Iceland, Norway and Sweden. In 2009, GLORIAD added Egypt, India, Singapore, Greenland and Vietnam with the Taj project.

([9]) The Americas Lightpaths project at Florida International University, http://amlight.net.

the initiatives of the Brazilian national network RNP (`www.rnp.br`) and the São Paulo regional network ANSP (`www.ansp.br`). It remains an important fact that progress in much of the underdeveloped and developing world remains slower than in the U.S., Europe, Japan, Korea and regions of Brazil that are deep into the information age, where state of the art networks, architectures and services continue to be deployed, passing relatively frequently and rapidly from one technology generation to the next.

A leading example of this issue is Africa, which has undergone striking progress in the last few years, as a result of 1) the arrival of a dozen major undersea cables to the West and East Coast of Africa, with connections to Europe, the U.S. (and soon Brazil), 2) the efforts of the Ubuntunet Alliance[10] that has been instrumental in creating 15 African national research and education networks (NRENs) and the development of national and cross border fibers on the continent, joined by the West and Central Africa Research and Education Network (WACREN[11])), and 3) the AfricaConnect initiative[12] of GÉANT and Terena (now the GÉANT Association[13])) in cooperation with Ubuntunet, to provide resilient connections to a dozen African points of presence (PoPs) to the GÉANT PoPs in London and Amsterdam.

1'2. *Key Research & Education Network developments in 2014–2015.* – The year 2014 was marked by a number of major developments in networking, both in support of the HEP community and beyond. The transition of the major continental optical network infrastructures from links based on wavelengths modulated at 10 Gbps (10G), to 100 Gbps (100G) wavelengths began in 2012 and was led by Internet2 and ESnet in the U.S. and GÉANT as well as SURFnet (Netherlands) in Europe. The migration of many national infrastructures to 100G core networks in Korea, Poland, the Czech Republic, Germany, Italy, Romania, China, Hungary in 2012–2014 is now well advanced. Similar developments, including some access connections at 40G or 100G, are expected in France, Italy, Japan and the Nordic countries starting in 2015. In parallel with these developments, in data center environment, 400G ports have begun to appear in the largest centers, although this has not yet had an impact on the HEP community as of this writing.

A major development of 2015 is the transition of Transatlantic network services supporting HEP from Caltech's U.S. LHCNet (a dynamically resilient $6 \times 10G$ network) to ESnet EEX[14] (the ESnet European extension) with 340G of resilient capacity, complemented by the ACE project[15] (a collaboration between GÉANT and Indiana

---

[10] The Ubuntunet Alliance, `http://www.ubuntunet.net/`.

[11] The West and Central Africa Research and Education Network, `http://www.wacren.net/`.

[12] See `http://www.africaconnect.eu/Project/Pages/Network.aspx`.

[13] The GÉANT Association has been formed by DANTE, the managing organization of the GÉANT network, and the Trans European Network Association TERENA, `http://www.dante.net/Media_Centre/News/Pages/DANTE-and-TERENA-join-forces.aspx`.

[14] W. Johnston and E. Dart, "ESnet capacity requirements: Projections based on historical traffic growth and on documented science requirements for future capacity", `http://www.es.net/assets/ESnet-capacity-projections-to-2022.pdf`.

[15] See `http://internationalnetworking.iu.edu/initiatives/ACE/index.html`.

University). In 2013–2015 the larger networks have been expanding their services to allow 40G and 100G access ports (most notably in Internet2 with 27 100G access ports as of this writing), and GÉANT with 26 100G links and the use of 500G "superchannels" in the core network, together with ESnet, and SURFnet. This trend is expected to expand to several other countries in the course of LHC Run2, between now and 2018.

A principal enabling technology is dense wavelength division multiplexing (DWDM), where the optical data transmission throughput supportable using multiple wavelengths of light on a single fiber pair has increased over the long term by an average of 20% per year, with technology generation changes in network links (from 10G to 100G for example) occurring typically once per 7 years. The introduction of 100G production links in both continental and transoceanic networks has removed the threat of capacity exhaustion in the global Internet (which was a major concern through 2012) on the major transatlantic routes for the foreseeable future, and for approximately the next decade on trans-Pacific routes. In the coming years we expect the cost premium of 100G links relative to 10G to decline, although the 100G/10G cost multiplier has remained in the $7\times$–$8\times$ range on the major routes in 2014. The cost of a 10G link across the Atlantic or Pacific has continued to decline at a typical rate (a three year CAGR) of -25% per year.

Beyond capacity, the range of services offered by the more advanced networks continues to expand. These notably include 1) LHCONE, a so-called virtual routing "fabric" (VRF) that has improved the throughput to and from several national Tier1s and Tier2s across ESnet, Internet2, GÉANT and many national and regional networks, 2) the use of dynamic circuits with bandwidth guarantees (in ESnet, Internet2 and SURFnet in the context of LHCONE), 3) providing a dedicated outreach group to engage with and teach the community high throughput methods (notably in ESnet), 4) the deployment of the de facto standard network monitoring toolkit PerfSONAR, and associated tools, to encourage high throughput (now deployed at more than 1200 sites), and 5) the use of SDN on many campuses in the U.S. and in Europe, perhaps most notably through Internet2's Innovation Campus program that now includes more than 20 campuses and 6 regional exchange points with 100G connections that also deploy a so-called "Science DMZ"([16]) to isolate large flows from general purpose campus traffic.

1˙3. *Networks for the LHC program*. – Despite the shutdown period of the LHC, during which no new raw data has been produced by the experiments, LHC related network activity has been significant. The LHCOPN has been expanded with the addition of two new Tier1 sites in 2013: KISTI in South Korea and K1-T1 in Russia. The LHCOPN traffic between CERN and all the Tier1 sites averaged 12 Gbps over all of 2013, with peaks in the 50 Gbps range. Traffic over the LHCONE was comparable in size, but increased as more sites were added during the year. The network maps of the LHCOPN and LHCONE networks are shown in fig. 3.

([16]) The Science DMZ is a portion of the network, built at or near the campus or laboratory's local network perimeter that is designed such that the equipment, configuration, and security policies are optimized for high-performance scientific applications rather than for general-purpose business systems or "enterprise" computing; https://fasterdata.es.net/science-dmz/.

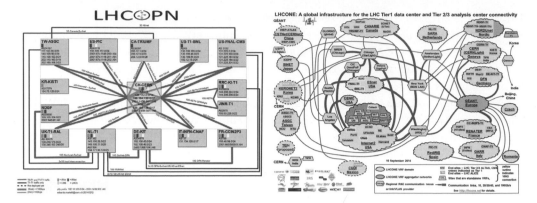

Fig. 3. – Core LHC Networking —The LHCOPN (left) and LHCONE (right) network maps. (Courtesy of Edoardo Martelli, CERN, and Bill Johnston, ESnet.)

The LHCONE multipoint service has been deployed widely, connecting eight Tier1 sites and over 40 Tier2 sites worldwide. It is built as a so-called Virtual Routing and Forwarding (VRF([17])) overlay on top of the NRENs' IP backbones, interconnected through Open Exchanges, as illustrated in the right-hand diagram of fig. 3. Figure 4 shows the network maps of four of the partner networks participating in both the LHCOPN and LHCONE: U.S. LHCNet (through January 2015), ESnet, GÉANT and Internet2. Networks currently providing this LHCONE-specific L3VPN service are ESnet, Internet2, CENIC, CANARIE, GEANT, NORDUnet, DFN and GARR, with more networks planning to join in 2015 Some sites, such as the Tier2 sites in Canada, operate their own VRF instance at the site border, connecting seamlessly into the L3VPN fabric. Several of the NRENs in Europe as well as Canada have expressed their satisfaction with the increased capacity provided by LHCONE in this way.

The LHCONE partners, led by SURFnet and ESnet, together with GÉANT and the Caltech network team, are also working on the development of point-to-point circuit based services that provide guaranteed bandwidth to a specified set of large flows. The plan is to deploy an experimental infrastructure and service in multiple domains in 2015. After initial testing within the participating NRENs, the plan calls for inclusion of a first set of end-sites as well as integration with the experiments' middleware. Excellent progress has been made in 2014–2015 in association with the ANSE project. This project plans that dynamic circuit services across LHCONE will be used by CMS' PhEDEx([18]) mainstream dataset placement and transfer system, moving from pre-production to production among a growing set of sites during LHC Run2. Similar developments for

---

([17]) See, *e.g.*, http://en.wikipedia.org/wiki/Virtual_Routing_and_Forwarding.
([18]) CMS' Physics Experiment Data Export system. See https://cmsweb.cern.ch/phedex/about.html.

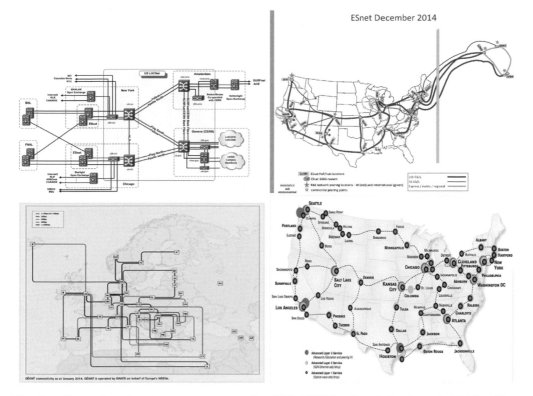

Fig. 4. – Examples of major partner networks: U.S. LHCNet (top left, through 2014), ESnet including the EEX "European extension" (top right), GÉANT (bottom left), and Internet2 (bottom right).

ATLAS, based on their PanDA([19]) workflow management system, also have begun as of this writing.

1'4. *LHC-Driven network traffic growth and impact.* – Even during LS1, the experiments have continued their very large scale use of computing, storage and networking resources. A recent snapshot, taken from the WLCG([20]) Dashboard (fig. 5) shows an hourly peak of 17.5 Gbytes per second (GB/s) including 14 GB/s solely among CMS sites. In ATLAS alone, the globally distributed data throughput since mid-2013 has amounted to a monthly average of 5 GB/s, or 40 Gbps. CMS' data movement during 2013–2014 amounted to a weekly average of 1.2 GB/s, with little change on average between 2013 and 2014.

([19]) PanDA, the ATLAS Production and Distributed Analysis workload management system. See `https://twiki.cern.ch/twiki/bin/view/PanDA/PanDA`.
([20]) See `http://wlcg.web.cern.ch/`. The snapshot shown was taken during the President's Day holiday in the U.S.

Fig. 5. – Worldwide LHC Computing Grid traffic snapshot among 170+ sites in 40 countries. The above snapshot was taken on the President's Day holiday in the U.S.

However, as shown below, the balance in network usage between CMS and ATLAS has changed recently with the increased usage of so-called "federated" or location-independent data access where physicists doing analysis are able to access data (with local caching) through such projects as CMS' AAA (Any Data, Any Time, Anywhere) project. Such use was a major focus in 2014 and is encouraged and increasing as we approach Run2[21]. A similar change in emphasis in the mode of use of networks is expected in the course of LHC Run2 for ATLAS, using their federated access tool "Fax".

While the monthly averages[22] observed in 2013–2014 were somewhat lower than the monthly peaks experienced during the Run1 data taking, the rates are much higher than in the period before the Higgs boson discovery. A recent trend (illustrated in fig. 5 above) is the occurrence of record data transfer peaks, in spite of the fact that LHC Run2, scheduled to start in March with first collisions in May, has not yet begun. This may be due in part to the availability of 100G links across the Atlantic, combined with the increased use of federated data access by many physicists, as explained above.

In any case, this presages the fact that the data flows over networks during Run2 will very likely be substantially greater than those observed during Run 1. Indeed, while the transition to the present generation of 100G core networks has been rapid, the progress of the HEP community's needs, and the ability to use the network infrastructure, together with other fields of data intensive science may be even faster.

This projected growth will be driven not only by the greater collision energy (13 TeV during Run2 *versus* 8 TeV in 2012), luminosity, pileup and event complexity, and the trigger rate, which all scale with the experiments' use of computing and storage (and

[21] See for example M. Girone, "CMS Experiment Status, Run II Plans, & Federated Requirements", Presentation at the UCSD XRootD Workshop, January 27, 2015.

[22] See R. Mount, "Computing in High Energy Physics", talk at the ICHEP 2014 Conference in Valencia, Spain, July 9, 2014, indico.ific.uv.es/indico/getFile.py/access?contribId= 113&sessionId=17&resId=0&materialId=slides&confId=2025.

which have tended to grow linearly in recent years), but also by the ongoing qualitative changes in their Computing Models. In addition to the traditional mode of preplacing data at the Tier1s and having Tier2s in the corresponding region access and analyze data there, the Run1 models have shown an increasing tendency towards inter-regional access, where Tier2s could request data from any Tier1, or in some cases from a Tier2 site in another region. During LS1 there is now a further evolution towards greater use of "location independent" access mechanisms with caching, where Tier2s and Tier3s can access and/or pull data from any other Tier1, 2 or 3 site.

The consequences of such use, the impact on networks, and the ways in which such complex flows can be tracked and managed, and controlled, have only just begun to be understood by the experiments. Network-awareness of the experiments' data processing and management systems is beginning to be addressed in small projects such as ANSE (Advanced Network Services for Experiments). Beyond the end of ANSE, that will conclude this year, a larger effort is needed to integrate these systems with network-resident services, such as dynamic circuits with bandwidth guarantees, and the programmable control and management of data flows using the newly emerging paradigm of Software Defined Networking (discussed further in sect. 1˙10).

The use of these emerging technologies, which is already under development, is important to manage and potentially limit the impact of an experiment's network usage, both on the world's networks, on the other experiments, and even on other data distribution and analysis tasks in the same experiment. A significant factor encouraging these developments is the availability of large scale testbeds (up to the 100G range), notably in Internet2[23], ESnet[24], the Netherlight Open Exchange point[25], and ANA-200G (discussed further in sect. 1˙7 below).

1˙5. *Network requirements for LHC Run2 and beyond*. – The projected growth estimates for transatlantic transfer rates over the next 5 years vary widely. The projected baseline growth is a factor of approximately two between 2013–2015 (LS1) and 2015–2018 (Run2), and is based on the foreseen growth in computing and storage resources. It should be noted that such estimates do not include the changes in Computing Models discussed above.

Other estimates indicate the potential for substantially greater growth. These include the historical and recent exponential growth trends in HEP network traffic observed in ESnet, as well as in case studies presented at the 2013 ESnet Requirements Workshop, and discussions of network needs at the 2013 Snowmass on the Mississippi meeting. A CMS case study of network needs for physics analysis during LHC Run2 presented by S. Dasu at that workshop led to a projection of a factor of up to 5, in a scenario where

---

[23] See "Advanced Networking", http://www.internet2.edu/products-services/advanced-networking/.
[24] The ESnet European Extension, http://www.es.net/assets/100G-testbed-v1.pdf.
[25] The Netherlight Open Lightpath Exchange, https://www.surf.nl/en/services-and-products/netherlight/index.html.

location-independent data access based on the AAA (Any Data, Any Time, Anywhere) system is used extensively.

When setting requirements, it is also important to contrast peak and average requirements. U.S. LHCNet, as well as many NRENs and Tier1 and Tier2 sites, observed many peaks of 5–10 GBytes/s lasting for minutes to many hours, corresponding to individual dataset transfers in the 1–100 Terabyte range. In addition to periods when a major data reprocessing campaign is underway (as seen in late 2012-early 2013), peak usage tends to occur during periods when the need to complete a large set of transfers is most urgent, especially when a major new result or a discovery is at hand (as in mid-2012 for example).

The ability to dedicate and guarantee capacity to the larger flows is thus beneficial to both the experiments and the network providers, by making both data analysis and network operations more predictable and manageable, and by allowing the most urgent tasks to be completed in a timely manner. This is the design philosophy behind the LHCOPN([26]) that mainly supports Tier0-Tier1 and Tier1-Tier1 operations, and similar considerations will need to be applied to the LHC Open Network Environment (LH-CONE)([27]), a facility that supports transfers among the Tier1s and Tier2 or Tier3 sites.

While it is generally agreed that ongoing evolutionary changes in the data and network management methods will carry the experiments successfully through the end of Run2 in 2018, greater changes are expected to be required by LHC Run3 and beyond, as the use of worldwide storage and CPU resources continue to grow and stress budgets. This was discussed at the Snowmass Community meeting for example, where longer term forward projections raised the prospect of the potential need for a two order of magnitude increase in the use of storage by the early 2020s compared to today. This led to a call for more forward looking R&D, towards intelligent, agile systems that can strategically and intelligently manage the combined use of resources (dedicated, opportunistically available, and cloud), and integrate the use of networks as a managed resource along with computing and storage in the experiments' overall workflow.

Projecting forward to LHC Run3 and beyond, ESnet estimates([28]) (as illustrated by fig. 6) that the average current use by HEP will expand by a factor ten, to approximately 200 Petabytes/month by the end of Run 2, roughly following the long term historical growth trend (observed since 1992), with nearly two-thirds flowing between Europe and the U.S. largely in support of the LHC program. An equally interesting projection is that the rapid growth of use by other U.S. DOE supported disciplines (namely Basic Energy Sciences, Biological and Environmental Sciences and Advanced Scientific Computing), will result in these fields outpacing HEP within the next 5 years. This means that the aggregate use of ESnet is expected to grow to 1 Exabyte (1000 Petabytes) per month by

---

([26]) The so-called LHC Optical Private Network (LHCOPN) is a series of dedicated links connecting the Tier0 at CERN to the Tier1 sites, with cross links as part of the overall resilience of the network. See `http://lhcopn.cern.ch`.

([27]) The LHC Open Network Environment that focuses on improving data operations to and among the Tier2 and some Tier3 sites. See `http://lhcone.web.cern.ch`.

([28]) See `https://my.es.net/network/eex`.

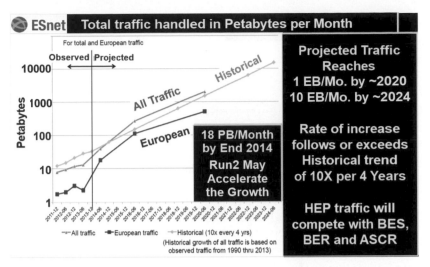

Fig. 6. – Network traffic handled by ESnet: Observed and projected to 2024. As shown the projected network use is expected to match or somewhat exceed historical trends.

2020, with 23% being exchanged with Europe, and an estimated 10 Exabytes per month by approximately 2024.

1˙6. *Evolution of Research and Education Networks*. – In general, R&E Networks have been evolving during 2014 towards increased deployment of 100G wavelengths in their backbones, which effectively has become the mainstream technology in the Wide Area Network. 100G has been deployed by ESnet, Internet2 and CANARIE in North America; SURFnet (nl), CESNET (cz), GARR-X (it), RENATER (fr), DFN (de) and RoEduNet (ro), as well as the GÉANT backbone in Europe; CERNET (cn) and KREONET (kr) in Asia; and AARnet in Australia. Many other NRENs are planning upgrades this year or next to a 100G-based core network, notably PIONIER in Poland and RNP in Brazil. 100 Gigabit Ethernet (100GE) is used today by many campuses and computing sites to connect their backbone routers. In the U.S., we also have seen the deployment of 100G both as an uplink technology and within the campus network.

The TERENA 2013 and 2014 compendia([29]) also clearly demonstrate the progress in the use of dark fiber infrastructure in the European NRENs, as well as the rapid deployment of cross-border dark fiber. Figure 7, extracted from the compendium, shows the state of deployment of cross-border fiber at the time of writing of the compendium. In the meantime, the Amsterdam-Geneva fiber has been lit with two 100 Gbps lambdas, in addition to the existing 40 Gbps ones. All European NRENs have at least part of their infrastructure built on dark fiber. In North America, the backbones of the Internet2, ESnet and CANARIE networks are largely built on their own dark fiber. Examples in Asia

---

([29]) Available online: http://www.terena.org/activities/compendium/.

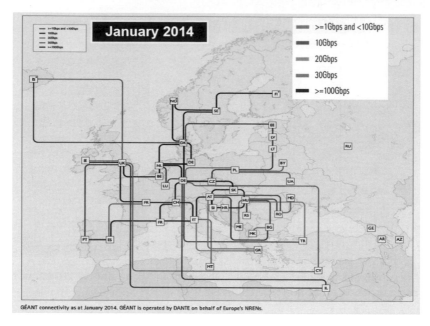

Fig. 7. – Cross-border Dark Fibre deployment in Europe. Picture from the 2014 TERENA Compendium.

include SINET4 and KREONET2. In the southern hemisphere, 90% of AARnet's, 68% of REANNZ's and 20% of Brazil's RNP network uses their own dark fiber infrastructure. Ownership of the fiber infrastructure provides a very cost effective, flexible and highly scalable option for supporting high bandwidth services, and is expected to increase in the NREN community in the future.

1'7. *Intercontinental networks*. – In May 2013, the first transatlantic 100 Gbps wavelength was deployed, and was used as an experimental resource by a consortium of six organizations: ESnet, Internet2, CANARIE, NORDUnet, SURFNet, GEANT, along with other partner networks including U.S. LHCNet. The Advanced North Atlantic 100G (ANA-100G) pilot([30]) See http://nordu.net/content/ana-100g interconnected exchange points in Amsterdam and New York, and is available to the large research community for evaluation on a time shared basis. In the context of HEP, the ANA-100G has been used by Caltech during its SC'13 demonstrations, as well as for data transfers between Caltech and CERN. BNL has carried out tests to CERN as well, with an aggregate throughput of ∼ 80 Gbps using two servers on each side of the connection, equipped with 40GE network interface cards (NICs).

([30]) The aim of the ANA-100G project is to try out the technology, operations and organization for inter-continental R&E networking by bringing the interconnection between continents on par with the intra-region transmission speeds of 100 Gbit/s.

In the spring of 2014, the ANA-100G Collaboration entered a new phase of the project which involved a resilient 100 Gbps production facility consisting of a ring of 100 Gbps links between four Open Lightpath Exchanges. This infrastructure is called ANA-200G, and was put into service in November 2014.

Another major development was the successful transition from U.S. LHCNet to ESnet EEX, completed by January 2015 in time for the start of LHC Run2.

In the Pacific, the Southern Cross cable system completed its upgrade in 2014 to support 40 and 100G wavelengths on both legs linking the U.S. with Australia and New Zealand.

1˙8. *Campus networking evolution.* – The data and computing center infrastructures at many Tier1, Tier2 and some Tier3 sites involved in the LHC program also have been undergoing rapid evolution to 40G and 100G technology, as well as to new methods (Science-DMZ, experimentation with the OpenFlow software defined networking protocol). Many universities in the U.S. have used NSF CC-NIE and CC-IIE grants to deploy 100G access links to their regional backbones. The concept of Science-DMZ has seen wider acceptance. It is based on a trust-based security model, where science computing infrastructure is separated from the general purpose campus computing equipment though a firewall but has direct connectivity to the high-performance network and subsequently the remote computing sites. Science-DMZ thus allows high throughput data movement between remote sites without disruption of the general purpose network traffic. This is important in the case of 100G networks because firewalls pose a serious performance bottleneck to data movement.

On the server side, 40 Gbps Network Interface Cards (NICs) have become widely available over the last two years, and are now providing the fastest data rates at many data centers today. High-end servers equipped with several 40GE interfaces and solid state storage have been used to demonstrate 80+ Gbps data rates via a 100G WAN infrastructure. The first such demonstration was accomplished with transfers between Salt Lake City and Caltech, during the Supercomputing 2012 conference. More recently, Caltech's test on a 100G path between Pasadena and CERN (including use of the ANA-100G link across the Atlantic) yielded a sustained throughput of 68 Gbps over ESnet early in 2014 and 97 Gbps over Internet2 later in 2014. The equipment used in these tests is suitable as a front-end for fast data caching in an infrastructure designed for remote data access.

100GE NICs are expected to appear widely on the market in 2015. They have been available since 2014, but the throughput achievable with data transfer applications that use them is only in the range of 50 Gbps. The 2015 generation of 100 Gbps Ethernet (100GE) interfaces is expected to be capable of reaching wire speed as more manufacturers come to market with products, competition intensifies, and firmware matures.

A particularly interesting use case of 100G networking is demonstrated by CERN: its remote computing site located at the Wigner data center in Budapest is connected through two 100 Gbps MPLS links. The Wigner data center is built following the same architecture as the main CERN data center, the location of the services running at any of the two sites transparently to the user. Each site can run independently from the other, adding to the resiliency of the CERN computing infrastructure. Further details are available in Annex 5 and at `http://home.web.cern.ch/about/computing`.

1˙9. *State of the art in high-throughput wide area networking.* – Advances in networking, server and storage technology naturally lead to increased expectations in the performance of a distributed system. Particularly relevant for the LHC data processing models is the achievable throughput in data transfers between two computing sites over wide area networks. As summarized above, today's servers can be equipped with multiple 40GE interfaces. Using a single pair of servers, 60 Gbps data rates have been achieved on the very long path between Caltech and CERN over ESnet, the transatlantic ANA-100G and CERN's 100G wave from Amsterdam to CERN. The limitations today are imposed by a combination of PCIe bus throughput and single-core processing of the data flows. One can thus expect that more parallelized implementations will lead to higher data rates per server in the future. Using multiple servers, BNL has recently achieved close to 80 Gbps memory-to-memory data rates between BNL and CERN over the transatlantic 100G network.

In November 2013, the Supercomputing conference exhibition was used by Caltech in close collaboration with several partner institutes([31]) to demonstrate high throughput data movement over 100G infrastructure. Located in the Denver Convention Center, the installation included several high-end servers equipped with SSD storage, and emulated a (very) well-connected storage site. Data was moved using Caltech's Fast Data Transfer (FDT) tool([32]) at 75 Gbps between Denver and DE-KIT, 90 Gbps between Denver and NERSC, and 40 Gbps between Denver and CERN. All these disk-to-disk results were obtained using multiple servers, and multiple streams.

During the SuperComputing 2014 (SC14) conference in New Orleans, an international team of high energy physicists, computer scientists, and network engineers led by Caltech, the University of Victoria, and the University of Michigan, together with a team from SPRACE São Paulo, FIU, Vanderbilt and other partners set new records for data transfer rates while using software defined networking (SDN)([33]) to control switchgear. The SC14 demonstration involved building up a Terabit network on the show floor consisting of sets of 10×100G optical links among the Caltech, iCAIR/LAC and Vanderbilt Booths. An optical ring was coupled with four WAN links and a fifth link to the Michigan Booth, as shown in the picture below. The ring was constructed using Padtec Lightpad optical

---

([31]) Vanderbilt, Victoria, CERN, São Paulo, Karlsruhe, Michigan, Johns Hopkins, Fermilab, BNL and ESnet.

([32]) FDT is a Java application for efficient data transfers which is capable of reading and writing at disk speed over wide area networks (with standard TCP) that runs on all major platforms; `http://monalisa.cern.ch/FDT/`.

([33]) "Towards Managed Terabit/s Scientific Data Flows," A. Barczyk, M. Bredel, A. Mughal, H. Newman, I. Legrand, R. Voicu, V. Lapadatescu (Caltech) and Tony Wildish (Princeton), paper presented at the 4th International Workshop on Network Aware Data Management. See `http://2014.ndm-meeting.org/`.

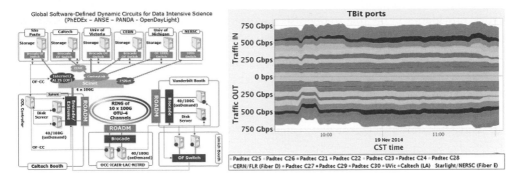

Fig. 8. – Layout (left) and terabit/s data flows (right) obtained at SC14. The wide area network traffic reached 400 Gbps during these demonstrations.

ROADMs, and the optical channels linking the booths were lit dynamically using SDN software from a team at UNICAMP in Campinas (Brazil).

The setup at the Caltech booth, with more than 1 Terabit/s of on-floor capacity and four 100G wide area connections, sustained 1.5 Terabits/s of throughput during an initial memory-to-memory trial and reached its main goal of 1.0 Terabits/s between storage and memory, including up to 400 Gbps over the wide area networks, linking the conference in New Orleans to Caltech, CERN, Victoria, Michigan, and São Paulo. The layout and some of the combined data throughput results are shown in fig. 8.

Software Defined Networks using OpenFlow

OpenFlow software modules were written by the Caltech team for the OpenDaylight (www.opendaylight.org; ODL) SDN Controller, with the goal of being able to steer designated sets of flows along preferred paths across complex multi-domain networks. The ODL controller included several flow path selection algorithms such as shortest path, round-robin, minimum bandwidth utilization path, etc. A subset of the systems at SC14 were controlled by the ODL software, thus enabling dynamic transfers between hosts. Further information on the intelligent SDN (Openflow)-driven path selection part of the demos can be found at[34].

In 2015, the team will further integrate network awareness and strategic network use to support data analysis by thousands of physicists who access data remotely with local caching, generating a large set of small flows with an entirely different traffic pattern in time. From the network point of view, the software-defined network (SDN) controller operations during SC14 marked a watershed in terms of coordinated operations among the network providers and the major science users. By limiting the aggregate set of flow allocations to a "high water mark," monitoring the flows and capacity in real time, and varying the mark as needed to adapt to changing conditions, the science programs and

---

[34] supercomputing.caltech.edu/docs/Experience_with_OpenDaylight_Controller_at_SC14.pdf.

network providers will be able to operate the network infrastructures at high throughput levels without saturation, and avoid the destruction of competing traffic.

CMS PhEDEx Data Transfers

This demonstration, during SC14, involved the installation and operation of a configuration emulating a complete Tier2 Center, and actual transfers of LHC datasets using CMS' PhEDEx data placement and transfer system and dynamic circuits([35]).

Dynamic Optical Lambda switching (Bandwidth on Demand)

The bandwidth on demand concept was demonstrated by stitching together various SDN pieces: PhEDEx, Monalisa, ODL and the Padtec Controller([36]).

The latest generation servers and networks deployed at SC14 and over the wide area represented a prototype of a state-of-the-art global-scale autonomous network system; it is a faithful representation of the global operations and cooperation that is inherent in global science programs handling hundreds of petabytes per year, such as the high energy physics experiments at the LHC.

The methods, tools and systems demonstrated in 2014 also represented a major step towards meeting the challenges of the future machine-to-machine communication-dominated world envisaged in the Internet of Things —with billions of data sources and sinks, and the multi-Petabyte to Exabyte scale data operations of the future High Luminosity LHC, as well as LSST and the Square Kilometer Array— to mention two of the biggest astrophysics data projects planned in the next decade.

In carrying out these demonstrations the HEP team worked together with laboratory groups engaged in network development from the DOE's Lawrence Berkeley National Laboratory, Fermilab, and Brookhaven National Lab. The team worked with many network partners as well, including DOE's ESnet, Internet2, CENIC, Florida Lambda Rail, MiLR and other leading U.S. regional networks, BCNET in Canada, leading exchange points including Starlight, AmLight, NetherLight, and CERNLight, along with GEANT, SURFNet and other European research and education networks, as well as the RNP national network and the ANSP (São Paulo) regional network in Brazil, on novel network system development and optimization projects focused on LHC and related applications for the last 15+ years.

1.10. *Global network trends and implications for ICFA and the SCIC*. – To put the developments in R&E networks and the networks supporting our field, as well as the observed and projected exponential growth in network requirements and our estimated

---

([35]) Further information on the PhEDEx part of the SC14 demonstrations can be found here `http://supercomputing.caltech.edu/cms-phedex.html`.
([36]) Further information on the optical bandwidth on demand (and dynamic network topology at the optical layer) can be found at `http://supercomputing.caltech.edu/padtec-switching.html`.

overall use (presented in the previous of sections of this report) in context, it is useful to consider the corresponding trends in worldwide networks, the Internet and the World Wide Web at large.

The number of Internet Users worldwide hit three billion in December 2014[37], including more than 650 million in China and 800 million elsewhere in Asia, including India. While this is a large number, it is important to note that this represents only a 40% penetration rate. Four billion people are thus without Internet connectivity. The annual rate of growth in 2014 was only 8%, down from 17% in 2004. A substantial part of this growth is through the use of mobile smartphones, and this is the dominant factor throughout the emerging economies in the developing world.

In order to address the challenge of the unconnected billions, Google, Facebook, Verizon, Qualcomm, HSBC and others are considering, and have invested in, several schemes, based on a constellation of medium or low earth orbit satellites, or balloons flying in the stratosphere, or unmanned autonomous solar powered aircraft with the ability to stay aloft for years[38].

Global IP traffic (the protocol that comprises the vast majority of the data transmitted on the Internet) grew to 60 Exabytes per month in 2014, and is estimated to continue to grow at a 21% compound annual growth rate (CAGR) reaching 132 Exabytes per month by 2018. Once again, this growth rate is far slower than in earlier years, when the traffic grew at the rate of $10\times$ every 5 years (a 60% CAGR) from 1992 to 2002, $20\times$ from 2002 to 2007 (an 83% CAGR) and $14\times$ between 2007 and 2013 in spite of the worldwide Great Recession in 2008–2010. It is thus unclear if these projections, taken from the Cisco Visual Networking (VNI) white papers[39] will hold in the presence of an ongoing worldwide economic recovery that is foreseen for the next few years.

Some of the main conclusions of the Cisco VNI study of June 2014[40] are abstracted here for convenience:

- Annual global IP traffic will pass the zettabyte (1000 exabytes) threshold by the end of 2016, and 1.6 zettabytes by 2018.

---

[37] Live as cumulative figures on the global number of Internet users, Facebook Users, Google+ users, Twitter users, the number of websites, the daily number of Emails sent, and other interesting or surprising statistics about the Internet, its energy use and its carbon footprint can be found at http://www.internetlivestats.com/.

[38] See slides 45–47 in the accompanying slide deck, from information provided by Les Cottrell.

[39] The projections in this section are taken from the Cisco Visual Networking Index (VNI) http://www.cisco.com/c/en/us/solutions/service-provider/visual-networking-index-vni/white-paper-listing.html, specifically from the white paper "The Zettabyte Era" —Trends and Analysis" http://www.cisco.com/c/en/us/solutions/collateral/service-provider/visual-networking-index-vni/VNI_Hyperconnectivity_WP.html.

[40] The projections in this section are taken from the Cisco Visual Networking Index (VNI) http://www.cisco.com/c/en/us/solutions/service-provider/visual-networking-index-vni/white-paper-listing.html, specifically from the white paper "The Zettabyte Era" —Trends and Analysis" http://www.cisco.com/c/en/us/solutions/collateral/service-provider/visual-networking-index-vni/VNI_Hyperconnectivity_WP.html.

– Global IP traffic has increased fivefold over the past 5 years, and will increase threefold over the next 5 years.

– Internet traffic during the busiest hour of the day is growing more rapidly than average Internet traffic. Busy-hour Internet traffic is estimated to increase 3.4 times between 2013 and 2018 when it will reach 1 petabit/sec, compared to 2.8 times for average traffic (to 0.31 petabits/s).

– Metro traffic will grow nearly twice as fast as long haul traffic, will surpass long-haul traffic in 2015, and will account for 62 percent of total IP traffic by 2018. The higher growth in metro networks is due in part to the increasingly significant role of content delivery networks (CDNs), which bypass long-haul links and deliver traffic to metro and regional backbones.

– Content delivery networks will carry more than half of Internet traffic by 2018.

– Over half of all IP traffic will originate with non-PC devices by 2018. PC-originated traffic will grow at a CAGR of 10 percent, while TVs, tablets, smartphones, and machine-to-machine (M2M) modules will have traffic growth rates of 35 percent, 74 percent, 64 percent, and 84 percent, respectively.

– Traffic from wireless and mobile devices will exceed traffic from wired devices by 2016.

– Global Internet traffic in 2018 will be equivalent to 64 times the volume of the entire global Internet in 2005. Globally, Internet traffic will reach 14 gigabytes (GB) per capita by 2018, up from 5 GB per capita in 2013.

– The number of devices connected to IP networks will be nearly twice as high as the global population by 2018. There will be nearly three networked devices per capita by 2018, up from nearly two networked devices per capita in 2013. Accelerated in part by the increase in devices and the capabilities of those devices, IP traffic per capita will reach 17 GB per capita by 2018, up from 7 GB per capita in 2013.

– Broadband speeds will nearly triple by 2018. Global fixed broadband speeds will reach 42 Mbps on average, up from 16 Mbps in 2013.

– Globally, IP video traffic will be 79 percent of all IP traffic (both business and consumer) by 2018, up from 66 percent in 2013. This percentage does not include the amount of video exchanged through peer-to-peer (P2P) file sharing. The sum of all forms of video (TV, video on demand [VoD], Internet, and P2P) will continue to be in the range of 80 to 90 percent of global consumer traffic by 2018.

– Internet video to TV grew 35 percent in 2013. It will continue to grow at a rapid pace, increasing fourfold by 2018. Internet video to TV will be 14 percent of consumer Internet video traffic in 2018, up from 11 percent in 2013.

– Content delivery network traffic will deliver over half of all Internet video traffic by 2018. By 2018, 67 percent of all Internet video traffic will cross content delivery networks, up from 53 percent in 2013.

– Globally, mobile data traffic will increase 11-fold between 2013 and 2018 (a 61% CAGR) reaching 15.9 exabytes per month (12% of the total traffic) by 2018, up from 3% in 2013.

Embedded in these statistics are a number of global cultural shifts in network traffic and the nature of networks in the world at large, which are taking hold with remarkable speed. The rise of mobile devices, and their increasing ubiquity, whether a smartphone, a hand-held or wearable device, has led to increasing reliance on them as connectors to an "always on" world, that will soon render traditional telephones and (non-smart) televisions entirely obsolete among the younger generations. The generational change is already well-advanced, with college students glued to their smart devices several hours per day[41], and during all their waking hours among a growing sector of the young population.

The overarching concept is that of the Internet (and the worldwide web) as more than a communications fabric, more than a source of information, and more than a means of education and economic development. They are becoming a utility that is an essential part of daily life in modern society. The trend is thus towards considering the Internet, the World Wide Web, and one's always on interface to it, as a basic requirement of modern existence if not a basic human right[42]. Indeed as networks, and the devices, services and systems they interconnect become increasing intelligent, the everywhere-and-always-available always-responsive Web (or its successor) will ultimately become a requirement for one's sanity, safety and identity, as an integral part of the fabric of our civilization.

The accelerating trend in this direction is driven by several factors, including the emergence of more intelligent networks (introduced in the following section), the rising tide of smart devices in our homes and throughout many areas of industry that send and receive data and can be remotely controlled or act autonomously (usually called the Internet of Things, or IoT[43]), and the rising predominance of machine-to-machine communication over the Internet over communications involving humans (the rise of the Internet of Everything, or IoE[44]), whereby regional and global information can be obtained from masses of so-called smart devices, and where these devices can potentially

---

[41] See for example http://www.sfgate.com/health/article/College-students-spending-hours-daily-on-5745673.php reporting on a study showing that college students are spending half their waking hours on smartphones, and http://www.bloomberg.com/bw/articles/2014-11-19/we-now-spend-more-time-staring-at-phones-than-tvs reporting that the time spent on mobile devices in the U.S. (3 hours per day) surpassed the time spent watching television for the first time the third quarter of 2014.

[42] The concept of Internet connectivity as a basic human right has been reported to the United Nations in May 2011, www2.ohchr.org/english/bodies/hrcouncil/docs/17session/A.HRC.17.27_en.pdf. See in particular the conclusions and recommendations on pp. 19–21.

[43] See for example the Internet of Things Council at http://www.theinternetofthings.eu/.

[44] There is no one vision of the potential applications and the issues, including the potential dangers of an Internet of Everything, particularly one that is even partly autonomous, and which seems increasingly within reach. For a sampling of articles see http://www.zdnet.com/topic/internet-of-everything/

be controlled in a coordinated fashion([45]).

Another important issue, related to the right of equal access to the Internet, is that of Network Neutrality. This issue has again come to the fore after decades of debate([46]), with the strong proposals in May 2014 by the Chairman of the U.S. Federal Communications Commission, that would define Internet service as a basic common utility (like electricity and water) rather than a non-essential service. The proposed rules would apply to broadband access, including wireless and mobile broadband. If enacted the proposed rules would:

– Keep Internet providers from blocking legal websites

– Prevent them from slowing down certain services, such as Netflix and other streaming video providers, based on the load presented to the networks by such data intensive services

– Ban Internet fast lanes and slow lanes. That means Internet providers would not be able to charge extra to streaming video providers and other users making intensive use of the network, for faster lanes to users' homes.

It is in this context that the work of the SCIC on Digital Divide issues, on behalf of the world scientific community as well as the at large world community, has an importance that both addresses an important set of issues for our field, while also going beyond the needs and well-being of our field alone.

1˙11. *Software Defined Networking.* – Software Defined Networking (SDN) is a major paradigm shift in network and data center operations which is being adopted by many R&E and commercial networks, as well as major network equipment vendors. The motivation is to replace many of the narrowly focused and rigid hardware-based proprietary services, by deeply programmable common software-driven services and methods that span across multiple vendor-platforms. Since SDN allows network administrators to manage network services through abstractions of lower level functionalities, this opens up a wide range of new concepts in network architecture, operation and management. The use of SDN also makes possible new forms of interaction between end-users' applications and networks, which are of direct interest to the LHC experiments as they hold the promise of more deterministic and better use of the available network resources, leading to higher overall throughput across the complex set of networks that serve the LHC program.

One of the powerful concepts that has driven the uptake of SDN is the fact that it decouples the "control plane" of the network that makes decisions about where the traffic is sent, from the "data plane" that forwards the traffic. Therefore, a logically centralized network controller (implemented as software that runs on a relatively low

---

([45]) With all the legal, ethical and moral issues that the IoE entails, which society has not begun to tackle.

([46]) See for example `https://www.ocf.berkeley.edu/~raylin/whatisnetneutrality.htm`. For the recent FCC rulings, which are currently being debated, see `http://www.fcc.gov/openinternet`.

cost server) can manage all traffic flows in a network. One of the protocols that enable the communication between the control and data plane is OpenFlow. Today, OpenFlow is maintained by the Open Networking Foundation (ONF) and supported by all major network equipment vendors. Moreover, OpenFlow and the OpenFlow controller integrate easily with homegrown network applications. Thus, it can be easily used to offer new network services also to end users.

Network intelligence in SDN is (logically) centralized in software-based controllers that maintain a global view of the network, which appears to applications and policy engines as a single, logical switch. This enables deep programmability of the network, new network architectures and concepts from both the network-provider and user point of view, as well as dynamism and agility in response to traffic pattern or policy changes. SDN is thus being developed in a way that is very well-aligned with the new class of globally distributed systems needed by our field in the coming years, as mentioned in the Introduction above.

SDN concepts have triggered a great deal of interest in the R&E networking space. The GENI program in the U.S., and the OFELIA project in Europe, have aimed at providing the supporting infrastructure to network researchers, based on OpenFlow. Internet2's AL2S infrastructure uses OpenFlow enabled switches and a custom controller for managing user traffic, and its Innovation Program of many SDN-enabled campuses and regional exchange points (also with 100G connections) has led a major sector of the academic community into the active development of SDN-based methods and concepts in support of their science. ESnet also is a major player in the SDN development space, working with key university and laboratory groups as well as key HEP projects such as ANSE and others. GÉANT also is hosting a number of SDN projects in Europe([47]).

1˙12. *The SCIC Network Monitoring Group: the PingER Project* ([48]). – Internet performance is improving each year with throughputs typically improving by 20% per year and losses by up to 25% per year. Most countries have converted from using Geostationary Satellite (GEOS) connections to terrestrial links. This has improved performance in particular for Round Trip Time (RTT) and throughput. GEOS links are still important to countries with poor telecommunications infrastructure, landlocked developing countries, remote islands, and for outlying areas. In some cases they are also used as backup links.

In general, throughput measured from within a region is much higher than when measured from outside. Links between the more developed regions including N. America([49]), E. Asia (in particular Japan, South Korea and Taiwan) and Europe are much better than elsewhere (3–10 times more throughput achievable). Regions such as S.E. Asia,

---

([47]) See http://www.geant.net/opencall/SDN/Pages/Home.aspx.

([48]) We reproduce here the Executive Summary of the 2014–2015 Report of the ICFA-SCIC Monitoring Working Group as prepared by R. Les Cottrell (SLAC) and Shawn McKee (Michigan).

([49]) Since North America officially includes Mexico, the Encyclopedia Britannica recommendation is to use the terminology Anglo America (U.S. + Canada). However, in this document North America is taken to mean the U.S. and Canada.

S.E. Europe and Latin America are 5–9 years behind. However, in 2009, Africa was ~15 years behind Europe, also Africa's throughput was 12–14 times worse than Europe and extrapolating the data indicated that it would further degrade to almost 60 times worse by 2026. Since 2009, due in large part to the installation of multiple submarine fiber optic cables to sub-Saharan Africa, there has been a significant improvement in Africa's performance. It now appears to be catching up, such that if the present improvements are maintained, it could catch Europe by around 2030.

Africa and South Asia are two regions where the Internet has seen phenomenal growth, especially in terms of usage. However, it appears that network capacity is not keeping up with demand in these regions. In fact many sites in Africa and India appear to have throughputs less than that of a well-connected (cable, DSL, etc.) home in Europe, North America, Japan or Australia. Further, the end-to-end networking is often very fragile both due to last mile effects and poor infrastructure (*e.g.* power) at the end sites, and also due to lack of adequate network backup routes. Africa is a big target of opportunity with over a billion people of which in 2012 only 15.6% are Internet users. It also had a 3607% (compared to 566% for the world) growth in number of Internet users from 2000–2012[50]. However, there are many challenges including lack of power, import duties, lack of skills, disease, corruption, and protectionist policies. In almost all measurements, Africa stands out as having the poorest performance. Further, Africa is a vast region and there are great differences in performance between different countries and regions within Africa.

There is a moderate to strong positive correlation between the Internet performance metrics and economic and development indices available from the UN and International Telecommunications Union (ITU). Given the difficulty of developing the human and technical indicators (at best they are updated once a year and usually much less frequently); having non-subjective indicators such as PingER that are constantly and automatically updated is a very valuable complement. Besides being useful in their own right these correlations are an excellent way to illustrate anomalies and for pointing out measurement/analysis problems. The large variations between sites within a given country illustrate the need for careful checking of the results and the need for multiple sites/country to identify anomalies.

For modern HEP collaborations and Grids there is an increasing need for high-performance monitoring to set expectations, provide planning and trouble-shooting information, and to provide steering for applications. As link performance continues to improve, the losses between developed regions are decreasing to levels that are not measureable by PingER. Though the measurements for RTT, jitter, and unreachability[51] are still correct, as the measured losses go to zero this also makes the throughput derivation unreliable. Alternative solutions to measuring the throughput are available, however they can be harder to install and absorb more network bandwidth. Examples

---

[50] Internet World Statistics available at `http://www.internetworldstats.com/stats1.htm`.
[51] A host is considered unreachable when none of the pings sent to it there is no response to any of the pings sent to it.

of other measurement projects using the more intense methods are the MonALISA([52]) project that uses the pathload([53]) packet pair technique as well as file transfers, and perf-SONAR([54]) that uses the iperf([55]) TCP transport mechanism. There is also a project in place at SLAC and LBNL under the perfSONAR umbrella to analyze and present data from production gridFTP([56]) transfers that are heavily used in the HEP community. These projects are becoming increasingly important for links between well-developed sites.

In the last year there have been the following changes:

– An invited article in February 2013 IEEE Spectrum on Pinging Africa. This was picked up by Al Jazeera and SlashDot among others.

– The network monitoring collaboration between SLAC and the University of Malaysia in Sarawak (UNIMAS) was extended to the University of Malaya in Kuala Lumpur and the Universiti Technologi in Johor Baru.

– Deployment of two new PingER Monitoring nodes in Malaysia, one in Dakar, Bangladesh and several in Pakistan.

– Case studies of the impact on the Sudan disconnecting from the Internet in September 2013, Syria going offline in May 2013, and routing of Internet traffic within S. E. Asia.

– Updating of the major figures and tables.

– Improved analysis and reporting tools.

– The number of hosts monitored, which started to decline in 2010, increased to an all-time high in 2013. We now monitor 170 countries having added Myanmar, Jamaica, Kuwait, Trinidad and Tobago. We monitor all countries with populations > 1000000 apart from Puerto Rico.

– A new project whose proposal is to publish PingER data in Linked Open Data([57]) Semantic Web([58]) standards has begun. Part of PingER data has been published in Resource Description Framework([59]) (RDF) format using an OWL ontology([60])

([52]) MonALISA, see `http://monalisa.caltech.edu`.
([53]) Pathload, see `http://www.cc.gatech.edu/fac/Constantinos.Dovrolis/bw-est/pathload.html`.
([54]) What is perfSONAR available at `http://www.perfsonar.net/`.
([55]) Iperf home page is available at `http://dast.nlanr.net/Projects/Iperf/`.
([56]) "The GridFTP Protocol and Software". Available `www.globus.org/datagrid/gridftp.html` and also see `en.wikipedia.org/wiki/GridFTP`.
([57]) Linked Data, see `http://en.wikipedia.org/wiki/Linked_data`.
([58]) Semantic Web, see `http://en.wikipedia.org/wiki/Semantic_Web`.
([59]) Resource Description Framework, `en.wikipedia.org/wiki/Resource_Description_Framework`.
([60]) Web Ontology language, see `http://en.wikipedia.org/wiki/Web_Ontology_Language`.

for network measurements and linked to other existing databases on the web. The data is also retrievable through a SPARQL[61] Endpoint, using structured SPARQL queries. Use cases were added as visualization examples to show how the data in this standard format can be useful.

– We completed a working version of Geolocation of Internet hosts using trilateration based on ping round trip times.

To quantify and help bridge the Digital Divide, enable worldwide collaborations, and reach-out to scientists worldwide, it is imperative to continue the PingER monitoring coverage to all countries with HEP programs and significant scientific enterprises. However, the funding for PingER is currently a major challenge. The ICFA SCIC Monitoring Working Group representatives met with Google to explore continued support for PingER. Google's interest is in the long term history of the Internet's performance. While promising, this will not resolve the PingER project's need for ongoing support, on which the SCIC, and its work on Digital Divide issues in particular rely.

2. – Conclusions and recommendations. Requests to ICFA

2˙1. *Conclusions*

– The extensive and efficient use of the world's national, continental and transoceanic networks by the HEP community has been a key factor in the Higgs boson discovery and the search for new physics throughout LHC Run1, and will continue to play a key role in the anticipated discoveries that may emerge during LHC Run 2.

– Our field's use of networks continues to grow exponentially, and so our field's awareness of its impact on the world's research and education networks is essential to our future success.

– Beyond major users, through the SCIC and other leading representative organizations in our field, we are now among the world's leading developers, working in an important inter-regional and interdisciplinary partnership with both leading research and education networks and industry partners.

– This provides a strong foundation for the development of the next generation Computing Model that we will need for our future, including at the High Luminosity LHC, and in the shorter term to meet the challenges of larger scale and more agile, coordinated use of limited network, as well as computing and storage, resources that may emerge during Run2.

– Changes to the LHC Computing Models are already well underway, but the common vision of the next generation Model has yet to emerge. ICFA has an important potential role to play in overseeing that the necessary studies are undertaken, that

---

[61] Search RDF data with SPARQL, see Resource Description Framework RDF.

a new common project is formed if needed, and that the future needs and requirements of the field in the networking and computing areas are recognized to be in the context of an emerging paradigm of intelligent networks and of a new class of network-integrated system.

– The need for attention in these areas has heightened the rising network needs of other data intensive fields, along with the fact that the major users in our field, as well as others at both major laboratories and universities, are gaining the ability to use networks at a rate that is greater than the rate at which the capacity of the networks is growing.

– Engaging in these developments has profound benefits, not only for our field, but for other fields of data intensive science. Building on the experience of our own field, our R&E network partners, and a few leading teams in astrophysics and other fields as well as computer and computational science, leading to common development of future systems for data intensive science, is an important direction. This would have profound benefits for all the fields and all the teams concerned, both in terms of working efficiency and budgets. The work of the Monitoring WG, led by Cottrell, is of special, central importance to the work of the SCIC, and to the field as whole.

– The Digital Divide activities of the SCIC, in tracking the world's networks, providing information and training on network monitoring and advanced network methodologies relies on the efforts of the Monitoring WG, and the singular effort of Les Cottrell and the students and visitors working with him in the PingER project.

– The impact of the work of this group is great, both within and beyond the bounds of the HEP community. Although the financial needs are relatively modest, it is apparent that the profound value of this work has been difficult to fully appreciate. If the funding needs are not met soon, the continuity of the Monitoring Group's work, which is a vital part of the work of the SCIC in meeting the charge it has been given by ICFA, will be at risk.

– We request ICFA's help in solving this ongoing problem.

2˙2. *Recommendations and requests*

– We recommend that ICFA consider and encourage the development of a new paradigm for network-integrated worldwide distributed computing for our field, leveraging the profound and rapid developments in networking described in this report.

– We request that ICFA consider effective ways to build an inter-regional, interdisciplinary collaborative effort in support of this goal, and to achieve the greater goal of more effective worldwide systems supporting the science goals of many data intensive fields.

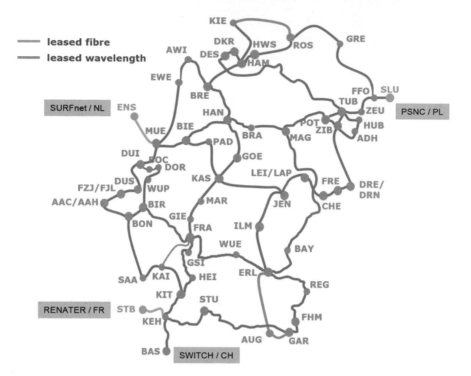

Fig. 9. – Dark fiber footprint of X-WiN including cross border fiber.

– We request ICFA's support and guidance in finding ways to improve the connectivity to several regions of the world that continue to lag behind, as made clear in this Report and the report of the Monitoring Working Group, in order to achieve greater equality of access to data and results. This is essential to give physicists in all world regions the opportunity to be strong partners in the global process of search and discovery, and to develop strong HEP groups for this purpose, thereby strengthening our field as a whole.

– We request that ICFA helps the SCIC find ways to provide the financial support needed by the Monitoring Working Group, so that its work can continue.

3. – Updates from Research and Education Networks by region

This section summarizes the main developments and the future directions as reported for 2014 by the R&E Networks. Not all of them are listed here; the full text of each report is included in the Annex document attached to this report([62]).

3`1. *Europe*. – In 2014 DANTE finalized the migration to the new pan-European GEANT 100G backbone. The two year GN3plus project commenced on 01 April 2013

([62]) See reports online at ICFA-SCIC website: http://icfa-scic.web.cern.ch/ICFA-SCIC/.

Fig. 10. – The GARR-X Progress backbone fiber network.

succeeding the four year GN3 project. The 7 year successor project GN4 will commence in Q2, 2015. The GÉANT network was the first to support a multi-terabit transmission using the industry's first commercially available 500 Gbps long-haul optical super-channels. The GÉANT network backbone now directly connects 17 major European cities in 16 countries across 12000 kms of fiber. Moreover, GÉANT IP service offers NRENs access to the shared European IP backbone at capacities of up to 100 Gbps or $n \times 100$ Gbps, subject to technical and commercial considerations. During 2014 total NREN IP traffic volumes have increased slightly over the course of the year to an average of 1 Pbyte/day, with the highest peak at 1.4 Pbyte in a single day.

DFN operates the X-WiN network, which provides network services for the German research community. In 2013 the DWDM equipment was migrated from a Huawei platform to ECI, which enabled the optical layer to support single wavelengths of up to 100 Gbps. DFN. The dark fiber footprint is presented in fig. 9. During second half of 2014, GridKA started the transition of T1-T1 traffic from LHCOPN to LHCONE. As a

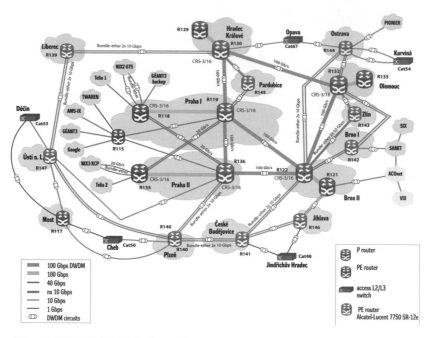

Fig. 11. – The CESNET2 IP/MPLS topology.

prerequisite, the IP access capacity of GridKA to X-WiN was upgraded to 100 Gbps. In addition, the LHCOPN T1-T0 capacity between GridKA and CERN will be upgraded early 2015 to two dedicated 10 Gbps circuits via GÉANT.

In Italy, the GARR-X network, implemented during 2012–2013, is being strengthened with a new deployment in four regions of southern Italy. The "GARR-X Progress" network, shown in fig. 10 featuring 4000 km of new backbone fiber, equipped with new Infinera DTN-X transmissive platform and new Juniper MX routing platform is now operational, providing 40G and 100G channels to GARR users. The project includes an additional number of fiber access links, summing up to 1300 km of new access fiber.

During 2014 the Tier1/Tier2 network of Italian LHC sites continued to evolve. INFN-CNAF T1 was upgraded to 4×10G, sharing the capacity between LHCONE traffic and LHCOPN connectivity, while INFN Frascati T2 obtained a dedicated 10G link. The high capacity (40 Gbps and 100 Gbps) channels made available by the GARR-X Progress project will boost the capability of the INFN centers in southern Italy to participate in the LHC experiment data. From the LHCOPN point of view, two international connections are continuing to carry the Italian Tier1 traffic: a 10 Gbps to CERN using GÈANT circuit services, for the direct Tier0-Tier1 traffic, another 10 Gbps to CERN built over a "cross border fiber" link across Italy, Switzerland. An additional 10 Gbps link to Karlsruhe used for Tier1-Tier1 interconnection to DE-KIT, IN2P3 and NL-T1 was cancelled during 2014, and its traffic steered onto the much larger LHCONE capacity. The LHCOPN backup path to CERN also uses the LHCONE capacity.

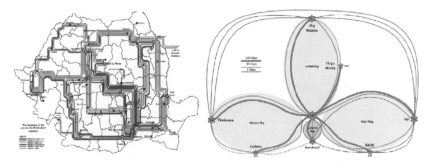

Fig. 12. – RoEduNet2 network: the topology of the lambdas for backbone (left) and the 100G rings connecting major cities (right).

The hybrid communication network CESNET2 is based on leased optical fibers deployed with DWDM transmission systems operated by the CESNET. The CESNET2 optical DWDM backbone operates two different types of DWDM technologies (Cisco ONS 15454 MSTP with the ROADM and open DWDM systems based on CzechLight). As shown in fig. 11, several upgrades have been performed in 2013–2014. The main network has been upgraded to 100G and new PE access routers with 100GE support have been installed in 9 (CESNET) PoPs. Access to the LHC Tier1 node in Karlsruhe has also been increased to 10G. Finally, connectivity has been established to the LHCONE VPN operated by the GEANT3 network.

In 2014, the computing power managed by MetaCentrum increased to 10000 processor cores (comprising 4500 owned by Masaryk University centre CERIT-SC and 4400 owned by CESNET). For its users Metacentrum provides temporary and semi-permanent storage capacity which was upgraded to 1100 TB. The high capacity distributed storage system consists of three geographically distributed nodes totaling approximately 21PB.

In 2014 SANET upgraded its metropolitan ring in Bratislava to 40GE. At the same time a completely new approach for L2 forwarding was introduced, which now utilizes TRILL protocol. SANET is planning to gradually upgrade its backbone and cross-border links to 40GE and introduce TRILL to all rings. In the near future, SANET is planning to increase its backbone capacity to 100 Gbps when 100G Ethernet will be economically reasonable.

The entire communication infrastructure of the Romanian NREN, RoEduNet, is based on dark-fiber, which has a total length of 5365 km, and DWDM equipment. The DWDM network, which is called RoEduNet2, facilitates the provisioning of bandwidth on demand based on traffic needs. The core of the network is based on 100 Gbps Ethernet, which connects the main PoP in Bucharest to all the other major PoPs in a star topology. The backup between major PoPs as well as the connectivity to all other smaller PoPs is realized via 10 Gbps circuits. The current topology and the redundant 100G links are depicted in fig. 12.

International RoEduNet connectivity consists of 3×10 Gbps to GEANT, TeliaSonera and Cogent. The first cross-border fiber was installed with Moldova, other two,

Fig. 13. – The PIONIER network topology. Shown are the Polish national dark fiber footprint in red, and cross-border fiber connections in green, including a DWDM link to Hamburg.

with Serbia and Bulgaria, being currently prepared. RoEduNet provides the LHCONE connectivity, via the GEANT VRF, for all the Grid communities and WLCG sites in Romania. In 2014 the connectivity with the HEP center in Magurele, near Bucharest, was upgraded from 10 Gbps to 100 Gbps.

The Polish R&E Network PIONIER consist of approximately 6500 km of dark fiber inside Poland and has international connections to research and education networks in Germany, the Czech Republic, Slovakia, Ukraine, Belarus, Lithuania and Russia. PIONIER dark fiber network interconnects 26 major university centers in Poland. A DWDM system is also installed on the fiber line to Hamburg, as shown in fig. 13. The system capacity allows to carry 40 channels up to 10 Gbps each. In Hamburg PIONIER is directly connected to the national research networks SURFnet and NORDUnet. PIONIER is also a member of the international virtual organization GLIF, the Global Lambda Integrated Facility. Additionally PIONIER is a member of the AMSIX exchange with 10GE access interface.

Fully renewed since late 2009, the current RENATER infrastructure in France is based on dark fiber. During 2014, RENATER deployed more than 20 extra lambdas, some of them being dedicated to HEP users. LHCONE peerings with GEANT were established in Paris and Geneva. The current topology and the current provisioned bandwidth between major PoPs is depicted in fig. 14.

3`2. *The Americas.* – Internet2 advanced its network in all three Layers, starting from the core optical network to IP network. The current map showing the optical, switched and routed infrastructure is shown in fig. 15. Internet2's Layer1 upgrade includes the acquisition of 16000 miles of dark fiber and the installation of 100 Gbps optical links

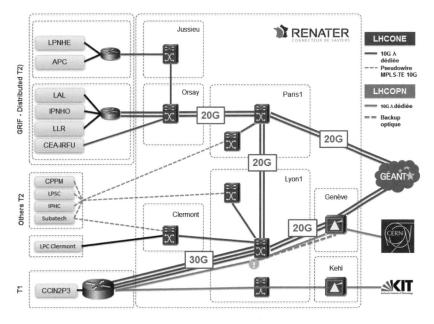

Fig. 14. – RENATER metropolitan infrastructure as of November 2013.

for a total of 8.8 Tbps in network capacity. In order to satisfy the diverse needs of the research community, Internet2 has devised a portfolio of services including Layer 1, Layer 2 (AL2S) and Layer 3 (AL3S) services. AL2S operates using the software-defined networking (SDN) framework OESS using OpenFlow.

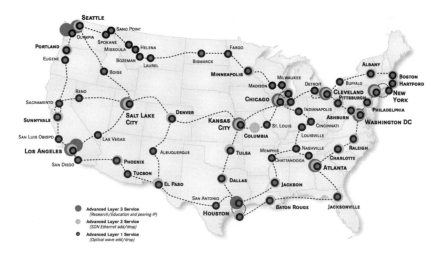

Fig. 15. – The Internet2 network infrastructure.

Internet2's Innovation Platform is based on three pillars: abundant bandwidth through deployment of 100GE national backbone, fewer bottlenecks through support of advanced concepts such as Science-DMZ, and a new class of control through. Internet2 is working on a several ongoing projects: NDDI for OpenFlow deployment, Internet2 NET+ for cloud solutions, TIER for open-source software development, Internet2 ION for dynamic circuit provisioning system, DYNES for channel allocation with bandwidth guarantee, and perfSONAR for network monitoring performance. In addition Internet2 is supporting two IRNC special projects: IRIS and DyGIR for scheduling dynamic circuits on IRNC ProNet infrastructure. Internet2 participated in the Super Computing Conference 2014, for which it deployed several 100G Ethernet links on its SDN-based Layer2 and Layer3 Service.

Internet2, in coordination with six of the world's leading R&E Networks and two commercial partners, deployed the first intercontinental 100 Gbps transatlantic link between North America and Europe in 2013. The 100 Gbps link, called the Advanced North Atlantic 100G Pilot project (ANA-100G) helped determine the operational requirements needed to effectively run 100 Gbps wavelengths between North America and Europe, modeling the same owned infrastructure approaches used terrestrially in Europe and North America to create bandwidth abundance and encourage utilization. In 2014, the ANA-100G project was expanded to include a second 100G along with terrestrial redundancy in the U.S. and Europe. This moves the project into a production phase.

As the first service developed on the NDDI, Internet2 has introduced the Open Science, Scholarship and Services Exchange (OS3E) to offer persistent VLAN services and a nationwide Layer 2 open exchange capability. The OS3E connects Internet2's regional network connectors with international exchange points and key collaborating partners via a flexible open-policy Layer 2 network.

The Dynamic Network System (DYNES) was an NSF-funded project to alleviate the issues of separate large data flows for science projects from general campus traffic, through the provisioning of dedicated traffic channels between participating end sites. The project focused on developing and deploying a nationwide "cyber instrument" spanning approximately 40 U.S. universities and 14 Internet2 connectors. A collaborative team including Internet2, Caltech, University of Michigan, and Vanderbilt University worked during the course of the project and is still engaged with regional networks and campuses to support large and long-distance scientific data flows for the Large Hadron Collider (LHC), other leading programs in data intensive science (such as LIGO, Virtual Observatory, and LSST), and the broader scientific community.

As shown in fig. 16, the traffic observed on Internet2's Innovation Platform grew rapidly between 2007 and 2014, including an 87% increase between 2013 and 2014 alone. This is likely due to the increased number of regional networks connected at multiple 100G to the AL2S platform for IP and Layer2 connectivity and in addition to the campuses taking advantage of the NSF CC-NIE grants which enabled them to bring 100G to the campus core.

ESnet's major advance in 2014 was the timely completion of the ESNet European Extension (EEX), shown in fig. 17, before the start of LHC Run2 in the second quarter

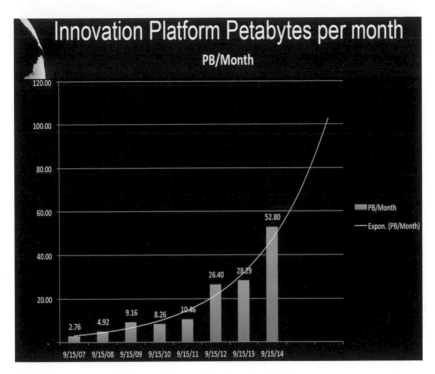

Fig. 16. – Internet2 Innovation Platform —growth in 7 years.

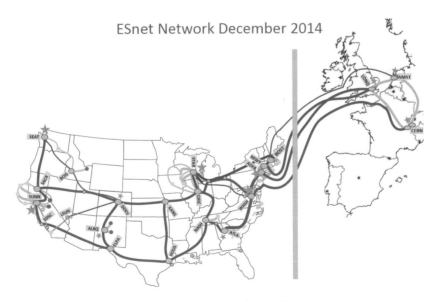

Fig. 17. – ESnet including the recently installed European Extension.

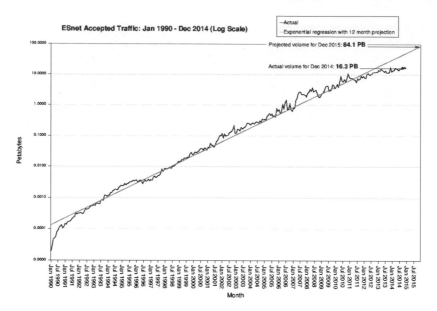

Fig. 18. – ESnet's traffic growth since 1990 through December 2014.

of 2015. EEX extends the ESnet's network footprint from U.S. to Europe at different locations including London, Amsterdam and Geneva (CERN) over four distinct fiber routes across the Atlantic. This has increased the capacity available to CMS and ATLAS.

DOE SC is one of the largest supporters of basic research in the physical sciences in the U.S. It directly supports the research of roughly 27000 scientists, postdocs and graduate students, and operates major scientific facilities at DOE laboratories that interact with national and international research and education (R&E) communities, as well as other Federal agencies and industry.

ESnet provides offerings to more than 40 SC research sites and their users, including the entire National Laboratory system, its supercomputing facilities, and its major scientific instruments. ESnet also connects to 140 research and commercial networks, permitting tens of thousands of DOE-funded scientists around the world to collaborate productively.

ESnet accepted traffic of typically 17 petabytes (PB) per month during the last months of 2014. This number has grown roughly 72% each year for over 20 years (see fig. 18). ESnet's fifth-generation architecture, ESnet5, consists of 100 Gbps backbone links, and the capability of scaling to 44 × 100 Gbps on the optical network. Traffic growth rates in the last couple of years have been lower, but ESnet anticipates a jump in 2015 when the LHC is turned back on after its long shutdown.

OSCARS, the open source software application allows users to create and reserve virtual circuits on demand or in advance. Using a Web interface or API, OSCARS gives users the ability to engineer, manage and automate the network based on the specific needs of their work with scientific instruments, computation, and collaborations. The automation of this complex process has reduced circuit setup time to minutes; previously it had often taken weeks, especially in the inter-domain case. Today, OSCARS circuits carry nearly half of ESnet's 100 PB of annual traffic; using OSCARS, approximately 5000 circuit reservations have been created for ongoing projects, experiments, and demonstrations.

CANARIE —The LHCONE L3VPN was very stable and successful during 2014, accounting for a significant fraction of the total traffic across CANARIE. A contributing factor to the stability was the initial design choices that avoided PBR and used VRFs at each LHCONE site where dedicated equipment was not available. LHCONE bandwidth across CANARIE was provision at $2 \times 10G$ circuits in 2014 and the LHCONE overlay network will be moved onto the new CANARIE 100G IP network as the first customer in March of 2015. Canadian T2s are beginning to observe occasional bottlenecks with 10G links into the LHCONE, particularly in the case where the LHCONE uplink is shared with other projects (UVic and Simon Fraser University). Investigation into adding a second 10G LHCONE link is being considered at most T2s. We also expect at least one Canadian T2 will move to 100G in 2015. TRIUMF will add $3 \times 10G$ capacity for LHCONE in early 2015, while considering 100G upgrade possibilities.

CANARIE is planning to phase out the SONET infrastructure because technological limitations prohibits its. The migration of SONET service into MPLS VPN service will start in early 2015.

During the 2014 Supercomputing Conference in New Orleans, UVic, Caltech and U Michigan demonstrated that a single server equipped with PCIe Solid State storage devices is able to drive LAN connections using $3 \times 40GE$ NICs at over 100 Gbps, and on the WAN at more than 70 Gbps. We expect that these configurations will be useful both a fast data caches at the edge of larger sites and as method to enable smaller sites to provide high bandwidth storage simply.

The Brazilian National Research and Education Network —RNP— first commissioned its Phase 6 IP backbone network in May 2011. The IP backbone subsequently underwent continual rounds of upgrades each year. Further significant upgrades took place in 2014, leading to the topology shown in fig. 19.

Major upgrades in 2014 include 1) the upgrade to 10 Gbps of former 3 Gbps circuits (provided by Oi) reaching the cities of São Luís and Belém from Fortaleza; 2) the upgrade from 3 Gbps to 10 Gbps of circuits (also provided by Oi) reaching Palmas, Cuiabá and Campo Grande from Goiânia and Curitiba; 3) the introduction of a new 10 Gbps link (provided by Telebras) between Fortaleza and Recife; and 4) the opening of landing points in Rio de Janeiro and Fortaleza of the 10 Gbps (LA Nautilus) submarine link formerly connecting São Paulo to Miami via the Atlantic, and the consequent incorporation into the backbone of the submarine links São Paulo – Rio de Janeiro and Rio de Janeiro – Fortaleza.

These changes have increased to 21 (out of 27) the number of PoPs served by 10 Gbps links, as well as greatly enhancing redundant 10 Gbps connectivity, and thus resilience, of the network (of these 21 PoPs, only São Luís and Belém do not count on redundant 10 Gbps connectivity, as the second circuit to Belém has capacity 3 Gbps). Of the remaining 6 PoPs, Teresina continues to have 2 redundant 3 Gbps connections, Porto Velho

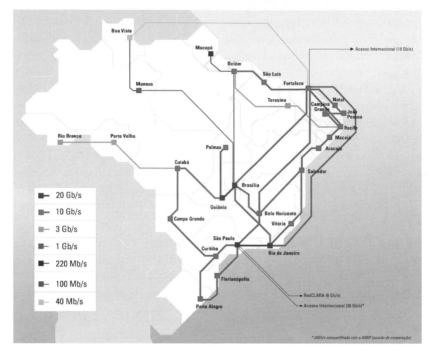

Fig. 19. – Configuration of the Phase 6 Ipê backbone of RNP in 4Q 2014.

and Rio Branco have non-redundant connections at 3 Gbps, Manaus has 2 connections at 1 Gbps and 100 Mbps, respectively, and Rio Branco and Macapá count on redundant connections of 100 Mbps. Improvements to the situation of nearly all of these PoPs are expected in the near future.

The future of the national infrastructure used by RNP has been much discussed in 2014, especially in relation to the perceived need to support 100G lambdas in the short term, and scalable capacity in the medium and long-term, for instance, in the BELLA project (see below). Thus RNP is actively seeking to acquire long-term rights in terrestrial fiber infrastructure to meet its coming needs, through agreements with other companies or organizations which already hold, or are prepared jointly to invest in, long-distance fiber assets within Brazil. Such agreements may involve the swap of RNP's existing stock of urban fiber (see the later section "Optical metro networks") or additional government investment. Similar considerations apply also to international connections, which are dealt with in the section "100G experiment and new submarine cables".

NSF and FAPESP are currently financing an experiment called OpenWave, whereby an operational submarine cable system between Brazil and Miami, currently using 10G lambdas, will be upgraded by the insertion of a 100G "alien wave" using Padtec equipment and a free part of the spectrum in one of the fiber pairs. This experiment is planned to begin during Q1 2015, and will continue for at least six months, or probably longer, if it is effective. The cable to be used connects Miami and Santos (São Paulo) and will provide

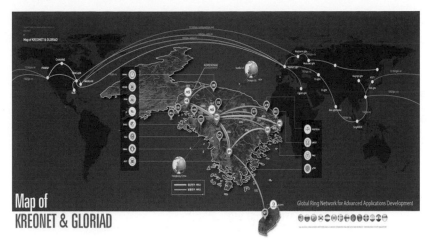

Fig. 20. – Current GLORIAD-KR international links (2014).

100 Gbps transport between AMPATH and the RNP and ANSP networks in São Paulo. All three networks are seeking to upgrade to 100 Gbps at least a part of their infrastructure, in order to be able to extend the submarine segment to real users at the endpoints.

3˙3. *Asia Pacific.* – In 2014 KREONET (see fig. 20) upgraded its domestic backbone network to 40–100 Gbps through the use of Alcatel and Ciena ROADMs. In 2015, KREONET has started to build a Software Defined Network on its backbone, and expects to have six SDN core nodes deployed by 2017 which will support advanced programmable network services with a new level of flexibility and application awareness.

In China, there are two Research and Education networks: CSTNET and CERNET2. CSTNET covers the whole country via 13 regional sub-centers to form the domestic backbone. The link from Hefei to CSTNET was upgraded from 155 Mbps to 1 Gbps in 2013. CERNET, or China Education and Research Network is the biggest NREN in China with a 100 Gbps backbone. This network connects 31 provinces, more than 200 cities, and over 2000 universities and institutes around China. Up to the end of 2014 nine 2.5 Gbps lines link ten major cities with Beijing as the hub. Another 21 middle-size cities and some important scientific labs are connected with access networks of 155 Mbps-1 Gbps.

CERNET2 is the second generation of the Education and Research Network in China and one of the Chinese Next Generation Internet (CNGI) core networks.

The backbone of the CERNET2 is 10–100 Gbps with more than 25 core exchange nodes and over 200 universities connected. CERNET2 has good connections through the Chinese next generation Internet Exchange Center (CNGI-6IX) with other Domestic next generation networks backbone as shown in figs. 21 and 22.

The CNGI-6IX NOC is located in Tsinghua University and links to North America, Europe and Asia-Pacific next generation network with high-speed bandwidth.

The Japanese High Energy Accelerator Research Organization (KEK) operates the HEPnet-J network to connect HEP laboratories in Japan, using L2VPN provided by

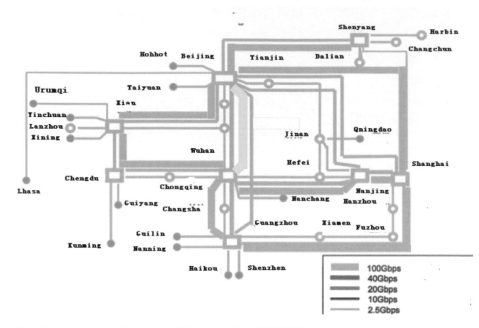

Fig. 21. – Current domestic network links inside CERNET.

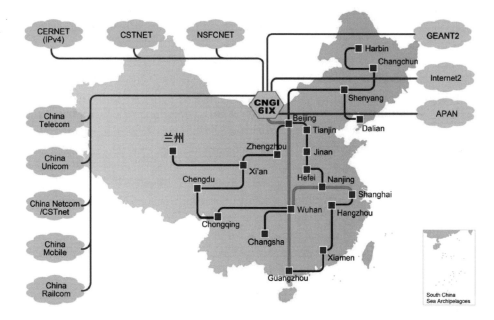

Fig. 22. – CERNET2 Domestic & International links.

SINET and the wide area Ethernet services. As most HEP laboratories and universities have connectivity to SINET, connectivity to the HEPnet-J is mainly provided by the SINET infrastructure.

As Japan Proton Accelerator Research Complex (J-PARC) and KEK work together, they are connected via another SINET L2VPN at 8 Gbps. This bandwidth is separate from two 10 Gbps between KEK and SINET. SINET will upgrade its infrastructure in FY2016, as SINET5. It will provide 40 Gbps and 100 Gbps connections at their data centers and a 100 Gbps link from Japan to U.S., and may have 10 Gbps links from Japan to Europe.

One of the largest user groups of this link is the Belle II experiment. The drill of computing activity for the Belle II experiment measures more realistic scheme using grid-ftp. In FY2013 and FY2014, they tested the performance over the Pacific Ocean and across the Atlantic Ocean. They achieved 9.5 Gbps between the U.S. and Europe, and 8.5 Gbps between Japan and the U.S. Another large group is the KOTO experiment at J-PARC. The experiment aims to find new physics in the CP violating decay, $K_L^0 \to \pi^0 \nu \bar{\nu}$. Since the beam operation for KOTO started in 2013, the bandwidth usage from J-PARC to KEK often has reached 8 Gbps. Both of them use the computing facility in KEK, and a bandwidth increase in the near future is essential.

The outbound traffic generated by the Belle II experiment is estimated to be above 20 Gbps, but the firewall system that can sustain a throughput of more than 10 Gbps is too expensive. Other LHC Tier1 and Tier2 sites met similar problems, and several have moving to LHCONE (as discussed in Section 1 of this report). Currently only the International Center for Elementary Particle Physics in the University of Tokyo is connected to LHCONE from Japan. Formerly this connection used the circuit between Tokyo and New York, and now they are using two connections to U.S. and one connection to Europe. Currently LHCONE traffic from ICEPP is activate only to GEANT, others are routed to the ordinary Internet. The diagram is shown in fig. 23.

SingAREN, the national research and education network in Singapore, is based on Gigabit Ethernet technology for most of its local and international connectivity. SingAREN has external peerings with AARNet, NICT, Internet2 and TEIN, all of them being 1 Gbps. The newly funded SingAREN Lightwave Internet Exchange (SLIX), which started in February 2013, aims to upgrade the network backbone to 100G. The new topology is depicted in fig. 24.

Pakistan Education Research Network (PERN)[63] is the solitary research and education network of Pakistan which was launched in 2002. Currently, hundred and ninety three (193) universities/ institutes/ campuses/colleges are connected to PERN utilizing about 9.45 Gbps Internet bandwidth with Internet bandwidth distribution hovering in between 16 to 600 Mbps. PERN is providing facilities such as Telemedicine, PERN to LHC, IPv6 research testbed and eduroam network services. PERN2 the current upgraded network and consists of variety of technologies including Gigabit MetroEthernet,

---

[63] http://www.pern.edu.pk.

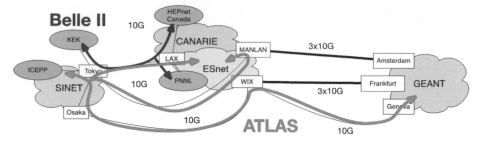

Fig. 23. – International circuits from SINET to U.S. in FY2013.

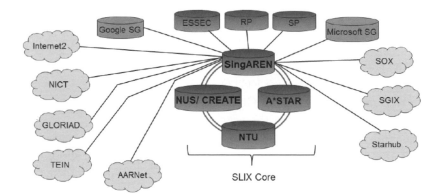

Fig. 24. – SingAREN-Lightwave Internet Exchange (SLIX) Network Connectivity, with 100G links in the core.

SDH, and DWDM (OADMs/OLAs) with a 10GE metro ring at the three main regional cities. 2014 highlights include: Installation of additional 6000 km fiber between 8 metro cities, gigabit connectivity to five distant universities, outreached to another 33 cities and overall increase in metro fiber by 853 km, Gigabit connectivity to additional seventy four (74) HEIs including colleges through acquisition of leased dark fiber, connectivity to twenty six (26) Colleges spread over 12 cities of the province of Punjab in collaboration with Higher Education Department, Government of Punjab.

With its increasing network capacity requirements, PERN is in the process of establishing the PERN3 backbone by 2016 (fig. 25). The plans includes to have 100GE backbone connectivity by 2016 (fig. 25) and upgrading current last mile links for higher education institutes to 10GE connections.

The National Knowledge Network in India (NKN), shown in fig. 26, was conceived as a multi-gigabit pan-India network with the aim to provide a unified high speed network backbone, with an emphasis on scalability and a robust network architecture. The initial phase of NKN was released to the users in April 2009 and to date it links 1357 institutes and leading national labs (out of 1500).

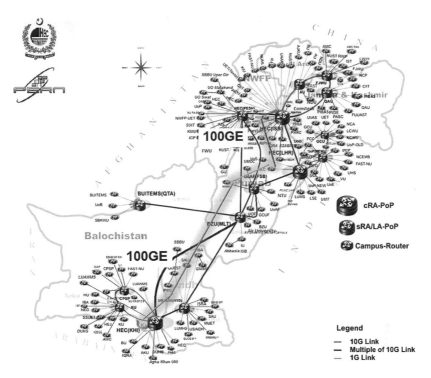

Fig. 25. – Pakistan Educational Research Network (PERN) 100GE by 2016.

As of 2014, the NKN backbone consisted of a mix of 2.5G and 10G supercore and core locations across different segments. Since then, a number of upgrades have been performed on NKN: many core links were increased to 10G, moved many institutions requesting higher bandwidth from 100M to 1G or $2 \times 1G$ links, migrated TEIN3 to TEIN4, enhanced TIFR-CERN International dedicated link to 10G, launched new NKN Cloud services and set up a remote Data Center for remote access at NKN premises in Delhi. In 2015 a new 10GE link is planned to connect NKN to the Internet2.

3˙4. *Africa*. – The UbuntuNet Alliance is a regional association of National Research and Education Networks (NRENs) in Africa. It was established in the latter half of 2005 by five established and emerging NRENs in Eastern and Southern Africa with, these are: MAREN (Malawi), MoRENet, (Mozambique), KENET (Kenya), RwEdNet (Rwanda) and TENET (South Africa). The driving vision was that of securing high speed and affordable Internet connectivity for the African research and education community in Gbps rather than in kbps.

The objectives of the Alliance are, on a non-profit basis, to

- Develop and improve the interconnectivity between Research and Education Networking (REN) Participants in Africa and their connectivity with research and education networks worldwide and with the Internet generally;

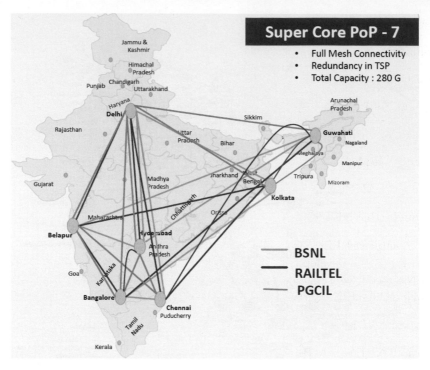

Fig. 26. – The network map of NKN India.

– Develop the knowledge and skills of ICT practitioners in these institutions; and

– Provide related auxiliary services to Research and Education Networking (REN) Participants.

3˙4.1. UbuntuNet Member NRENs. Participation is open to NRENs throughout Africa. Interested NRENs or NRENs in construction are invited to download and complete the Membership Application Form and send it to the Secretariat. The following NRENs have been recognized as participants in the Alliance:

– DRC: Eb@le

– Ethiopia: EthERNet

– Kenya: KENET

– Madagascar: iRENALA

– Malawi: MAREN

– Mozambique: MoRENet

– Namibia: Xnet

- Rwanda: RwEdNet

- Somalia: SomaliREN

- South Africa: TENET

- Sudan: SudREN

- Tanzania: TERNET

- Uganda: RENU

- Zambia: ZAMREN

- Burundi: BERNET [New]

3˙4.2. UbuntuNet NRENs in Development. The Alliance also recognizes Project teams working towards the development of NRENs in their countries. The following NRENs and NRENs-in-construction have either interacted with UbuntuNet Alliance or attended the Council of Members Meetings as Observer Members

- Botswana NREN

- Burundi NREN

- Lesotho NREN

- Mauritius NREN

- Swaziland NREN

- Zimbabwe NREN

The Alliance will pursue EIGHT strategic objectives during 2014–2018 in an effort to address the identified priority issues and thereby enhance its contribution towards achieving its institutional and societal visions. These are:

a) Sustainable and operational NRENs in all countries in the membership region established.

b) A reliable Alliance operated broadband backbone network reaching every member NREN established.

c) Robust broadband interconnections with other regional RENs operationalized.

d) Broadband Internet to member NRENs at a compelling charge provided.

e) Institutional Relevance and Business Health enhanced.

f) Effective communication and advocacy to reach out to NRENs, communities of practice and policy makers implemented.

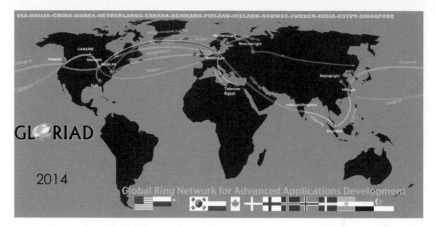

Fig. 27. – The GLORIAD topology map as of January 2014.

g) Increased and effective support for regional and global communities of practice (COP).

h) A fully interconnected Africa based on collaboration among Regional RENs in the continent.

3˙5. *Interregional networks and organizations*. – The Global Ring Network for Advanced Applications Development (GLORIAD) is a network-enabled community providing advanced collaborative services to scientists, educators and students around the world. GLORIAD's operations and governance are decentralized, serving to foster the continuous, flexible, community-driven innovation required for modern science infrastructure. GLORIAD provided and upgraded a large number of links to various partners, *e.g.* between Chicago and Seattle, to KISTI in Korea, and between Korea and Hong Kong. In 2014, GLORIAD established a PoP at Vancis facility in Amsterdam connecting the newly lit 10GE R&E connection from Russia and 10GE connection to Netherlight exchange. Moreover, GLORIAD open-sourced and published InSight([64]), a new set of network measurement and monitoring tools that focus on multi domain performance analysis. Finally, GLORIAD created a new and improved version of the Distributed Virtual Network Operations Center (dvNOC), that provides an unprecedented view into the performance of individual network flows by analyzing packet retransmits, distance (RTT), jitter and routing of every significant flow across the network. It addresses three key areas of advanced networking: virtual network management and performance monitoring, cybersecurity in a rapidly changing cyber environment, and dissemination of data through interactive visualization interfaces via a Suite of monitoring and measurement tools, automated alerts, web-based interfaces and integrated databases. The current network map, showing the global ring structure, is shown in fig. 27.

([64]) https://insight.gloriad.org/insight/.

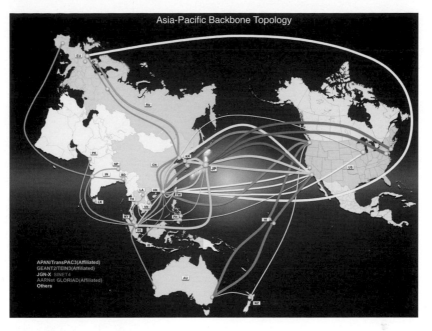

Fig. 28. – The APAN network in 2014.

GLORIAD's hybrid network of multiple technologies provides up to 12.5 Gbps, and allows appropriate and dedicated services to all of our network users according to their research and education needs. Rich bandwidth and redundant network paths provide excellent reliability. GLORIAD has the capability to link to or peer with all international advanced computing networks. The network is composed of hybrid technologies that serve the most diverse user group. Network services include Layer 1 optical lambda lightpaths for big science projects and experimental networking research, Layer 2 switched Ethernet services especially well-suited for fundamental capacity building and reliability/redundancy, and Layer 3 routed high-bandwidth service with peering capability based on the needs of the users.

GLORIAD's daily traffic typically involves over a million significant flows and over 14 terabytes of data. GLORIAD measures performance through a series of automated queries to determine such factors as top users, applications, volume of traffic, and packet loss, which can hinder performance. Every second of every day GLORIAD serves a user community distributed across over 15 million research and education IP addresses.

APAN, the Asia Pacific Advanced Network, refers to both the organization representing its members and to the backbone network that connects the research and education networks of its member countries/economies to each other and to other research networks around the world. The APAN organization itself does not (at this stage) "own" any circuits in its own right. The circuits are generally owned by the respective APAN Members, though in some cases international partners (such as TransPac) fund international circuits to the APAN region, and in other cases international partners contribute to the

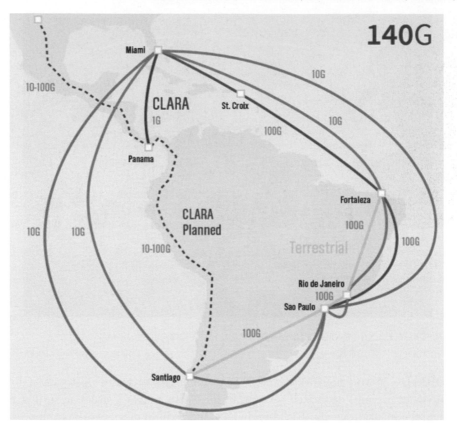

Fig. 29. – AmLight Connections Interconnecting R&E networks in U.S.-Latin America.

cost of circuits to developing countries (*e.g.*, the TEIN program) or to the cost of international links from APAN members to the global REN environment, like the GLORIAD program. The current map of the APAN network (November 2014) is shown in fig. 28.

Americas Lightpaths (AmLight) serves as the foundational network infrastructure to enhance the research and education traffic between the U.S. and Latin America. It is supported through a grant from NSF-IRNC program and a cooperative partnership between organizations in U.S. and South America. AmLight operates high-performance network links between the U.S. and Latin America, spanning four (4) geographical locations called AmLight-Andes, AmLight-East, AmLight-West and AmLight-Central. AmLight Andes serves as the primary path for the U.S. astronomy community in northern Chile, and is upgrade to 10G link. In 2014, OpenWave project was officially kicked to deploy an experimental 100G alien wave between the U.S. and Brazil within a live hybrid submarine network, using Coherent Differential Quadrature Phase Shift Keying (DQPSK) technology. OpenWave consists of the following four 100G segments: Miami-St. Croix (STX): 2400 km; St. Croix (STX)-Fortaleza: 4200 km; Fortaleza-Rio: 3500 km; Rio-Santos: 400 km.

Fig. 30. – Locations of PingER monitoring and remote sites as of December 2013. Red sites are monitoring sites, blue sites are beacons that are monitored by most monitoring sites, and green sites are remote sites that are monitored by one or more monitoring sites.

Potential impacts from the results of OpenWave are facilitating academic access to submarine spectrum. Another potential impact is bringing a new resource to science and education, preparing for future science demands, such as the Large Synoptic Survey Telescope (LSST), which is expected to push to the limits of 100 Gbps network connections, bridging the southern and northern hemispheres. OpenWave brings together the efforts of FIU via the AmLigjht project; Brazil via the ANSP and RNP; the LAN Nautilus submarine cable system operator, FLR, Internet2 and PadTec (the optical equipment manufacturer), see fig. 29.

4. – Network monitoring report for 2014

The full report from the ICFA-SCIC Monitoring Working Group, as compiled by R. Les Cottrell and Shawn McKee, is available online at: `http://www.slac.stanford.edu/xorg/icfa/icfa-net-paper-jan15/report-jan15.doc`.

PingER uses the ubiquitous "ping" utility available standard on most modern hosts and provides low intrusiveness ($\sim$10–100 bits/s) RTT, jitter and reachability information. The low intrusiveness enables the method to be very effective for measuring regions and hosts with poor connectivity. Since the ping server is pre-installed on all remote hosts of interest, minimal support is needed for the remote host (no software to install, no account needed etc.). There are more than 10000 monitoring/monitored-remote-host pairs in over 170 world countries, so it is important to provide aggregation of data by hosts from a variety of "affinity groups". PingER provides aggregation by affinity groups such as HEP experiment collaborator sites, region, country, Top Level Domain (TLD), or by world region etc. The world regions, as defined for PingER, and countries monitored are shown below in fig. 30.

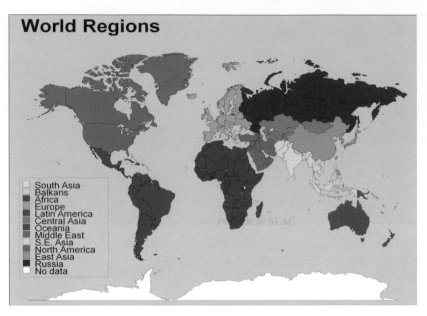

Fig. 31. – Major regions of the world for PingER aggregation by regions, countries in white are not monitored.

Internet performance is improving each year with throughputs typically improving by 20% per year and losses by up to 25% per year. Most countries have converted from using Geostationary Satellite (GEOS) connections to terrestrial links. This has improved performance in particular for Round Trip Time (RTT) and throughput. GEOS links are still important to countries with poor telecommunications infrastructure, landlocked developing countries, remote islands, and for outlying areas. In some cases they are also used as backup links. In future, developing techniques such as weather balloons[65] and solar powered drones[66] etc.[67] may assist in in providing much reduced latencies and hence performance to remote areas.

The world regions, as defined for PingER, and countries monitored are shown below in fig. 31. The growth in the number of active sites monitored by PingER from SLAC for each region since 1998 is shown in fig. 32.

Initially the main regions monitored were North America, Europe, East Asia, and Russia. These were the regions with the main HEP interest. Starting in 2003–2004, the increased number of hosts monitored in developing regions such as Africa, Latin America, Middle East and South Asia is very apparent. In the last year (2014), the number of hosts

---

[65] See http://www.google.com/loon/.
[66] See http://motherboard.vice.com/read/google-will-beam-gigabit-internet-from-solar-powered-drones.
[67] See http://www.nytimes.com/2015/01/22/business/google-hopes-to-take-the-web-directly-to-billions-lacking-access.html?_r=1.

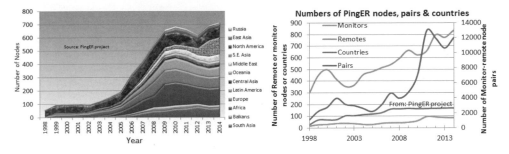

Fig. 32. – On left the number of sites monitored from SLAC by region at the end of each year 1998–2014. On right the growth in PingER monitoring hosts, remote hosts monitored, countries monitored & monitor-remote site pairs.

monitored by SLAC has increased from 717 to 794 mainly driven by the collaboration with Malaysia, and an increase in the hosts in S. E. Asia including Malaysia.

An interesting statistic is given by the yearly throughput trends, presented in fig. 33.

Looking at the data points one can see that East Asia and Oceania are catching Europe, Russia is 6 years behind Europe and catching up, Latin America and the Middle East are 7 years behind and falling further behind, S. E. Asia is also 7 years behind but is catching up, S. Asia and Central Asia are 11 years behind and keeping up, Africa is 14 years behind Europe. However as seen in the fig. 33: Extrapolations on the throughput data in 2008–2009 Africa was 12–14 years behind Europe. Since 2008 the improvement

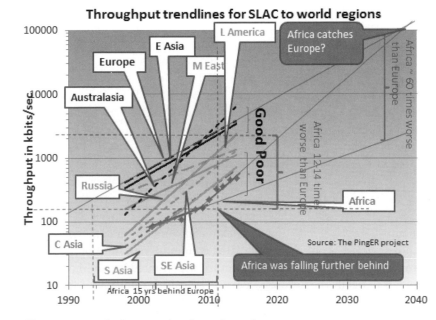

Fig. 33. – Figure extrapolations on the throughput data.

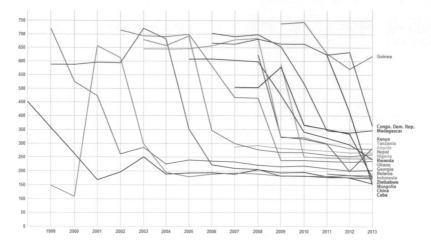

Fig. 34. – Time series of minimum RTT measured from SLAC to various countries since 1998.

is a factor of 3 in 5 years and at the current rate it could catch up with Europe by around 2040. This remarkable improvement is largely a reflection of the impact of the multiple terrestrial links installed since 2008([68]), initially driven by the soccer world cup. However, there is some evidence that the rate of catch up has fallen off in 2013 and 2014.

Looking at the minimum RTT as a function of time for many countries since 1998 seen in fig. 34, one can clearly see, by the precipitous drop in minimum RTT, when monitored hosts in various countries moved from GEOS satellite connections to terrestrial connections.

It can be seen that China shifted to a terrestrial link in 2001, Georgia in 2003, Indonesia and Belarus in 2004, Mongolia in 2006. Although Ghana received terrestrial connectivity in 2001, the nodes we were monitoring did not shift to a terrestrial connection until 2007. Rwanda, Kenya, Zimbabwe and Madagascar are some of the countries that started using terrestrial connections in 2010 due to the Soccer world cup in Africa. Cuba and Congo shifted to terrestrial link this year. RTT to Cuba first decreased to around 400 ms in 2012 as the link in one direction switched to terrestrial and then reduced to 170 ms in 2013 after completing the switch of both link directions to terrestrial 26A.

Within the last 15 years, because of improvements in default OS TCP stack settings, new protocols, hardware, firmware and software, this gap has decreased but still remains in 2014. Because of HEP's critical dependence upon networks to enable their global collaborations and grid computing environments, it is extremely important that more end-user focused tools be developed to support these physicists and continue to decrease the gap between what an expert can achieve and what a typical user can get "out of the box". Efforts continue in the HEP community to develop and deploy a network measurement and diagnostic infrastructure which includes end hosts as test points along end-to-end paths in the network. This is critical for isolating problems, identifying

---

([68]) African Undersea Cables, see http://manypossibilities.net/african-undersea-cables/

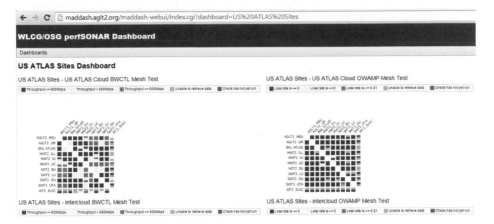

Fig. 35. – Example MaDDash display for one of the HEP perfSONAR-PS cloud.

bottlenecks and understanding infrastructure limitations that may be impacting HEP's ability to fully utilize their existing networks.

In fall of 2012 the Worldwide LHC Computing Grid (WLCG) formed an Operations task force to guide the deployment and configuration of the perfSONAR-PS Toolkit at all WLCG Tier-1 and Tier-2 sites worldwide. This decision was made in great part based upon both the success in using perfSONAR-PS in the U.S. and within the LH-COPN as well as the increasing need to better integrate networks within the HEP global Cyberinfrastructure.

The perfSONAR systems in WLCG are intended to run full-mesh tests for both throughput and latency with all other WLCG Tier-2's and the Tier-1. The latency role is assigned to the first node (typically designated with a "1" in the DNS name) by convention while the throughput role is assigned to the second node. An example of such a full-mesh tests is presented in fig. 35.

While perfSONAR has evolved to be more robust over time, there are still cases where it has problems and fails to gather the needed metrics. To address this we have created a simple-to-deploy infrastructure monitoring system based upon OMD (Open Monitoring Distribution; http://omdistro.org) which is a single RPM install of Nagios and many integrated applications. This has allowed us to quickly find infrastructure issues and better support end-sites when they have problems. We have created service checks for all perfSONAR services (by host type) as well as checks on registration information like admin name and email, latitude and longitude and program version. See fig. 36 for a view of OMD summarizing the WLCG perfSONAR host status.

Efforts to ensure commonality in both monitoring and provisioning of networks have seen a significant increase in activity in HEP during 2014. Originally, the GLIF([69])

([69]) "Global Lambda Integrated Facility", see http://www.glif.is/.

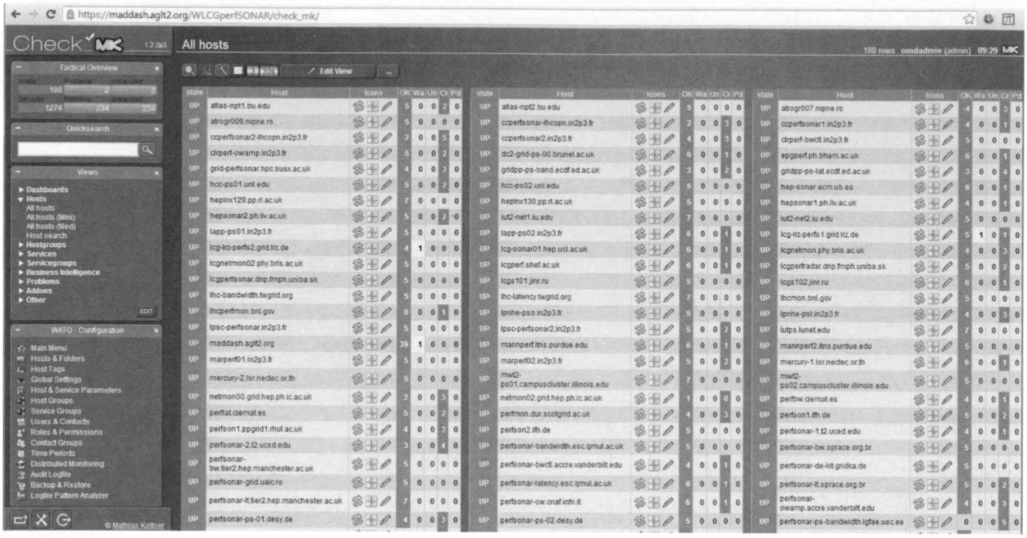

Fig. 36. – OMD Check MK screenshot showing some of the monitored perfSONAR hosts in WLCG.

and DICE([70]) communities were both working toward implementing "managed" network services and the corresponding monitoring that will be needed to support their efforts. During 2014 there were a number of new or expanded initiatives within global HEP:

- The WLCG community completed deploying perfSONAR-PS toolkits at sites to provide needed network visibility for users, site-admins and eventually higher-level services.

- The Open Science Grid (OSG) focused on provisioning network monitoring within OSG to become the definitive source of networking information for OSG sites as part of their year-2 planning for networking.

- Previous ATLAS-initiated perfSONAR-PS deployments within national regions in the U.S., Italy and Canada, were augmented by new national deployments in France, Germany, Spain, Taiwan, Russia and the UK and now include all four LHC experiments.

- The Worldwide LHC Computing Grid (WLCG) continued work on network issues via the networking committee chaired by Michael Ernst.

- The WLCG perfSONAR-PS deployment taskforce, chaired by Simone Campana and Shawn McKee, focused on deploying perfSONAR at all WLCG Tier-2s world-wide and integrating their registration and measurements within the WLCG monitoring framework. Non-compliant sites are being ticketed as of December 2013.

([70]) "DANTE-Internet2-CANARIE-ESnet collaboration, see www.geant2.net/server/show/conWebDoc.1308.

The goal is to have a single infrastructure providing network monitoring for WLCG as opposed to potentially many disparate systems per experiment or region.

There is interest from ICFA, ICTP, IHY and others to extend the monitoring further to countries with no formal HEP programs, but where there are needs to understand the Internet connectivity performance in order to aid the development of science. Africa is a region with many such countries. The idea is to provide performance within developing regions, between developing regions and between developing regions and developed regions and strive for more than 2 remote sites monitored in each major Developing Country. The results should continue to be publicized widely. The assistance from ICFA and others is needed to find sites to monitor and contacts in the developing and the rest of the world, especially where we have ≤ 1 site/country. A current list of countries with active nodes can be found at `www-iepm.slac.stanford.edu/pinger/sites-per-country.html`.

5. – Glossary

AutoBAHN: A GEANT2 research project to develop a control plane for bandwidth on demand provisioning in hybrid network environment. Continued as research activity leading to service deployment during GN3. See, *e.g.*, `www.geant2.net/server/show/nav.2240`.

Baud rate: Baud rate of a data communications system is the number of symbols per second transferred, `en.wikipedia.org/wiki/Baud`.

CBF: Cross-Border Fiber —Dark fiber link across country boundaries.

Dark Fiber: From provider point of view: deployed fiber link without attached transmission equipment. As opposed to leasing wavelength services, leasing dark fiber allows the customer to attach his own equipment, thus determining parameters such as wavelength capacity, number of wavelengths in use, etc. This practice, becoming common among R&E networks provides more flexibility to the customer, but bears potentially additional overhead and costs, as all transmission equipment, including amplification and regeneration hubs must be maintained.

DRAC: Nortel Networks, Dynamic Resource Allocation Controller, `www.nortel.com/corporate/news/collateral/ntj1_project_drac.pdf`.

DRAGON: Dynamic Resource Allocation via Gmpls Optical Network, `dragon.maxgigapop.net/twiki/bin/view/DRAGON/Overview`.

DWDM: Dense Wavelength Division Multiplexing, an optical technology used to increase bandwidth over existing fiber optic backbones.

FEC: Forward Error Correction, error control and correction scheme where the sender adds redundant data (as overhead) which is used by the receiver to detect and correct transmission errors.

GT/s: 1 GT/s means 109 or one (U.S./short scale) billion transfers per second. Commonly used with reference to PCIe BUS.

IEEE 802.3: IEEE set of standards defining the Ethernet. 802.3ba is the upcoming 100 Gbps Ethernet standard, www.ieee802.org/3/ba/.

LHCOPN: The LHCOPN is the private IP network that connects the Tier0 and the Tier1 sites of the LCG. https://twiki.cern.ch/twiki/bin/view/LHCOPN/WebHome.

MPLS: Multiprotocol Label Switching, en.wikipedia.org/wiki/Multiprotocol_Label_Switching.

NORDUnet: A joint collaboration between the five Nordic National Research and Education Networks, www.nordu.net/ndnweb/home.html.

OC-768: Optical Carrier 768, a standard for optical telecommunications transport, further reading visit iec.org.

OSCARS: ESnet On-demand Secure Circuits and Advance Reservation System (OSCARS), www.es.net/oscars/.

OTN4: Optical Transport Network Standard, wide area transport of that 100G traffic, www.oiforum.com/public/documents/OIF-FD-100G-DWDM-01.0.pdf.

PBT: Nortel's Provider Backbone Transport (PBT), adapted and revised by IEEE as Provider Backbone Bridge Traffic Engineering (PBB-TE), approved networking standard, IEEE 802.1Qay-2009, en.wikipedia.org/wiki/Provider_Backbone_Bridge_Traffic_Engineering.

ROADM: A reconfigurable optical add-drop multiplexer (ROADM) is a form of optical add-drop multiplexer that adds the ability to remotely switch traffic from a WDM system at the wavelength layer. This allows individual wavelengths carrying data channels to be added and dropped from a transport fiber without the need to convert the signals on all of the WDM channels to electronic signals and back again to optical signals. See en.wikipedia.org/wiki/Reconfigurable_optical_add-drop_multiplexer.

SURFNet: The National Research Network organization in The Netherlands, www.surfnet.nl/en/Pages/default.aspx.

VPLS: Virtual private LAN service (VPLS) is a way to provide Ethernet based multipoint to multipoint communication over IP/MPLS networks. See en.wikipedia.org/wiki/Virtual_Private_LAN_Service.

Proceedings of the International School of Physics "Enrico Fermi"
Course 192 "Grid and Cloud Computing: Concepts and Practical Applications",
edited by F. Carminati, L. Betev and A. Grigoras
(IOS, Amsterdam; SIF, Bologna) 2016
DOI 10.3254/978-1-61499-643-9-261

Towards an OpenStack-based Swiss national research infrastructure

P. Kunszt and M. Eurich

ETH Zürich, Clausiusstrasse 45, 8092 Zurich, Switzerland

S. Maffioletti

Universität Zürich, Grid Computing Competence Center
Winterthurerstrasse 190, 8057 Zurich, Switzerland

D. Flanders

FMI- Maulbeerstrasse 66, 4058 Basel, Switzerland

T. M. Bohnert and A. Edmonds

ZHAW - Obere Kirchgasse 2, 8400 Winterthur, Switzerland

H. Stockinger

SIB Vital-IT - Quartier Sorge, 1015 Lausanne, Switzerland

A. Jamakovic-Kapic and S. Haug

University of Bern - 3012 Bern, Switzerland

P. Flury and S. Leinen

SWITCH - Werdstrasse 2, 8004 Zurich, Switzerland

E. Schiller

University of Neuchâtel - Rue Emile-Argand 11, 2009 Neuchâtel, Switzerland

Summary. — In this position paper, we describe the current status and plans for a Swiss national research infrastructure. Swiss academic and research institutions are very autonomous. While being loosely coupled, they do not rely on any centralized management entities. A coordinated national research infrastructure can only be established by federating the local resources of the individual institutions. We discuss current efforts and business models for a federated infrastructure.

1. – Introduction and overview

Switzerland, as a country, is organized in a very decentralized manner, which has a deep impact on the organization of research and education. At the federal level, there is the national supercomputing center, CSCS in Lugano, the national research network SWITCH and several institutes of research and technology of the ETH Domain. At the cantonal level, there are ten universities, nine universities of applied sciences, and several specialized institutions for research and education. The organizational and funding structures are very heterogeneous. Today, infrastructure provisioning happens exclusively on the institutional level. We believe that the scientific research community, as well as resource providers, may greatly benefit from a coordinated, federated national research infrastructure.

There exist various architectures of federated clouds [1] such as hybrid, broker-based, aggregated, and multi-tiered. The hybrid architecture allows a private cloud to cooperate with a public one by using specific drivers for cloud bursting. For example, OpenNebula [2,3] can cooperate with Amazon (Amazon EC2 driver), and Eucalyptus [4]. StratusLab [5], an OpenNebula-based cloud infrastructure, provides a toolkit to integrate the most recent cloud management technologies. In the broker-based model, the broker coordinates the resources of several public clouds. There are a few online broker sites such as BonFire (`www.bonfire-project.eu`), Open Cirrus (`opencirrus.org`), and FutureGrid (`futuregrid.org`).

The Reservoir system [6] provides an infrastructure that may automatically deploy tasks of one organization in the clouds of other partners having spare capacities. A multi-tiered architecture is an interesting option for large companies with geographically distributed resources. Such resources are usually strongly coupled as they serve as sub-services of the same entity. However, we believe that none of these models serve our specific needs adequately for Swiss higher education and research.

There are several examples of past Swiss national initiatives working towards the goal of setting up services to address the needs of several scientific user communities. The Swiss Multi-Science Computing Grid project [7] provided services mainly to the Swiss High Energy Physics community and enabled that community to participate in the European Grid Initiative (EGI). In the life sciences domain, the SyBIT project [8] of the Swiss Initiative for Systems Biology, SystemsX.ch, makes use of the computing and storage infrastructure of all participating institutions. Infrastructure is not organized in a coherent manner, as SyBIT is focusing on bioinformatics support, not infrastructure.

The funding for these efforts is project-based, and is aimed to create infrastructure and services in tight cooperation with a user community. However, it is currently unclear what will happen to the services, infrastructure and all the other additional value created (mostly in the form of specialized know-how) after their funding expires. The user communities still require services beyond their lifetime.

An example of how long-term sustained funding can be set up, is given by the Vital-IT group [9] of the Swiss Institute of Bioinformatics SIB. Vital-IT provides services for bioinformatics in life sciences, coordinating bioinformatics infrastructure and resources for several universities in the Western part of Switzerland. Vital-IT is funded by the participating universities, through federal funds and to a large extent by second and third parties (industrial and academic research grants). Researchers are advised to request these charges as part of their project grant proposals as "bioinformatics consumables".

Very recently, the Swiss government has initiated a project to work out a strategy for the development of a sustainable set of services for research, education and digital archiving communities. The individual sustainability models for the services developed are to be established in this project.

In this paper, we describe the current Swiss Academic Compute Cloud project that we use to prototype a federated Swiss infrastructure for research computing. We also summarize our current ideas about necessary policy and accounting models that have to be established to allow for a sustainable distributed Swiss research infrastructure. This should solve the remaining open issue of sustainable operation.

1˙1. *Cloud definitions.* – We believe that it is necessary to specify our own definition of "cloud" since the term has been used in many, sometimes conflicting contexts.

We expect the following properties from a service with a "cloud" attribute:

Self-serviced A consumer has immediate access to resources and can unilaterally access computing capabilities, such as server time and network storage.

On-demand As needed, at the time when needed, with the possibility of automatic provisioning. No need to do the full investment planning upfront.

Cost transparent Accounting of actual usage is completely transparent to both the user and service provider, which is measured in meaningful terms.

Elastic, scalable Capabilities can be elastically provisioned and released, in some cases automatically, to scale rapidly up and down, matching demands.

Multi-tenant The providers computing resources are pooled to serve multiple consumers, with resources dynamically assigned and reassigned according to consumer demands. Ideally, for the customers, other tenants are invisible.

Programmable services The services expose a public programmable API that can be used to drive any aspect of the service programmatically.

These properties are technology-agnostic; the way we define cloud services has a consequence on how we expect the services to be exposed to the consumer and what kind of business model and usage policy is in place.

We also use the terms Infrastructure as a Service (IaaS), Platform as a Service (PaaS) and Software as a Service (SaaS) to define different fundamental types of services offered to researchers and educators. All these service types are considered to be part of the cloud ecosystem, they can be built on top of each other or directly on the underlying infrastructure.

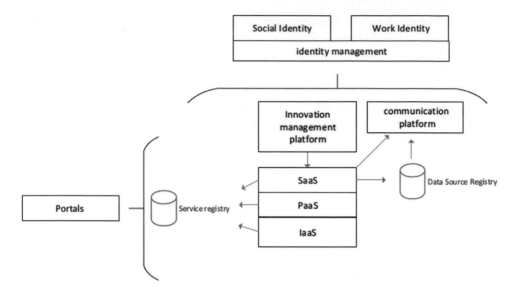

Fig. 1. – Architecture of the digital ecosystem.

2. – Ecosystem architecture

The development of a robust *digital ecosystem* is the key to maintain competitiveness of Swiss research. Researchers need easy access to resources for their work and to maintain collaborations across institutional boundaries. We propose the establishment of an open informatics platform, which can be used to create the digital ecosystem by using clouds as an innovation enablement technology for sharing all types of resources.

The architecture of the digital ecosystem is based on cloud services, but at a very high level, it can be divided into the following elements (see fig. 1):

- Identity management (authentication of social and work identities)
- Social platform (information of interest to the researcher)
- Ideation platform (process of developing new services)
- Service Portals (access to resources)

This will provide a platform for researchers, research institutions, societies, and associations to rely on cloud services so that they can focus their energies in areas of value creation. One such example is FASEB [10] (Federation of American Societies in Experimental Biology), which supports individual researchers and societies with tasks common to all of them.

In terms of *identity management*, every member of an institution of higher education in Switzerland has already an identity in a Shibboleth-based federated identity management infrastructure [11]. However, this infrastructure needs to be extended with additional services like inter-institution group management, to meet the needs of the full ecosystem.

Social and *ideation platforms* are instruments aimed to channel researcher requests, needs and ideas into a discussion network, in which problems (expressed in terms of challenges) are evaluated and discussed, and where solutions are agreed, designed, implemented, and then added to the service portals as part of the available service portfolio.

Service portals are a generic model to introduce new technology that can be offered and adapted to meet the needs of a variety of researchers. The services introduced will be based on use-cases delivered by researchers or by the ideation process.

3. – The Swiss Academic Compute Cloud Project

The Swiss Academic Compute Cloud Project (SwissACC) has been set up to keep and extend the currently established Swiss-wide computational science platform composed of resources and services of various types (local clusters, grid and cloud infrastructures) as well as the excellent know-how for user and application support.

Researchers who previously could concentrate on topic-specific skills now find themselves confronted with complex IT issues outside the scope of their expertise. While computing was initially a specialism of interest to some researchers, now it has an impact on everything from materials science to drug design and digital cultural heritage. Even when research is not based on processor calculations, the availability of large dataset and Big Data that can be mined for trends is occurring in almost all fields. Despite excellent work by local IT departments, there is a need for specific support of eScience, and a need to have a more coherent approach across the Swiss research community. To meet these needs, multiple Swiss universities have established scientific IT support units to meet local needs. These units, while very similar in their mission, have different profiles and focuses depending on their local needs and capacities. However, no single support unit can currently cover all types of services to fully meet the eScience needs of all their researchers. From a researchers point of view, there is a problem when a service or form of support is required that the local eScience Support unit is not specialized in or unable to provide. In addition, there are still many Swiss universities and institutes that do not have any such service unit providing eScience support, usually because they lack critical mass or resources to operate one. We aim to address these issues by establishing a Swiss National eScience Support Team which leverages the collective eScience support of Swiss academic institutions as well as coordinates eScience services for inter-institutional research projects.

Research communities can profit from this platform either to address their computational needs, or to make use of the platform for collaboration purposes in national and international projects. It provides IaaS, PaaS and SaaS services to communities and helps to build their own service portals or tools.

The project builds upon previous initiatives at the national level such as the Swiss Multi Science Computing Grid (SMSCG) [7], the Academic Compute Cloud Provisioning and Usage [12], VM-MAD [13], GridCertLib [14], RS-NAS [15]; and international projects like EGI [16], Chemomentum [17], and PRACE [18].

The primary goal of SwissACC is to sustain and keep together the research communities that have been brought to distributed infrastructures in the previous Grid and Cloud projects. The secondary goal is to increase the number of supported research communities. A large community can profit from mutual benefits due to economies of scale as they gain more experience and receive more feedback, improving the overall quality of the provided services.

The final goal is to provide a sound basis for decision making on infrastructure models, like in-house vs. outsourcing, and on technologies, like running a cluster, a virtualized infrastructure, or going to a public cloud provider.

The project is composed of infrastructure providers, service providers and user communities that have very close and regular interaction with each other. This allows the project to continuously improve the services and to focus on items that users really need and use. The user support is set up using a collaborative distributed support model, helping scientists in bringing their small and large-scale data analysis pipelines to a flexible cloud-like platform that can easily be shaped to accommodate their needs.

The current infrastructure supports user communities who already solve research problems with help of computational processing. Virtualization techniques from *e.g.* the VM-MAD [13] and AppPot [19] projects and a powerful toolbox for job management on heterogeneous infrastructures (GC3Pie [20]) allows us to set up a standardized procedure for enabling new research communities. These technologies have allowed us to start supporting new users and communities with relatively little effort. However, it is not enough to just virtualize a certain application; there have to be several middleware layers to assure that this application can scale, *e.g.* make use of necessary infrastructure services like storage, and is easy to use by the end user.

The SwissACC project currently supports over 20 applications [21] from the domains of life sciences, earth sciences, economics, computer sciences, engineering, cryptography and physics. Table I lists the applications supported, which we intend to extend throughout the duration of the project.

3˙1. *Infrastructure for SwissACC.* – The SwissACC project has currently access to 5 OpenStack cloud installations at the ETH Zurich, the University of Zurich, SWITCH, the Zurich University of Applied Sciences and the HES-SO site in Geneva. These clouds are relatively small: they range from 100 to 400 CPU cores each, but with relatively good memory and storage.

The project also has access to the Swiss National Grid infrastructure, an aggregation of relatively large clusters, as this is part of the LHC Computing Grid infrastructure.

The OpenStack versions of the various installations are not identical. The coordination does not involve upgrades being rolled out simultaneously across all sites, and we believe it is not necessary to aim for such strong coordination as long as interoperability can be maintained. The OpenStack distributions being used are also not identical. Some are based on Ubuntu, others on Red Hat, Scientific Linux or Fedora.

The choice of OpenStack as a reference cloud software stack has emerged as an evaluation done in a predecessor project, the Academic Cloud Provisioning and Usage project [12]. There, the ETH Zurich and the University of Zurich evaluated the available

Table I. – *Applications on SwissACC.*

Institution	Applications	Characteristics	Research field
IMSB/ETHZ	Rosetta, TPP, HCS pipeline	2-3 users, 152k jobs, 300k walltime hours during last 12 months	Life sciences/ proteomics
IBF/UZH	gpremium	1 user, 916k jobs, 238k walltime hours (1.5.2011–1.7.2012)	Economics/ financial models
GEO/UZH	GEOTop	4-8 users, 37k jobs with 11k walltime hours since June 2012	Earth sciences
UniBE/UniNE	A4-Mesh	15 users, real-time data collected since June 2013	Environmental research/ hydrogeological modeling
Lacal/EPFL	gcrypto	1-4 users, 16k jobs, 32k walltime hours during last 6 months	cryptography
UNIL/Vital-IT	Selectome	1 production user. 71k jobs, 190k walltime hours during last 12 months	Life sciences/ phylogeny
UniGE	MetaPIGA	execution model still to be defined.	Life sciences/ engineering
LHEP/UniBe	ATLAS	Several (international) users, ca 27k jobs/month with 239k walltime hours	High energy physics
WSL/SLF	CATS, Alpine3D, SwissEx	CATS: 1 user, 1month, 2300 jobs, 38k walltime hours SwissEx: cyclic analysis (30′ frequency) processing data from 3 IMIS stations	Earth sciences/ climate modeling

cloud solutions and set up several pilot cloud installations. OpenStack has been evaluated against other public open cloud stacks (like OpenNebula, Eucalyptus, CloudStack [22]) as well as commercial cloud solutions (Flexiant, StackOps, HP CloudSystem Matrix, etc.).

Commercial cloud solutions are usually very mature, with several layers of well-tested software built into themselves, leveraging these companies' experience in operating large-scale automated infrastructures. These layers make them very complex and not easy to maintain without proper training. Therefore, such systems should be optimally bought directly from the company including expert support, preferably by an on-site full-time specialist.

Lacking the funding for such a system and the expert, we chose OpenStack as the open cloud software stack, since currently it has the largest community and commercial support. However, OpenStack is not yet fully mature as a production system. It is already usable and there are very large installations running it (for example at CERN), but the expectations of what is possible and what the challenges are need to be set correctly, also towards the users. We have exposed a lot of stability and security issues, that are being addressed in newer releases. For example, the accounting and quota management functionality is still largely in development. Our recommendation to our partner resource providers is therefore to slowly ramp-up cloud services offered to the researchers, with proper training and expectation management, initially being mostly for testing and educational purposes. With the right high-level middleware like GC3Pie [20], the free OpenStack solution is already adequate for many use-cases. For more reliable services and more complete installations, a commercial OpenStack-compliant solution might be considered, as offered by Rackspace, Red Hat, etc.

In terms of cloud coordination for technology and adoption, we have initiated a dedicated interest group for cloud computing in the Swiss Informatics Society [23].

4. – Cloud charging models for federated infrastructures

In order to exploit economies of scale, *i.e.*, the consolidation of resources, the institutions need to be able to provide services to each other at a cost. However, there is currently no model and in fact no sufficient legal basis that would allow the institutions to charge each other for their respective incurring service costs. We are therefore proposing several cloud-like business models for the provisioning of services by higher-education centers, allowing for many different charging models for them to choose from, in the hope of starting a process that will eventually allow a much tighter cooperation than is possible today.

Also as part of the Academic Cloud Provisioning and Usage project [12], we tried to gain insights into service consumers' and providers' needs as a basis for a pricing strategy of cloud-based services and for future decision-making. Information was gathered by interviewing research groups currently using central computing services.

The interviews revealed that academic service consumers currently perceive cloud services as a playground for testing, experimenting, and training students. However to date, most academic service consumers do not fully perceive the added value that the cloud computing model can provide. Some groups say they would use cloud services if they were available at a competitive cost. Currently, these cloud-based services are not necessary due to existing private infrastructures or service providers. These service providers do, however, see several advantages that a cloud model could provide in the future, such as flexibility, provisioning of additional services, time to service, self-serving aspects and increased automation, elasticity, and a more balanced workload.

There are three basic pricing schemes that are acceptable for academic consumers of cloud-based services:

"Pay per use" Service consumers are charged a fee according to the time and volume of a computing service that has been consumed.

Subscription The service consumer pays a fee on a regular basis for the usage of a service. Subscriptions allow services to be sold as packages.

"Pay for a share" In this approach service consumers buy a share in order to get a corresponding amount of service.

It is of course possible to offer several of the three models above simultaneously or in a mixed form, for example adjusting the pay-per-use pricing on a pre-subscription volume, as it is already done by Amazon.

The interviews revealed that academic service consumers care little about pricing strategies. They want to focus on science and research. Foremost, they just want services that work. They expect an easy approach and want the university to clear all of the obstacles from their paths. From their perspective, the "per pay use" and subscription approach can only work if there is a way to get funding for it.

From the service providers' perspective, there is no pricing scheme that outperforms any of the other schemes. Each of the three pricing schemes has certain advantages and disadvantages. The usefulness of one approach can depend on the length of time a given service is needed. Pay per use qualifies best for a short-term service demand that lasts no more than three months or as an addition for peak usage on top of a subscription or share. The subscription scheme might be a good solution for mid- to long-term commitments. The pay for a share approach may be most suitable for long-term commitments, *i.e.*, for more than two years. In our definition of cloud we of course favor the pay-per-use model as it fits the operational-expense-only model best. However, until the funding obstacles for such a model are overcome (both on the provider and the consumer side), we need the other schemes at least during a transition phase, the length of which is to be determined.

Finally, many academic service consumers do not know much about cloud computing and in fact do not care much about what computing resources are used. They just need some powerful computing services in order to do their research. Therefore, the pricing scheme should be simple, yet fair and transparent. In this context, subsidization can play an important role to clear inconveniences out of the service consumers' way. The institutions might set up a subsidization scheme, providing the researchers with free access to resources, or other means for the researchers to pay for cloud-based services.

To the funding agencies, we propose to introduce an "informatics consumable" concept based on the experience of the Vital-IT competence center. The idea is that projects simply put in a line item called "informatics consumables", requesting funding to be spent on the available research computing infrastructure to meet their computing and storage needs. Obviously, the evaluation process applied by the funding agencies should take the amount of requested informatics consumables into consideration and the process should check back with the infrastructure providers to find out whether the request is technically sound and whether the requested consumables are adequate. In the Vital-IT model, such consumables also apply to user support services and to standardized data analysis services performed by bioinformaticians at the competence center, providing expertise to projects in this domain that do not have the project partners to perform a standardized analysis of their data.

5. – Summary and outlook

We have presented the current efforts to maintain a federated research computing infrastructure in Switzerland, with details on our thoughts for sustainability and funding models.

We are working towards a sustained national infrastructure model based on federation concepts where researchers can easily gain access to the necessary resources and support persons through local contacts at their individual institutions. Sustainable funding models have been presented but they still need to be refined, accepted and put in place by funding bodies and institutions to have a lasting, sustained effect on the Swiss research landscape.

Given the high expectations that cloud technologies set, there are certain risks that we need to be aware of and address properly. Based on our experience with federation in the context of Grid technologies, we know that it is very important to get actual scientific users on board early, to set expectations correctly and to immediately use new technologies and services.

Our goal is to advance scientific research by lowering the barriers to usage and adoption of information technologies in general. In an ideal scenario, a scientist has the choice to select from a large array of easy to use tools and services to perform his or her research. He or she should also be able to easily publish new scientific services based on their individual research or to contribute to the existing community of tools and services. Such frameworks and services need to be intuitive, resilient to failures, provide meaningful error messages, and integrate with social media to interact with other scientists and service supporters in the right context.

REFERENCES

[1] Rafael Moreno-Vozmediano, Rubn S. Montero and Ignacio M. Llorente, *IEEE Comput.*, **45** (2012) 65.
[2] Borja Sotomayor, Rubn S. Montero, Ignacio M. Llorente and Ian Foster, *IEEE Internet Comput.*, **13** (2009) 14.
[3] Rafael Moreno-Vozmediano, Ruben S. Montero and Ignacio M. Llorente, *IEEE Trans. Parallel Distrib. Syst.*, **22** (2011) 924.
[4] Nurmi D., Wolski R., Grzegorczyk C., Obertelli G., Soman S., Youseff L. and Zagorodnov D., *The Eucalyptus Open-Source Cloud-Computing System*, in *Proceedings of the 9th IEEE/ACM International Symposium on Cluster Computing and the Grid, CCGRID '09, 18-21 May 2009* (IEEE Computer Society) 2009, pp. 124–131, doi: 10.1109/CCGRID.2009.93.

[5] StratusLab.stratuslab.eu/.

[6] ROCHWERGER BENNY, TORDSSON JOHAN, RAGUSA CARMELO, BREITGAND DAVID, CLAYMAN STUART, EPSTEIN AMIR, HADAS DAVID, LEVY ELIEZER, LOY IRIT, MARASCHINI ALESSANDRO, MASSONET PHILIPPE, MUNOZ HENAR, NAGIN KENNETH, TOFFETTI GIOVANNI and VILLARI MASSIMO, *IEEE Comput.*, **44** (2011) 44.

[7] The Swiss Multi-Science Computing Grid project, www.smscg.ch.

[8] The Swiss Systems Biology Initiative, www.sybit.net/.

[9] Vital-IT: bioinformatics competence center of the SIB Swiss Institute of Bioinformatics, www.vital-it.ch/, www.isb-sib.ch.

[10] Federation of American Societies for Experimental Biology, www.faseb.org.

[11] Authentication and Authorization Infrastructure (AAI), www.switch.ch/aai/support/presentations/.

[12] KUNSZT PETER, MAFFIOLETTI SERGIO, MESSINA ANTONIO, FLANDERS DEAN, MATHYS SANDRO, MURRI RICCARDO *et al.*, Academic Cloud Provisioning and Usage Project, https://wiki.systemsx.ch/display/cloudresult.

[13] TYANKO ALEKSIEV, SIMON BARKOW, PETER KUNSZT, MAFFIOLETTI SERGIO and MURRI RICCARDO, *Christian Panse: VM-MAD: a cloud/cluster software for service-oriented academic environments*, arXiv:1302.2529 [cs.DC].

[14] MURRI RICCARDO, MAFFIOLETTI SERGIO, KUNSZT PETER and TSCHOPP VALERY, *J. Grid Comput.*, **9** (2011) 441.

[15] GORINI CLAUDIO, MAFFIOLETTI SERGIO, KUNSZT PETER, TACCHELLA DAVIDE, BALAZS CSABA, BRIAND CHRISTOPHE, MURRI RICCARDO, MESSINA ANTONIO and CORBEIL LUC, Remote Scalable Network Attached Storage Project.

[16] The European Grid Infrastructure, www.egi.eu/.

[17] *Grid services based environment to enable innovative research*, cordis.europa.eu/search/index.cfm?fuseaction=proj.document&PJ_RCN=8505182.

[18] PRACE Research Infrastructure, http://www.prace-ri.eu/.

[19] MURRI RICCARDO and MAFFIOLETTI SERGIO, *Batch-oriented software appliances*, arXiv: 1203.1466 [cs.DC].

[20] MAFFIOLETTI SERGIO, MURRI RICCARDO and MESSINA ANTONIO, *GC3Pie: A Python Toolkit for Job Management on Heterogeneous Infrastructures*.

[21] MAFFIOLETTI SERGIO *et al.*, *Applications on the Swiss Multi-Science Computing Grid*, www.smscg.ch/WP/applications/.

[22] Apache CloudStack project, cloudstack.apache.org/.

[23] Swiss Informatics Society, www.s-i.ch/fachgruppen-und-sektionen/cloud-computing/.

International School of Physics "Enrico Fermi"

Villa Monastero, Varenna

Course 192

25 – 30 July 2014

Grid and Cloud Computing:
Concepts and Practical Applications

Directors

FEDERICO CARMINATI
PH Department
CERN
1211 Geneva 23
Switzerland
tel: ++41 22 7674959
fax: ++41 22 7668505
Federico.Carminati@cern.ch

LATCHEZAR BETEV
PH Department
CERN
1211 Geneva 23
Switzerland
tel: ++41 22 7674537
fax: ++41 22 7669706
Latchezar.Betev@cern.ch

Scientific Secretary

ALINA GRIGORAS
PH Department
CERN
1212 Geneva 23
Switzerland
tel: ++41 22 7671470
fax: ++41 22 7668377
alina.gabriela.grigoras@cern.ch

Lecturers

ARTUR BARCZYK
California Institute of Technology
1200 East California Blvd
CA 91125, Pasadena
USA
Artur.Barczyk@cern.ch
arturb@caltech.edu

IAN BIRD
IT Department
CERN
1211 Geneva 23
Switzerland
tel: ++41 22 7675888
fax: ++41 22 7668782
Ian.Bird@cern.ch

VINCENT BRETON
LPC
Campus des Cezeaux
24 avenue des Landais
F-63177, Aubiere Cedex
France
tel: ++33 47 3407219
fax: ++33 47 3264598
breton@clermont.in2p3.fr

DIRK DUELLMANN
IT Department
CERN
1211 Geneva 23
Switzerland
tel: ++41 22 7674937
fax: ++41 22 7669289
Dirk.Duellmann@cern.ch

IOSIF LEGRAND
PH Department
CERN
1211 Geneva 23
Switzerland
tel: ++41 22 7676366
fax: ++41 22 7679480
Iosif.Legrand@cern.ch

MIRON LIVNY
Computer Sciences Department
University of Wisconsin
1210 W. Dayton St.
WI 53706-1685, Madison
USA
tel: ++1 608 2620856
fax: ++1 608 2629777
miron@cs.wisc.edu

SERGIO MAFFIOLETTI
University of Zurich
Winterthurerstrasse 190
8057 Zurich
Switzerland
Tel: ++41 44 635 4222
Fax: ++41 44 635 6888
sergio.maffioletti@uzh.ch

DAVIDE SALOMONI
INFN-CNAF
Viale Berti Pichat 6/2
I-40127, Bologna
Italy
tel: ++39 051 6092753
fax: ++39 051 6092746
davide.salomoni@cnaf.infn.it

HARVEY NEWMAN
California Institute of Technology
1200 East California Blvd
CA 91125, Pasadena
USA
tel: ++1 626 3956656
fax: ++1 626 5849304
newman@hep.caltech.edu
norma@hep.caltech.edu

Students

OLGA DATSKOVA — University of Houston, USA

SEBASTIEN FABBRO — University of Victoria, Canada

ANDRES GOMEZ RAMIREZ — Johan-Wolfgang-Goethe Universität Frankfurt, Germany

MORITZ KRETZ — University of Heidelberg at Mannheim, Germany

SAKHILE MASOKA — Meraka Institute, South Africa

DMITRIY MAXIMOV — Budker Institute of Nuclear Physics, Russia

SAMUELE RILLI — Università di Camerino, Italy

ARTURO RODOLFO SANCHEZ PINEDA — Università di Napoli "Federico II", Italy